The Sweet Sixteen

The Journey that Inspired
the Canadian Women's Press Club

LINDA KAY

McGill-Queen's University Press
Montreal & Kingston • London • Ithaca

Legal deposit second quarter 2012
Bibliothèque nationale du Québec

Printed in Canada on acid-free paper that is 100% ancient forest free
(100% post-consumer recycled), processed chlorine free

This book has been published with the help of a grant from the Aid to
Research Related Events (ARRE) program at Concordia University.

McGill-Queen's University Press acknowledges the support of the
Canada Council for the Arts for our publishing program. We also
acknowledge the financial support of the Government of Canada
through the Canada Book Fund for our publishing activities.

Library and Archives Canada Cataloguing in Publication

Kay, Linda, 1951–
The sweet sixteen : the journey that inspired the Canadian Women's
Press Club / Linda Kay.

Includes bibliographical references and index.
ISBN 978-0-7735-3967-9

1. Canadian Women's Press Club – History.   2. Women journalists –
Canada – Biography.   3. Women in journalism – Canada – History –
20th century.   4. Women and journalism – Canada – History – 20th
century.   I. Title.

PN4912.K39 2012   070'.0820971   C2011-907835-X

Set in 10.2/13.5 Adobe Caslon
Book design & typesetting by Garet Markvoort, zijn digital

CONTENTS

THE SWEET SIXTEEN

List of Press Corps Members travelling to St Louis
(including penname and affiliation in 1904)

Grace Denison (1854–1914)	Lady Gay	*Saturday Night*
Kate Simpson Hayes (1856–1945)	Mary Markwell	*Manitoba Free Press*
Kathleen Blake Coleman (1856–1915)	Kit Coleman	*Mail and Empire*
Cécile Laberge (1860–1948)	Cécile Laberge	*Le Soleil*
Robertine Barry (1863–1910)	Françoise	*Le Journal de Françoise*
Léonise Valois (1868–1936)	Attala	*Le Canada*
Margaret Graham (1870–1924)	M.G.	*Halifax Herald*
Antoinette Gérin-Lajoie (1870–1945)	A.G.L.	*L'Événement*

Amintha Plouffe (1870–1962)	A. Plouffe	*Le Journal*
Marie Beaupré (1873–1942)	Hélène Dumont	*La Presse*
Anne-Marie Gleason (1875–1943)	Madeleine	*La Patrie*
Alice Asselin (1877–1954)		*Le Nationaliste*
Katherine Hughes (1877–1925)	K.H.	*Montreal Daily Star*
Gertrude Balmer Watt (1879–1963)	Peggy	*Woodstock Sentinel-Review*
Mary Adelaide Dawson (1880–1932)	M.A.D.	*Toronto Evening Telegram*
Irene Currie Love (1881–1945)	Nan	*London Advertiser*

ACKNOWLEDGMENTS

I have tapped sources from across the country in my research. I am so grateful to those who have shared their recollections, their knowledge, and their time.

In particular, I want to thank Dr Norman Fergusson, former executive director of the Nova Scotia Teachers Union, who escorted me to the birthplace of Margaret "Miggsy" Graham in Upper Musquodoboit outside Halifax and generously shared his own research, begun forty years ago, on the "mother" of the Canadian Women's Press Club. Accompanied by town resident and guide Ross Graves, we visited a tiny restored cemetery in Upper Stewiacke where Miggsy's great-grandfather and father are buried.

Thanks, also, to Miggsy's granddaughter, Margalo Grant Whyte of British Columbia, who, through telephone conversations and e-mail, helped me piece together aspects of Miggsy's life.

Edmonton filmmaker Tom Radford spoke to me at length about his strong-minded grandmother Gertrude Balmer Watt. I cannot thank him enough for fleshing out her character and personal history. And heartfelt thanks go to Mary Liley, a volunteer with the Oxford County Branch of the Ontario Genealogical Society, who got to the bottom of what had remained, before Ms Liley's intervention, a mysterious dispute between Gertrude Balmer Watt and Kathleen "Kit" Coleman. It is mysterious no more.

For hard facts on Katherine Hughes, I'm deeply indebted to writer-researcher Juliette Champagne, my Edmonton guide and a valuable source of information, and to veteran Edmonton broadcaster and historian Tony Cashman, whose knowledge of Canadian history is encyclopaedic and who provided many tips about the feisty Hughes. Éloi DeGrâce, archivist for the Catholic Archdiocese of Edmonton, located on short notice for my perusal the correspondence of Katherine Hughes. Merrily K. Aubrey, Alberta author and historian, helped me trace Hughes's steps in Edmonton. Rob Carstensen of Edmonton Visitor Services escorted me to Father Albert Lacombe's mission and chapel in St Albert, Alberta, where Hughes spent time researching her highly praised biography on the missionary priest. Pádraig O Siadhail, associate professor of Irish studies at St Mary's University in Halifax, and author of a wonderful magazine article on Hughes, kindly responded to my inquiries; and James O'Regan, the great-grand-nephew of Katherine Hughes, sent along by e-mail genealogical links to his family tree.

Alison Fraser of Tourism Regina proved an able guide as she escorted me to the locations where Kate Simpson Hayes worked and worshipped in Regina, and, for crucial information about Hayes, I relied heavily on an authoritative master's thesis penned in 1996 by Constance Anne Maguire at the University of Regina. Although I did not have the opportunity to meet Maguire, her research opened a window that provided wide avenues of inquiry. I also found valuable leads in *No Daughter of Mine*, a book by the late Kay Rex, who astutely tracked the club's rise and fall.

I am deeply thankful, as well, to Raymonde Marchand Paré, niece of Alice Asselin and daughter of Eva Le Boutillier Marchand, who kindly welcomed me into her home in Montreal to speak about her family; to André Asselin, grandson of Alice Asselin, who made time to speak with me in his Montreal law office and generously loaned me a book on the Le Boutillier family roots; and to Christine Asselin, great-granddaughter of Alice Asselin, who graciously acquired information related to the family history on my behalf.

Anne Carrier of Quebec City, researcher for the *Dictionary of Canadian Biography*, freely shared her extensive doctoral research on Robertine Barry and on numerous occasions provided her keen observations. The descendants of Cécile (née Hone) Lefevbre Laberge Léger helped me round out her persona: my thanks to her great-grandson Charles DesBaillets and great-granddaughters Danielle Badeaux Edgell and Suzanne Badeaux. Josée Sarazin, archivist for the Congrégation de Notre-Dame, and Carole Gélinas, development officer at Villa Maria high school, helped me uncover information about the elusive Marie Beaupré, including a crucial reflection on her life written in her own hand. Jo-Anne Colby of the Canadian Pacific Archives patiently answered repeated queries about Windsor Station and the railway car *Trudeau*, on which the Sweet Sixteen travelled to St Louis.

Through devoted research, Anne Gow, assistant at the public library in London, Ontario, helped me retrace the path in downtown London where a young Irene Currie Love once walked. Cynthia Cooper, curator, Costume and Textiles, at the McCord Museum of Canadian History in Montreal, discussed with me the clothing the women wore during the trip to St Louis. And Robert C. Fisher, archivist with Library and Archives Canada, whom I met at the beginning of this long journey, when the Canadian Women's Press Club celebrated its one hundredth birthday in 2004, helped me get my facts straight from the start.

My gratitude also goes to Concordia librarian Sonia Poulin, who answered calls of distress with unstinting good humour and, on many occasions, helped me locate research material. And my immense gratitude as well goes to two formidable editors: journalist and former Concordia colleague Sheila Arnopoulos, who read the first draft of the book and made many perceptive and exceedingly helpful comments; and acquisitions editor at McGill-Queen's University Press Mark Abley, who pointed out many places in the manuscript that needed polish.

Last but not least, by any means, I want to thank my research assistant and former Concordia journalism student, Alexandre Paquin, for his meticulous attention to detail and for his help with translations of sometimes excessively florid prose as all the French texts written by the women on the trip have been translated into English for the purposes of this book. I am certain that Alexandre will one day write a book that will contribute to Canadian press history.

THE SWEET SIXTEEN

Introduction

Sixteen. Eight English Canadians and eight French Canadians,
but all sisters by thought and by pen, united in heart and soul even
before knowing each other … Ah! The good example we set there!
– Anne-Marie Gleason, *La Patrie*.[1]

The sixteen women who reported on the St Louis World's Fair in 1904 and
created the Canadian Women's Press Club (CWPC) on a railway car during
the excursion stood out at a time when most women had few rights and
played no role in public affairs. Women in Canada did not have the right to
vote in federal or provincial elections. They could not hold office. There was
a strong prejudice against women professionals and a matching belief that
no woman should work after marriage. The image of a woman at home was
the measure of respectability.[2] Opposition to higher education for women
was widespread.[3] Holding a job as a journalist and forming a national club
for women professionals was an audacious move that made a resounding
political statement.

Only a few dozen Canadian women worked as journalists at the turn of
the last century. They were hired to write and edit a so-called "Woman's
Page," which usually ran in the Saturday edition of the newspaper and was
expressly designed to attract women readers. The page followed a familiar pattern, interspersing the writer's personal observations with fragments
of poetry and prose clipped from other publications while weaving in local
society news and letters from readers (published with a reply). Given that

the first female journalists aspired to be serious writers, the Woman's Page presented them with an early vehicle for literary expression.

The first women journalists did not cover hard news, nor were they hired to do so. They were talented writers and brought strong writing skills to an outlet that paid. Using pseudonyms, they created intriguing personae for themselves. Wide exposure on the leading newspapers of the day turned several women into stars, but that prominence also presented a paradox. Born in the Victorian age, they walked a fine line with editors and readers between representing the new woman, open-minded and venturesome – which they were – while at the same time maintaining conventional societal norms that promoted marriage and motherhood as a woman's true calling.[4]

As these pioneers evolved in the journalistic milieu, they developed the classic "nose for news" we associate with journalists today. They worked hard to transcend the boundaries imposed on them by editors who thought women were only interested in reading about the domestic realm. Many early women journalists had trained to become teachers, an acceptable career option open to unmarried women of that era, and they carried that approach into their writing style, seeing themselves as tutors and guides for their readership on all matters.

Covering a world's fair would have been a coup for any journalist in 1904, but for the sixteen Canadian women on the trip to St Louis, the assignment represented a professional milestone. Writing for the women's pages, female journalists were largely limited to reporting upon social events and answering readers' queries about etiquette and moral conduct. They rarely had the opportunity to travel for their work and write about the bigger issues of the day.

And the Louisiana Purchase Exposition, commonly known as the St Louis World's Fair, was one of the biggest stories of the year. It commemorated the one hundredth anniversary of what historians deemed the best real-estate deal ever made, as France ceded more than 800,000 square miles to the United States at bargain prices. The land would form parts of fifteen states and two Canadian provinces. Most important, it would allow for western expansion in both countries.

The exposition, which attracted 20 million visitors and provided a stage for the first Olympic Games held in North America, rated among the top three news interests in 1904, according to the *National Magazine*, an American monthly publication. The others were the war between Japan and Russia, which began in February 1904, and the US presidential campaign, which would pit Republican incumbent Theodore Roosevelt against Democrat Alton B. Parker.[5] The sixteen Canadian women who travelled to St Louis witnessed two of the top three events – the exposition, of course, but also a portion of the presidential campaign, which was an unscripted part of their trip.

Their journey to St Louis, with stops in Chicago and Detroit, widened their scope as journalists, allowing them to see first-hand parts of Canada and the United States. The fair alone, with more than sixty nations participating, exposed them to a global scene they had little chance to encounter in their routine work and introduced them to the newest products and innovations from around the world.

The trip would also legitimize them as professionals since they were treated with the same deference as male representatives of the press at a time when women journalists were marginalized by their male colleagues. Most important, the trip marked the formation of the CWPC, laying a foundation upon which female journalists in Canada, separated by vast distances, could come together and build credibility and status in the decades ahead.

At some point during the voyage, the sixteen women and their patron George Ham, publicity director for the Canadian Pacific Railway (CPR), concluded that the combined pen power in the railway car should not be allowed to dissipate at the end of the trip. Ham prodded the women to form an association. Together, French- and English-speaking journalists created the CWPC, the first women's press club in the world to embrace a national membership. The CWPC would eventually become the longest-running national press club for women in existence.

From the beginning, the CWPC had three concrete aims: to promote and protect the professional interests of its members, to advance Canadian national sentiment in the publications for which its members wrote, and to encourage high standards of literary excellence in newspaper writing. At a time when there were no journalism schools in Canada and when women had only limited access to higher education, the club served as a surrogate for instruction and information. Club members learned about the profession from each other and, most significantly, with the help of free passage on the railway, were able to learn first-hand about Canada's history, its geography, and its inhabitants.

The little businesswomen's club quickly grew large. Branches spread across the country so that the women could meet in the regions on a regular basis. At its peak in the late 1960s, membership in the national organization reached nearly seven hundred. In order to gain admittance, applicants had to prove they wrote for newspapers or magazines and that they were paid for their work. The CWPC became so influential that prominent political figures and even prime ministers Lester B. Pearson, John Diefenbaker, and Pierre Trudeau either made appearances or spoke at its general meetings.

Club members included Canada's earliest feminists. Emily Murphy, the first female magistrate in the British Commonwealth, and author Nellie McClung, both of whom led the movement to have Canadian women recognized as "persons" under the British North America Act, joined the club early on. So did Lucy Maud Montgomery, author of the most popular book ever written by a Canadian, *Anne of Green Gables*.

I first learned about the CWPC when it celebrated its one hundredth birthday with a weekend party in Ottawa, an event both momentous and bittersweet. The club formally disbanded that weekend in June 2004. Remaining members had not been able replenish the ranks to keep the national club a going concern. In fact, membership began declining precipitously in the 1970s, when women entered journalism in greater numbers and decided that they did not need a club devoted to women's interests in order to advance in the field.

On that centennial anniversary weekend, I became intrigued by the story of a club forged on a railway car – a quintessential Canadian beginning. As a journalist myself, I was also curious about my predecessors. I had entered the profession at a time when women were welcomed, if not completely accepted. I knew nothing about the uncommonly talented women who had paved the way for my peers and me in the late 1800s and early 1900s. They were daring women in so many ways, defying societal norms and completely contravening the stereotypical image of a Victorian woman.

In researching the birth of the CWPC, I found lore and legend on the trip's origin but little information on the group, particularly the French-speaking contingent that formed fully half of the participants. So scant was reliable information on the club's formation and earliest days that, when club executives attempted a Herculean effort to assemble an authoritative history for the CWPC's fiftieth anniversary in 1954, Kathleen Mathers, editor of the Golden Jubilee publication and a meticulous researcher, almost threw up her hands in frustration as she confronted conflicting accounts of the number of women on the trip, their names and pennames, and their newspaper affiliations. "I'm ready to jump off a bridge over the St Louis crowd!" Mathers exclaimed in a letter to Mae Clendenan, corresponding secretary of the club at the time.[6]

I had similar feelings when attempting to bring all sixteen women and their trip to life. My starting point became the articles they had written about the St Louis excursion over one hundred years ago. Using their own words, I attempted to piece together the trip and the lives behind the bylines, travelling from Prince Edward Island to Alberta to retrace their steps, scouting archives for private papers, and tracking down descendants.

Tracing the bylines proved, in itself, a monumental effort. Female journalists at that time used a nom-de-plume, and some of the women on the trip used several. For example, Kate Simpson Hayes, in addition to using the penname "Mary Markwell," also wrote under the name "Yukon Bill." Anne-Marie Gleason wrote as "Madeleine" and "Myrto." Irene Currie Love used the pennames "Nan" and "Margaret Currie." Verifying the true identity of the women writing in newspapers at the time became a knotty problem. Additionally, the women on the St Louis trip were writing for a total of thirty-four publications in Canada and the United States, using pseudonyms that may never be tracked back to the writer with absolute assurance. What is more, the passenger list for the St Louis trip was less than authoritative.

Léonise Valois, for example, was listed simply as "Miss Valois, Ottawa." It took months to verify that she was actually from Quebec and wrote for a Montreal newspaper.

CPR publicity director George Ham dubbed the group he took to St Louis "the Sweet Sixteen," but he readily acknowledged that the cliché he used to describe them was purely his own invention since "some of them didn't think they were [sweet]."[7] Indeed, they were a strong and intrepid bunch, possessing so much ability that most merit a full-length biography. The group included the first woman to work full time for a newspaper in Quebec, the first woman to be an accredited war correspondent, the first woman to publish a volume of poetry in Quebec, the founder of a highly popular magazine that later became the French version of *Chatelaine*, and the author of a book lauded by the *New York Times*.

Six of the group never married – five of them French-Canadian. Three divorced or separated at a time when doing so bordered on scandalous. Two others married, had a long journalism career, but never had children. Only one woman in the group had a child, a lasting marriage, and a long productive career as a journalist. In some ways, the struggles these women faced resonate for contemporary young women who, more than a century later, wonder how to combine meaningful work with marriage and motherhood.

In writing this book, I sought answers to many questions. Who were these enterprising women breaking new ground in the profession? What did they see and do on that pivotal excursion to St Louis? What subjects did they choose to write about? How did that choice reflect their linguistic and cultural identities? How did their distinct identities merge and emerge as they crossed the border into another country? How did the trip affect them personally and professionally? How did they, in turn, influence the profession of journalism? What does their experience tell us about women journalists in Canada at the turn of the twentieth century, when women were first gaining a place in the field? What does their experience tell us about society in Canada in that era? And last, could the businesswomen's club they formed over one hundred years ago hold lessons of value for women today?

In the pages that follow, I attempt to bring their story to life.

Demanding Equal Rights

It is a big fair. Big in every sense of the word. The intention was big –
it is being carried out on big lines, and the man, woman or child who
can, and doesn't, see the wonderful things to be seen, will miss one
of the big things which the world has to show.
– Kate Simpson Hayes, *Manitoba Free Press*, 2 July 1904

Margaret Graham walked briskly into the Montreal headquarters of the
Canadian Pacific Railway at Windsor Station in early June 1904. The Ottawa correspondent for the *Halifax Herald*, covering matters of interest to
women from the political heart of the nation, belonged to a select group of
female journalists employed by newspapers in Canada at that time.

Some fifty women listed "journalist" as their occupation in the federal
census of 1901. Considered stars in their day, they often drew readership
numbers as high as any male journalist. Margaret Graham, age thirty-four
and a powerful writer, had been with the *Halifax Herald* nearly seven years.
Many factors led to her hiring, not the least of which was timing.

Newspapers were wildly popular in Canada in the early 1900s. Two circumstances in particular contributed to their popularity: literacy had become
widespread in Canada, and, at the same time, the population of Canadian
cities had expanded rapidly. Over a million people – one in five Canadians –
lived in a city at the turn of the last century, and the daily newspaper had become indispensable to the city dweller.¹ The Montreal newspaper *Le Monde*
declared the newspaper to be "un article de première nécessité, comme le

pain et la viande."[2] In Toronto, the story was the same. As early as 1883, the average Toronto family bought two newspapers a day.[3]

Once underwritten by political entities or religious groups that espoused their own causes, most daily newspapers by the late 1800s were mass circulation journals attempting to appeal to a large audience. But without political or religious backers to fully fund a costly enterprise that was growing more sophisticated technologically, newspapers needed advertising revenue to stay afloat. Advertisers were eager to court women as the force behind most family purchases, so editors hired female writers expressly to attract female readers.[4]

In 1886, Sara Jeannette Duncan became the first woman to break the gender barrier as a full-time employee at a newspaper in Canada. Hired by the *Globe* in Toronto – and later to become an acclaimed novelist – Duncan ushered in a new era for female writers in Canada, who were, for the first time, avidly recruited by astute editors and publishers across the country as these practical businessmen began to realize the economic value of including a "woman's voice" in the newspaper.

Margaret Graham was certainly the beneficiary of the burgeoning move among big city editors to cater to female readers. On that June day in 1904, when Graham climbed the stairs at Windsor Station headquarters in Montreal and strode confidently down the long corridor leading to the offices of CPR publicity director George Henry Ham, she may have felt empowered by the clout she commanded as a journalist. She had just snared an important interview with the wife of Prime Minister Sir Wilfrid Laurier.

With self-assurance, she prepared to address the CPR publicity chief, whose affability was legendary. Described as "a large body of superfine humanity entirely surrounded by the Canadian Pacific Railway," George Ham's jovial nature and wry sense of humour made him one of the most popular men in the country at the time.[5] But Margaret Graham, dubbed "Miggsy" by family and friends, was not in the mood for jokes. She had a serious mission.

Entering Ham's office, she greeted Ham's assistant, Kate Simpson Hayes, a tall and distinguished-looking woman in her late forties wearing wire-rimmed glasses, who, under the penname "Mary Markwell," wrote a lively and light-hearted weekly column aimed at women for the *Manitoba Free Press*. Newspaper work did not pay well, and many female journalists worked a second job or freelanced widely. Kate Simpson Hayes did both. She sent her clever column to Manitoba by telegraph each week while at the same time working in Ham's office in downtown Montreal assisting the CPR's massive publicity effort to encourage immigration to the Canadian west.

By 1900, Canada had 17,600 miles of rail, counting trunk lines and feeder lines.[6] To understand the enormous investment that had been made in railways in Canada in an extremely short span, consider that, in the 1850s, the country had only sixty-six miles of track. But by 1867, when the articles of Confederation were signed and British Columbia had been promised a rail connection with the east, there were already fifteen different railway companies operating on 2,495 miles of track in a frantic race for dominance.[7]

In 1904, the year that Margaret Graham appeared in George Ham's office, the CPR was pre-eminent among railways with its transcontinental line completed in 1885, but competitors were still actively jockeying for territory in the west. The CPR responded by adding even more track.[8] The competition ultimately doomed the CPR's rivals. The Canadian Northern was taken over by the government in 1917 to become the first big section of the Canadian National Railways, and a similar fate awaited the British-backed Grand Trunk Railway in 1920.[9]

But at the time Margaret Graham strode into the CPR headquarters, the railway was intent on establishing supremacy by making sure there was enough traffic to support its growing line. Luring Canadians to move west was part of the strategy. More important, the railway sought to entice immigrants, predominantly from the United States and Britain. Kate Simpson Hayes had been hired to promote that effort, and it was not easy. The CPR had to spend millions erasing the country's image as a frozen wasteland, a vision perpetuated when Rudyard Kipling published a poem in 1897 entitled "Our Lady of the Snows" – his code name for Canada. Ironically, the content of Kipling's poem was highly favourable, but the damage was done.[10] George Ham and Kate Simpson Hayes had to work diligently to counter the portrayal.

In Ham's office that day, Margaret Graham wasted no time telling the railway executive the reason for her visit. You take newspapermen to all your functions, she told him, whether it be steamship landings, hotel openings, sight-seeing tours, or world's fairs. What about women? Why, Graham wanted to know, weren't newspaperwomen accorded the same rights as men?[11]

In his 1920s memoir, Ham sketched out his version of the fateful encounter. Graham, a "champion of women's rights," began to "cyclonically" tell him that the CPR had transported men, free of charge, on various excursions, while "women had altogether been ignobly ignored." She then demanded to know "why poor downtrodden females should thus be so shabbily treated." When she finished, indignation blazing from her eyes, Ham politely motioned for her to take a seat: "Sit down, Miggsy, sit down and keep cool."[12] But Margaret Graham was accustomed to speaking her mind and fighting for equal treatment. Born in 1870 and raised in difficult circumstances with few material resources, she had nevertheless achieved what few women of her era could hope to attain.

Her father died of lung disease when she was four, leaving a wife and six children destitute in the rural hamlet of Upper Musquodoboit, Nova Scotia, southeast of Truro and about an hour's drive from Halifax. The sparsely populated area is still dotted with farms, haystacks, and dairy cows even today. The Graham household split up by necessity. While Margaret Graham and her mother stayed together, living with relatives, her brothers and sisters were parcelled out to members of the extended family.

At age fifteen, Graham enrolled in Normal School in Truro for teacher training, a predictable path taken in that era by respectable young women whose families lacked the financial means to support them and who would have to support themselves until they got married. After a year's training, she became a teacher.

From the time of Confederation until the First World War, novice elementary school teachers throughout Canada were mostly teenagers like Graham. Salaries for these teachers were low, workloads were heavy, and working conditions were often intolerable. In rural areas, many teachers boarded with a family. In winter, they were expected to open the school-house at dawn, light a fire, and teach children of all ages. Female teachers drew an average salary of around $300 a year, a third less than men, and, as a rule, school boards sought out the least experienced teachers rather than the most competent in order to pay the lowest wages.[13]

Teaching in Lawrencetown, about twelve and a half miles from Halifax, and perhaps growing dissatisfied with her working conditions or simply growing restless, Margaret Graham applied to be a missionary, emulating, in a sense, her great-grandfather, the Reverend Hugh Graham, a highly respected Presbyterian minister who had come to Nova Scotia from Scotland in the late 1700s. Likely because of her distinguished pedigree in Presbyterian circles, her application was accepted, and, in 1889, when she was only nineteen, Graham undertook what was to be a blustery and distressing boat voyage to the Caribbean island of Trinidad to serve as a missionary-teacher with the Presbyterian Synod. Her work with 170 pupils at the San Fernando Indian School, on the southwestern part of the island, would have lasted five years under normal circumstances and could have extended far longer had she chosen, but Graham's stay was cut short after a year and a half. She injured her back when she was thrown from a horse and returned to Canada to recuperate.[14]

Her return was to have long-term consequences and lasting benefits for Canadian women. Teaching again in Nova Scotia, Graham emerged as an outspoken leader with strong ideals and convictions. At a meeting of the provincial Education Association in 1895, she proposed a motion giving women the right to vote at the school board meetings. It failed, but her suggestion that Nova Scotia teachers form a union had traction. "It seems to me that the time has come when we teachers should organize ourselves into some sort of union, similar to the societies existing in the medical, legal and other professions," she said at the Education Association meeting in October of 1895.[15]

An executive committee was struck to explore the matter, but the committee did not include Margaret Graham. She enjoyed planting the seeds for revolutionary endeavours but moved on before they could be implemented.

It would be a pattern that would repeat itself. Even at that pivotal Education Association meeting, Graham had already been toying with the idea of leaving the teaching profession altogether. As early as 1894, she had begun writing book reviews for the *Sun* (New York). Her older brother Whidden worked as a journalist in New York City, writing about economics and politics for newspapers and magazines. Graham visited him in his Upper West Side apartment and, perhaps at his urging, decided to try her hand at writing as well.

Her book reviews for the *Sun* display a keen intellect, breadth of knowledge, and strong writing skills. Her versatility is apparent as she effortlessly moves from reviewing a tell-all book – *Life in the Tuileries under the Second Empire* – to a weighty tome on Virgil penned by a professor from the University of Florence. Reviewing the third volume in a series about American heads of state, *The Messages and Papers of the Presidents*, she ably tackles subject matter of a political nature: "The first six Presidents were men of social distinction in their respective States, and, with the exception of Washington, all of them had been liberally educated. This was not the case with Jackson or with Van Buren. The 'Van' in the name of the eighth President conveys an erroneous impression as to the class of the New York community from which he sprang."[16]

By the time she wrote that book review, Margaret Graham's teaching career was over, replaced by journalism. She began writing for the *Halifax Herald* in the summer of 1897. Her first major assignment involved reporting on the Christian Endeavour Convention, a worldwide movement of evangelical Christians meeting in Windsor, Nova Scotia. She didn't just report on the convention: she included the history and geography of Windsor in her article as well as a description of the schools and businesses in town.[17]

The *Halifax Herald* later made Graham its correspondent in Ottawa, where she commented on legislation relevant to women and interviewed the wives of prominent politicians, including Laura Bond Borden, married to then opposition leader and future prime minister Robert L. Borden. She had heard that Laura Borden had "ideas, lots of them," so she began her interview with an abrupt question she had never before asked the wife of any lawmaker in Ottawa: do you believe in women's suffrage? "I do not," came the unhesitating reply. "To my mind a wife is or should be in the truest sense of the word a helpmeet, and the wife of a politician can and ought to be a help and inspiration to her husband in a thousand ways without actually entering the political arena herself."[18]

Margaret Graham then attempted to engage Laura Borden in conversation about the work women did for various causes, encouraging her to put forth her own ideas on issues. "I don't want to borrow all your ideas," she told Borden, "I only wished to know that you have ideas and interests outside your own life. This it is that makes any person worth writing about." She told Borden she thought it important that Canadian women hear more from political wives than descriptions of table decorations, centrepieces, and gowns. "Not that I at all minimize the value of these things," Graham wrote with velvet-glove sarcasm, "but the constant mention of them every time you entertain at luncheon, dinner or receptions naturally gives the people far distant from the Capital the idea that you are mere butterflies. I know otherwise of course." Her gentle prodding drew little reaction from Borden, and Graham came away from the interview reminded of the way that Sara Jeannette Duncan, the first full-time female journalist in Canada, described the heroine of her just-published novel about political life in Canada: *The Imperialist*. Wrote Duncan: "She had several kinds of cleverness, one of them being a particularly nice way of doing her hair." Commented Graham: "This applies to Mrs Borden."

Margaret Graham's articles were smart, funny, incisive, and instructive. She clearly saw herself as an educator, particularly when it came to teaching readers the history and geography of Canada, a pedagogical role many early female journalists viewed as their mandate. In fact, at the turn of the twentieth century, female journalists saw themselves as tutors and guides for their female readers, believing that the "Woman's Page" in the newspaper served as a university of sorts for women who had limited access to higher education, particularly in Quebec.[19] Indeed, according to Robert M. Stamp, editor and contributor to *Canadian Education: A History*, "The question of higher education for women was a most explosive one in the late nineteenth century" (333). The *Canada Educational Monthly* argued against it in 1883: "Co-education at the University College [University of Toronto] is not possible nor yet desirable. The presence in the class-room of ladies, albeit most sober and demure, would not, we fear, be very inducive to study. There are very few young people quite indifferent to the presence of the opposite sex."[20] When universities did offer women an education in the last decades of the century, they made sure classes took place "beyond the walls of the established colleges," creating separate classes for women away from the male students.[21]

Sitting in George Ham's office in June of 1904, Margaret Graham tried to convince the railway man that women merited equal treatment. She told Ham that, contrary to what he might think, women journalists did attract a large readership and that the CPR would benefit from taking press women to the World's Fair.

Ham considered the idea and then issued a challenge: find twelve women who could get assignments from their newspaper to cover the Fair and he'd take them all to St Louis himself.[22] Graham could hardly believe her ears. As Ham exited the office, leaving the petitioner gasping, Graham turned to Kate Simpson Hayes for immediate assistance. "Mary," she said, using her colleague's familiar penname, "we've got to dig up twelve women writers."[23]

Hayes readily agreed. Despite a considerable age difference, Kate Simpson Hayes and Margaret Graham shared remarkably similar backgrounds. They were both Maritimers, they had both suffered the loss of their father at an early age, they had both attended Normal School for teacher training, and they had both worked initially as teachers. However, given there was fourteen years difference between them, the ascent of Kate Simpson Hayes to journalism's highest ranks appears even more remarkable than does Graham's climb to the top. When Hayes attended Normal School in the 1870s, Graham was a toddler. Opportunities for working women were far fewer for Hayes than for Graham, and opportunities to work on a newspaper as a salaried employee did not yet exist.

By 1904, the year of the St Louis World's Fair, career opportunities for women were still extremely limited. Women made up about 13 percent of the workforce in Canada at the time, with domestic service accounting for 40 percent of those paid female workers.[24] Middle-class women were just starting to be hired as secretaries and office support staff. Nuns monopolized the nursing profession in Canada,[25] and other professions (with the exception of teaching) were largely off-limits. Indeed, Kate Simpson Hayes began her working life in a rural schoolroom.

Baptized Catherine Ethel Hayes, she was only twelve when her father died in a logging accident in Wisconsin, where he had taken a job in hopes of recovering from financial ruin after the foreclosure of his general store in Dalhousie, New Brunswick. The youngest of three daughters, Hayes studied to become a teacher after her father's death and moved to Ontario to teach in a private school. She then ventured further west to Prince Albert, North West Territories (in present-day Saskatchewan), where she took a job as a governess. It was there she met, and in 1882 married, Charles Bowman Simpson, who was from a prominent Ontario family. The couple had two children in short order, but, just as quickly, their marriage unravelled. It was rumoured that Charles was a drunk, and perhaps an abusive one.[26]

In a courageous move for a woman at the time, Kate Simpson Hayes left her husband, from whom she later obtained a legal separation,[27] and took her little boy and infant girl to Regina in 1886. She would never formally divorce Charles. Indeed, divorce was extremely rare in Canada. In 1900, only six hundred people were divorced out of a married population of 1,833,000.

Regina was a boomtown when Hayes moved there and must have seemed filled with promise. The area had been a no-man's land until CPR surveyors arrived in May of 1882 and found just three settlers living in a spot distinguished only by a mound of buffalo bones. These bones were piled high and had been placed there by Aboriginal people who believed that the buffalo would always return to where the bones of their ancestors lay, thus ensuring a steady food supply.[28] By the time the rail track reached the place called Pile of Bones in late August 1882, the tiny settlement had been renamed "Regina" in honour of Queen Victoria and, almost overnight, had been transformed. A hodge-podge of temporary and permanent shelters had sprung up south of the CPR depot, and, in a matter of weeks, Regina could boast eight hotels, two blacksmith shops, two laundries, two bakeries, a drugstore, a jewel-ler, two doctors, six lawyers, four lumberyards, and a population exceeding eight hundred.[29] It was named the capital of the North West Territories in March 1883.

Even though it hummed with activity when Kate Simpson Hayes arrived, Regina was certainly not a sight for sore eyes. The town was a flat expanse, bereft of any greenery, even a tree. But for Hayes, a single mother with two little children to support, the barren landscape presented a slate wiped clean. Here she could make a fresh start. She worked in a millinery shop at first and then opened a hat shop of her own – a prudent move, it seems, since women of the era did not leave the house without wearing a hat. She played the organ at St Mary's Roman Catholic Church. She recited verse at the Literary and Musical Society, which she helped create, and she recruited members of the North-West Mounted Police to sing in the operettas and concerts that she produced.[30]

Kate Simpson Hayes also revived her literary talent. At age sixteen she had been recruited by the editor of the *St Croix Courier* in St Stephen, New Brunswick, to write poems and short stories for children after he had seen a school play she had written. She had taken the penname "Ivy" and received the grand sum of one dollar per year for her efforts.[31]

In Regina, Hayes submitted a poem to the *Leader* in July 1888 using the penname "Elaine," the name of her young daughter. The newspaper was owned by Irish immigrant Nicholas Flood Davin, a Canadian politician and former journalist who had once dressed up as a priest so that he could gain entrance to the jail where Métis leader Louis Riel was being held and then interview him. A member of Parliament and a noted orator who sometimes addressed the House of Commons in French,[32] Davin was also an attractive bachelor who would prove a powerful influence on Hayes's life. (See illustra-tion 1.)

She wrote three more poems over the following months for the *Leader* and then started submitting feature stories to the paper. Davin suggested she use the penname "Mary Markwell."[33] She closed her millinery shop and, with Davin's help, secured a job with the territorial government in 1890, becoming the first librarian for the Legislature, a full-time position that guaranteed much-needed financial stability while she wrote on the side.

Her most notable writing endeavour in the last decade of the nineteenth century was an eclectic collection that combined poems, short fiction, and a Christmas play into a book entitled *Prairie Pot-pourri*. Published in 1895, it established her reputation as a gifted and clever writer.[34] Inscribed on the title page, perhaps as a homage to Davin, she wrote: "To the early days and the weary ways / Enshrined in the sunset land; / To a kindly voice that bade grief rejoice / And the clasp of a friendly hand."

Kate Simpson Hayes captured her adopted home through the book's characters. A story entitled "An Episode at Clarke's [sic] Crossing" uses the main character to draw a contrast between the barely civilized old west and the bustling new territory.[35] In her portrayal of Peter Larue, Hayes may have been alluding to Métis leader Gabriel Dumont, who ran the ferry crossing at Batoche, not far from present-day Clark's Crossing.

Old Peter Larue was indisputably the caliphate of the plains; an authority on any subject that might be introduced in any of the four languages; English (broken), French, Sioux and Cree (which he would seldom use). Daddy Pete, as he was called, had but one grandchild, the daughter of his son Modèste, and the old man doted on his human flower with a love and devotion almost beyond belief. Daddy Pete was the sole link between the early days – when no footfall save that of the moccasined hunter trod the prairie and the buffalo swept across the plains in droves, like black clouds – and fast encroaching civilization with its noisy railways, its awkward river ferries, its improvements that came creeping on like an incoming tide, wiping away all the old landmarks, sweeping away old-time associations, and making a new era in the West. With the innovations, Daddy Pete (being an aristocrat by nature) would have nothing to do.[36]

In 1900, Hayes embraced journalism full time with the *Manitoba Free Press* in Winnipeg, then the largest circulating paper in the west. She brought to her weekly column on the Woman's Page the same creative touch and the same ear for dialogue that she exhibited in her short stories.

She was a formidable writer who created a cheery persona for herself in print, but Kate Simpson Hayes was also a living contradiction. As Mary Markwell, she praised a woman's place within the domestic sphere and venerated the role of wife and mother. But Hayes herself led an unconventional existence that contravened the Victorian standards of the time, not only because she had left her husband, raised her children alone, and worked outside the home, but also because her personal life would certainly have been thought scandalous had it ever been made public. She had two children out of wedlock with Nicholas Flood Davin and gave up both at birth, hiding their existence from the world.

At age forty-eight, Hayes might have been dispensing conservative advice about house and hearth to her readers in a folksy humorous way, but on the day Margaret Graham walked into George Ham's office, Kate Simpson Hayes faced great difficulties and a heart-wrenching dilemma she dared not disclose in her column – or anywhere else, for that matter. Straining to meet deadlines for her Manitoba readers while "wild with neuralgia and grocers' bills," she suffered from painful spasms in her throat and neck, a condition probably caused by emotional stress.[37] While she was responsible for supporting her family, other factors likely caused her anxiety as well. She had lost her long-time lover Davin to suicide three years before, and she was also closely guarding the secret of their illegitimate children – something that would have life-long repercussions.

That day in Ham's office, when Graham turned to Hayes to help round up the requisite twelve journalists for the trip to St Louis, Hayes pitched right in. The first call went out to the leading French-speaking journalist in town, Robertine Barry, more commonly known by her pseudonym "Françoise," who had started her own newspaper and given many women journalists in Quebec their first break. Barry readily signed onto the St Louis venture and assured Hayes she would find others to fill the ranks.

Calls then went westward, where Hayes had long-standing connections. She reached out to the leading female journalist in English Canada, Kathleen "Kit" Coleman, the social conscience of Ontario, according to *Maclean's* magazine, whose clever and wise comments on manners and morals were as avidly read, the magazine noted, by Toronto charwomen as by Lady Zoé Laurier, the prime minister's wife – not to mention by the prime minister himself.[38] When the legendary writer for the *Mail and Empire* (Toronto) agreed to participate in the St Louis venture, the roster quickly began to fall into place.

Margaret Graham and Kate Simpson Hayes, assisted on the French side by powerhouse journalist Robertine Barry, soon exceeded the required twelve bodies that Ham had set down as a condition. In fact, they lined up sixteen women to make the excursion. They reported their success back to Ham, who was already warming up to the idea. As he must have quickly surmised, the CPR could tap a new audience by courting these female journalists writing for female readers. In turn, those readers could entice their male partners to explore Canada. At the turn of the century, the country provided cheap and plentiful land for immigrants who were willing to farm it. For ten dollars, a pioneer could acquire 160 acres.[39] Ham likely saw the impending trip as a great opportunity to lure Americans to Canada. "Miggsy's idea appealed to me," Ham wrote in his memoir, "and we arranged for a party of sixteen – sweet sixteen, though some of them didn't think they were – to visit St Louis."[40]

Unwittingly, Graham, Hayes, and Barry were about to usher in a new era for female journalists in Canada, a big push forward. For the first time, women would be accorded the same rights and privileges as their male counterparts, even though it would be decades before their status in the field would be comparable. Kate Simpson Hayes made this very point in a column for the *Manitoba Free Press* when explaining to her readers how the idea for the trip had been hatched. Using her alter ego, Mary Markwell, she employed her trademark wit and folksy style to poke fun at the lowly status of women journalists at the time, pointing up the underlying realities they faced in trying to do the same job as men:

The Canadian Pacific railway (always to the fore in things gallant), said to itself, theirself, themself, "We have taken press men here, there, and everywhere, and why have we not taken press women?"

A little press woman standing by said: "Because, forsooth, women are nowhere recognized. We work, we labor, we travel on railways and pay full fare. [Is it] our fault we are born in petticoats instead of trousers?" And the answer of the railway was: "Gather together the women of the pen; bid them be at Windsor Station at ten-of-the-clock on the evening of June 16th, and we, the Canadian Pacific railway, will take the press women to the St Louis fair."[41]

The French Connection

She resembles Balzac by her gift of depicting, in a few well-chosen
strokes, a character or the physiognomy of a generation, and can
be compared with Georges Sand for wealth of imagination, the
contagious emotion that fills her work. Her whole style bears the
impress of truth, nobleness and elegance.
– *La Revue du Monde Catholique* (Paris)[1]

Robertine Barry had enthusiastically promised Kate Simpson Hayes that she
would gather a group of female journalists from Quebec for an expenses-paid
trip to the St Louis World's Fair. With brisk efficiency, this path-breaking
journalist – a columnist, a publisher, a literary figure, and an advocate for
women's rights – quickly mobilized and made good on her pledge.

Eight French-Canadian women would be boarding the train bound for
St Louis the night of 16 June 1904. The numbers were an ironic coincidence.
In their haste to assemble the requisite group of travellers, Kate Simpson
Hayes, Margaret Graham, and Robertine Barry recruited an even split.
Half the women had French roots in Quebec, the other half had English
roots outside Quebec. The number eight would figure providentially during
the trip, as would the French/English divide, which would reverberate in
decisions taken by the women later on.

By any measure, the French-speaking women hurriedly enlisted by
Robertine Barry formed an impressive group. They were a cross-section of
the cultural elite in Quebec. A few were experienced journalists; others were

novices. But Barry felt they were all capable of writing a story about the World's Fair for a newspaper or magazine either inside or outside Quebec since several wrote well in English, as did she herself. Using her extensive contacts, she planned to help the novices place their articles.

Considered the godmother of female journalists in Quebec,[2] Robertine Barry was a vivacious woman with curly brown hair who charmed those she met with a blend of vitality, intelligence, and good humour. She was not only an inspiration and a role model as the first woman to be hired full-time by a Quebec newspaper, *La Patrie*, but, in her capacity as editor and publisher of her own newspaper, *Le Journal de Françoise*, which she had started two years before the trip to St Louis, Barry served as a mentor to many women by generously providing a home for their work. At the time of the trip to St Louis, she was forty-one years old and among the most famous women in the province. Her personal calling card, an item widely used by middle- and upper-class women to proffer invitations to fancy teas called "at-homes," simply bore her penname "Françoise," a testament to her celebrity.

Born in 1863, Robertine Barry was the eighth of thirteen children who grew up in privileged circumstances in a bilingual household in Les Escoumins, a tiny Quebec community founded in 1846 on the north shore of the St Lawrence River. Her father, John Barry, born in Ireland, worked in logging camps in the Saguenay when he first arrived in Canada and later assumed managerial positions in the forestry industry. John Barry grew wealthy and influential in Les Escoumins, serving as mayor, justice of the peace and small claims commissioner, and holding an honorary title as vice-consul of Sweden and Norway.[3] He married Barry's mother, Aglaée Rouleau, in 1851 when she was twenty and he was thirty-five.

From her mother, Barry may have inherited a lively spirit and the ability to rock the boat gently. A family anecdote has Aglaée being chastised by the local priest in August 1861 for wearing a fashionable crinoline to church. Deeming the crinoline unseemly, the priest refused to give her communion at mass. Deeply embarrassed, Aglaée made her unhappiness known. It took the intervention of the archbishop and the appointment of a new priest before the matter was settled to the family's satisfaction.[4]

The Barrys gave their daughter the best education available to girls in that era. At age ten, Robertine Barry entered the Couvent Jésus-Marie elementary school across the river from Les Escoumins in Trois-Pistoles, where the family had moved, and she later boarded with the Ursulines in Quebec City, where she not only learned to sew and embroider but also studied math, chemistry, physics, and history. She developed a love of music at the convent, where she played the harp, organ, and guitar and, in a nod to her future career, wrote several articles for the school newspaper.

After graduation, Barry briefly considered taking the veil with the Sisters of Charity in Halifax, who taught music and literacy skills to young and old. Her decision to try convent life was not unusual: many young women in Quebec contemplated it. But Barry was most probably influenced by a decision taken by her closest sibling, Evelyn. Born twenty months apart, the sisters had been inseparable as youngsters,[5] but on 29 January 1890, Evelyn took her vows and became a nun.

At the turn of the twentieth century, 6 percent of all single women over age twenty in Quebec became nuns. Many more women than men turned to the religious life. In 1901, one male out of 720 Catholics in Quebec chose a religious vocation; one woman out of 216 Catholics in the province did so. By 1911, an even greater number of women chose a religious vocation: one woman out of 173 Catholics became a nun.[6] Not all of them took the veil for religious reasons, according to Marta Danylewycz, author of *Taking the Veil: An Alternative to Marriage, Motherhood, and Spinsterhood in Quebec, 1840–1920*. Convents, according to Danylewycz, presented large numbers of Quebec women with opportunities for professional and self-development that, at the time, were generally unavailable elsewhere in Canada.[7]

According to Danylewycz, in addition to providing a communal and supportive setting, convents provided an "esteemed alternative to motherhood" in a society that seemed to value women only "as procreative beings." Because the clergy had a prominent role in the province running hospitals and orphanages, convents gave women in Quebec a chance to rise to positions of authority and power unmatched in secular society. The religious community valued initiative and resourcefulness and also encouraged talented women to develop their literary and artistic side. In essence, Danylewycz argues, the religious life offered women in Quebec a career.[8]

But after her stint at the Sisters of Charity in Halifax, Robertine Barry knew she was not meant for the religious life. In the past, she had tried to obtain newspaper work, but nothing had materialized.[9] So, in 1891, she sent an article to Honoré Beaugrand, the former mayor of Montreal, a writer and founder of the newspaper *La Patrie*.[10] The article tackled an issue she would revisit for the rest of her life: the importance of an education for girls. In it, she tilted swords with a male columnist for a rival newspaper who frowned on mandatory instruction for girls and instead longed for "a small hearth, a simple roof, the grass of the meadow and a woman who is not scholarly." His words, Barry wrote, reminded her of a vulgar proverb: bête à manger du foin (dumb enough to eat hay).[11]

Beaugrand put the article on the front page of *La Patrie* on 30 April 1891 and, soon after, made Robertine Barry, at age twenty-eight, the first full-time female employee of a newspaper in the province, handing her the opportunity to write a weekly column for the front page of his four-page broadsheet. For her byline, Barry took the penname "Françoise" to honour St François de Sales, patron saint of the day that her sister Evelyn took her vows.

Beaugrand probably relished being the first newspaper owner in Quebec to employ a woman. He liked to take risks and defy convention. Anti-cleric in a very Catholic province and avant-garde in a conservative society deeply steeped in tradition, he had worked as a journalist for Franco-American newspapers in the United States and married an English Protestant.[12] *La Patrie* was an irreverent newspaper frowned upon by the clergy.[13] Assigning Barry to write "Chroniques du Lundi" (Monday Chronicles) was a bold move on Beaugrand's part since few women were writing a general column – and no woman was featured on the front page of a newspaper in Canada.

In "Chroniques du Lundi," Barry broached a variety of topics meant to appeal to both men and women, demonstrating a broad range of interests and a lively writing style, and sometimes incorporating fictional prose within the column. In her first year with the paper, she wrote about influenza; the history of carnivals; a visit to the city by actress Sarah Bernhardt (whom she later met personally); the romance between the crown prince of Romania and the lady-in-waiting to the queen; a visit to a child with supposed healing powers (whom Barry viewed as a quack); and the place of women in society – a topic she visited again and again, prompted to do so, in one case, by a question posed by a British magazine that asked husbands if they were proud of their wives' attire.

Robertine Barry's "Chroniques du Lundi" had a long life, even by today's standards, appearing once a week from September 1891 until March 1900. It provided a potent platform for Barry, who lobbied for higher education for women, the establishment of public libraries in Quebec, and general improvements in the condition of women. She was the first in Quebec to openly encourage women to earn their own living with or without a husband.[14]

Perhaps she realized how mighty a pen she wielded when she returned home after vacationing in Halifax during the summer of 1895. She had seen an old bell for sale in the window of a Halifax pharmacy. On closer inspection, she was astonished to find that it was the same bell that had been stripped from the fortress of Louisbourg after the British takeover in 1758. The British had completely destroyed the French preserve in what is today Cape Breton: the magnificent fort on view today is a modern rebuilding of the original. The bell carried a hefty price tag of $100. At the time, a loaf of bread cost five cents, fabric sold for as little as twenty-five cents a yard, and a fine men's suit from the Montgomery Ward's catalog cost fifteen dollars; the bell cost the equivalent of around $2,000 in today's dollars.[15] But Barry convinced the owner of the pharmacy to put it aside anyway, and she vowed that, in time, she would raise the money to pay for it.

Returning to Montreal inflamed with patriotic fervour and French pride, Robertine Barry used her column in *La Patrie* to organize a fundraising campaign to buy the bell. "We must reclaim this bell," she urged her readers.[16] Money accumulated until finally the bell was secured and displayed briefly in the offices of *La Patrie* before being donated to the Chateau de

Ramezay, constructed in 1705 as a home for Montreal governor Claude de Ramezay and now a museum. The bell remains there today.

Around the same time as she was being saluted for her contribution to French patrimony, Barry cemented her reputation with the literati by publishing a collection of short stories and sketches "dealing with daily life, the traditional beliefs, the joys and sorrows, the loves and dislikes of the Canadian habitant."[17] *Fleurs champêtres* met with critical acclaim. She was now a newspaper columnist and a respected writer of fiction, and, in the 1890s, she presided over a weekly literary salon in her home.

Robertine Barry unabashedly promoted Canadian literature and contemporary writers, many from Quebec. In *La Patrie*, she was among the first to champion now-legendary poet Émile Nelligan, an exceptionally handsome young man who wrote 168 poems in a brief span of three years. Barry and Nelligan forged a close friendship, though she was sixteen years his senior. They frequented the library at the Fraser Institute, now called the Fraser-Hickson Institute and one of Montreal's first libraries,[18] which carried reading material that was frowned upon by the Roman Catholic Church.[19]

Whether Nelligan regarded Barry as an older sister, a guardian angel, or a potential lover is a question raised by his poetry. The answer is inconclusive. Nelligan suffered a mental breakdown in 1899, was institutionalized in August of that year, and remained institutionalized for the rest of his life. In the span of a few months, from the end of 1898 to early 1899, he wrote five poems inspired by Barry, the so-called Françoise Cycle: "Rêve d'artiste"; "Beauté cruelle"; "Le vent, le triste vent de l'automne"; "À une femme détestée"; and "À Georges Rodenbach."[20] He gave these poems to her.

Robertine Barry published "Rêve d'artiste" in *La Patrie* in September 1899. And in March 1904 she published it once again in the pages of *Le Journal de Françoise* – the paper she founded, owned, and operated.[21] While "Rêve d'artiste" (A Poet's Dream) shows the artist's craving for a relationship with his intellectual muse, "À une femme détestée" (To a Woman Scorned) indicates a falling out between them. Barry did not publish the later poems in the cycle until long after they had been written.[22]

Here is the first verse of "Rêve d'artiste," with a translation by scholar P.F. Widdows from his book *Émile Nelligan: Selected Poems*:

> Parfois j'ai le désir d'une soeur bonne et tendre,
> D'une soeur angélique au sourire discret:
> Soeur qui m'enseignera doucement le secret
> De prier comme il faut, d'espérer et d'attendre. (46)

> Sometimes I crave a sister, sweet and good,
> An angel sister with a quiet smile:
> A sister who will teach me in her gentle style
> To hope, to wait and to pray as I should.

In 1897, Honoré Beaugrand sold *La Patrie* to Joseph-Israël Tarte. Robertine Barry remained on staff and, that same year, became director of "Coin de Fanchette," the Saturday Woman's Page in the paper, ushering in the era of the "lonely hearts column" in the Province of Quebec. Her new direction seems to have sown the seeds for the newspaper she would later start on her own, as did the chatty gossip column entitled "Causerie fantaisiste" to which she contributed from September 1898 to March 1900.

Robertine Barry closed her nine-year career at *La Patrie* with a series of letters addressed to both women and men and written during her nearly six-month stay in Paris for the Universal Exposition in 1900. Her dispatches appeared under the title "Lettre de Françoise." She had become so prominent by the turn of the century that she represented the women of Canada at the exposition. The trip may have taken a toll on her health, however. Shortly after returning to Montreal in the fall, Barry contracted typhoid fever and spent two months in the Royal Victoria Hospital in a life-threatening battle with the disease.

By the spring of 1902, she felt sufficiently recovered to launch an endeavour she had been dreaming about for years. She began publishing *Le Journal de Françoise*, an audacious move for any individual, let alone a woman.

Subtitled "Le Gazette Canadienne de la famille," *Le Journal de Françoise* was a general culture publication that provided a potent vehicle for female readers and writers in an era when, in Quebec, literature written by women for women was virtually non-existent.

While female literary figures in Britain and the United States were emerging, female writers in Canada had a difficult time gaining acceptance, and nowhere was this more true than in Quebec. Novels were regarded as dangerous reading material for women in the province, and literary women were accused of seeking personal fame, which was contrary to ideals of female reticence.[23] In a government-sponsored brochure listing the accomplishments of Canadian women in 1900, only three French-speaking women were among the sixty Canadian female novelists, and only three French-speaking poets were among the eighty-seven poets.[24] Robertine Barry was part of the effort to develop literary and artistic culture in Quebec.[25]

Barry carried her forthright opinions from *La Patrie* to *Le Journal de Françoise*, which she published the first and third Saturday of each month. A year's subscription cost two dollars, strictly payable in advance, as indicated on the masthead. Some readers lived in France, where a subscription cost fifteen francs. *Le Journal de Françoise* became an important cultural publication of the period not only for the richness of its content but also for its staying power.[26] New publications of that era routinely expired after a brief existence, sometimes after only a few months, but Barry's endured for seven years against formidable odds.[27]

Robertine Barry continued to promote home-grown writers and poets after leaving *La Patrie*. In the first issue of *Le Journal de Françoise*, writing what would today be called a mission statement, Barry said she wanted her journal to be literary, instructive, and entertaining. A typical issue of the publication routinely featured a poem on the front page and a short story inside; a column, often issue-oriented and signed by Françoise; an article about fashion; a page for children; and an article about etiquette by Quebec's then famous expert on manners, Madame Marc Sauvalle, author of *Les Mille questions d'étiquette*.[28] (See illustration 2.)

On the morning of 16 June 1904, Robertine Barry left the townhouse she shared with her widowed mother on St Denis Street in Montreal, around the corner from Carré St-Louis, and went to her office at 80 rue Saint-Gabriel, a location then at the corner of St James Street in present-day Old Montreal.[29] Lawyers, bailiffs, and the city fire commissioner also had offices in the building. No doubt Barry was mindful of the work that remained before she left town for ten days. The 18 June issue of *Le Journal de Françoise* was ready, but she worried about assembling copy for the 2 July issue, which would be prepared in her absence by her youngest sister Blanche, who had been writing and editing the children's section under a penname since the paper started. Barry poured her heart and soul into her publication, and, because she sometimes worked to the point of exhaustion, friends worried that it took a tremendous toll on her health.

Opening the door to Room 12 in the office building on rue Saint-Gabriel, Robertine Barry faced a desk piled with notices advising her of upcoming literary events in the city. Montreal's cultural life was flourishing around the turn of the century: the city sparkled with music and theatrical productions, and talented artists were plentiful.[30] As a journalist and noted writer of short stories, Barry was part of the cultural scene herself, as were several of the women whom she had recruited for the trip to St Louis.

As she prepared to leave for the world's fair, Robertine Barry had reached the pinnacle of her career and her life, attaining more than she had ever imagined possible. She was a woman of influence in many realms. She had been a journalist for more than a decade and a persuasive force. In a recent issue of *Le Journal de Françoise*, she had thanked subscribers for the donations that had enabled the establishment of a French section of the library in Waterloo, Quebec.

Not only had Robertine Barry been a powerhouse in the field of journalism, but she had also made her mark in literature, where many female journalists longed to leave an impression but were unable to do so. Caught up in the daily struggle to earn a living, many women journalists at that time put literary aspirations on hold in order to deal with the day-to-day grind. Barry, though, managed to be proclaimed as both a literary figure and a leading journalist. A few months before the trip to St Louis, she had been named an officer of the Académie Française in recognition of her contribution to French culture.[31] When she signed her name, she proudly appended her new title: R. Barry (Françoise) Officier d'Académie.

Having filed stories from the Universal Exposition in Paris four years earlier, Robertine Barry felt a tremendous sense of confidence and satisfaction as she readied for the St Louis venture. At the train station later that evening she would greet a group of French-speaking women whom she knew either professionally or through long-standing family connections. By publishing their work, she had already helped some of them gain a foothold in journalism. Others she hoped to help in the future. Convinced of her ability to make things happen, she had high hopes that all the women whom she had recruited would publish after their trip.

There is no doubt that Robertine Barry made a strong and lasting impression on the women who left that night on the train for St Louis. Fifty years after the trip, a fellow traveller looked back on the excursion and remembered Barry fondly. Peggy Watt was in her seventies when, upon request, she committed her memories to paper, stretching back five decades to recall when she was one of sixteen women who travelled to St Louis to cover the World's Fair. "I can't forgo the temptation to single out Françoise," Watt wrote, "a brilliant journalist who ran her own paper and who captivated all of us with her charm, ready wit, and sheer joy of living."[32]

All Aboard

He was more than a friend. He was the father of the press club.
We were always his girls.
– Irene Currie Love.[1]

Windsor Station bustled with more activity than usual the night of 16 June 1904. A large crowd gathered to wish a hearty bon voyage to the party of female journalists who were leaving on their trip.[2] Canadian Pacific Railway publicity agent George Ham enthusiastically greeted the women and their well-wishers. Ham loved his role as the public face of the CPR and never stopped devising ways to draw attention to the company. The newspapers, he knew, would carry reports of the evening's send-off in the next day's morning editions, and he smiled inwardly at the prospect.

Six feet tall and wearing his trademark felt bowler hat, George Henry Ham, at fifty-six, exuded amicability as he ambled among the women journalists, who were attired in their finest clothes, their upswept hairdos and elaborate hats adding inches to their height. In 1904, hats were an essential, often with veils attached. The women also wore floor-length skirts and tailored suit jackets with a loose blouse underneath called a shirtwaist, a practical and comfortable option for a working woman and quite a departure from the fitted bodices previously worn under dresses. Revealing the ankle was still taboo, but skirts were just starting to rise enough to show the tops of shoes.[3]

Dressed in his customary suit of plain grey tweed, Ham was usually weighted down with cigars for male journalists on press trips,[4] but gifts of a different nature awaited this party of women and he couldn't wait to show them off. He had arranged for a stylish new sleeper car to transport the female journalists to St Louis, with an escort of three CPR officials. The genial C.E.E. Ussher, general passenger agent of the road, would board along with Ham in Montreal, while assistant general passenger agent A.H. Notman would join the party in Toronto.

Kate Simpson Hayes made light of the manner in which the three railway men had been recruited for the trip. "The men fled at mention of a carload of 'Angels!'" she wrote in the *Manitoba Free Press*. "They had carried live weight hogs, western cattle, baled hay, gallons of beer, firewood, Chinamen and Injuns, and were ready to do duty again, but take a carload of women across the way betwixt Montreal and St Louis? No siree! Every man-Jack of 'em defaulted."[5]

Only one man had the nerve to accept the assignment. That man, wrote Hayes, was George Ham. "He said: 'I am bald-headed. My will is made. I have been through wars and rumours of wars. I have lived on pemmican and served through a Fenian raid and two rebellions, my life is of little value, let me go!'" Seeing his resolute attitude, C.E.E. Ussher came forward as well and said: "Let me go, too. I have had it foretold in the Book of Fate that I am to be the victim of a fearful encounter; let it come now!" Watching his colleagues make a courageous sacrifice, A.H. Notman stepped up to join his fellows: "Let me go! I am afraid to allow two unattended officials to go into this danger. Let me go to watch over the two brave sons of the iron way!"

The heroic railway men and their charges would make the trip in the sleeper car called *Trudeau*, the newest on the line, part of a series of six cars built in 1903 and all named for CPR stations beginning with the letter "T." Trudeau station, at the time, was situated on the Heron Bay subdivision in northern Ontario.

The new cars were richly appointed. *Trudeau*'s plush seats were uphol-
stered in a tasteful *vert réséda*, a mix of olive and emerald green, a small
detail that would certainly have appealed to faithful followers of fashion at
that time as the colour was in the height of style. Interior walls of the car
were panelled in mahogany, and spacious bathrooms at either end of the
sleeper were roomy and modern. *Trudeau* contained a smoking room (designated for "gentlemen" since few "ladies" dared smoke in public at the time)
as well as an enclosed stateroom that offered extra sleeping berths, a cushy
sofa, and a private toilet. The car had seating capacity for sixty, allowing
ample room for the women to spread out. At night, the seats folded down
to create a bed on the lower level, while a bed on high could be pulled down
from the ceiling wall. All the amenities made *Trudeau* a palace on wheels, "a
little masterpiece of elegance and good taste," as one presswoman described
it.[6] (See illustration 3.)

Ham looked at his watch and began counting heads: eleven women were
departing from Montreal and five more would be picked up along the route
at stops in Toronto, Woodstock, and London. He was eager for the trip to
get under way. He had already traversed the same terrain with a group of
male journalists earlier in the spring, and, while he regularly travelled across
the continent every year, Ham knew this excursion would be different. With
this batch of journalists, the CPR could reach a new audience, predominantly
female. Since women made most purchasing decisions for the family, stories
written by the presswomen on this trip – stories that would circulate around
North America – might entice readers south of the border to explore their
northern neighbour. And they would at the very least expose thousands of
readers (and potential clients) to the joys of long-distance travel on the CPR.

Ham's own path to the CPR began in Trenton, Ontario, where he was
born in 1847. His father was a country doctor who gave up medicine to study
law. It was suggested that young George also study law after graduating
from university, but, instead, he turned to newspaper work on the *Whitby
Chronicle* in the town in which he had been raised. His decision to shun the
law profession, as Ham humorously noted in his memoirs, was tied to a visit

he made to his grandfather as a youth. The older man wished to make his will without the knowledge of the rest of the family, so he asked George to draw up the document. George did as requested, but he wasn't sure he had used the proper legal terminology. To make certain, he rode eighteen miles by horseback to see a lawyer whom he knew through his father. "He pronounced the will to be perfectly legal," Ham remembered, "and, having all of $2.00 in my pocket, I rather ostentatiously asked him his fee. 'Nothing,' he smilingly replied. 'Nothing at all – we never charge the profession anything – never.'" The young man pondered the ease with which he'd drawn up a will with no training at all: "I thought if it was so blamed easy to be a lawyer, I wanted something harder."[7]

That "something harder" turned out to be newspaper work. After brief stints at small papers in Ontario, in 1875 Ham headed west to Winnipeg, where he worked for the city's earliest newspapers. He also dabbled in Winnipeg politics as a city councillor and as a school board trustee. A defender of the CPR and its policies in his writing, Ham probably drew the attention of railway boss Sir William Van Horne through his newspaper columns.[8] In 1891, Van Horne offered him a job, and, before the term had been invented, Ham became the first "PR man" for the railway.

On the night of 16 June 1904, George Ham led the presswomen onto the platform at Windsor Station in preparation for the ten o'clock departure. Robertine Barry, whom he certainly knew by reputation if not personally, introduced him to the seven other women who were representing the French press. The contingent belonged to a segment of French-Canadian society notable for its contributions to culture. Most of the women were part of the artistic elite in Montreal, the members of which formed a tight circle and knew each other through family ties or professional connections.

Half the women in the French-speaking contingent were published journalists, but half were not. Nevertheless, even the novices had secured bona fide credentials, no doubt through Robertine Barry, and they planned to cover the World's Fair as journalists. For the most part, the newspapers for which they worked were organs of the Liberal Party or the Conservative Party, and, at the turn of the last century, the provincial members of these parties were not distinguishable from their federal counterparts.[9] The Liberals were in power in Quebec at the time (as they were federally) and they remained at the helm provincially until 1936.

On the railway platform that evening, Robertine Barry presented the Quebecers to George Ham. Just shy of her forty-fourth birthday and the oldest woman in the French-speaking contingent, Cécile Laberge represented the Quebec City daily newspaper *Le Soleil*, created in December 1896 by Liberal Party backers. Laberge's coverage of the St Louis World's Fair for *Le Soleil* marked her first venture as a reporter.

Likewise for Antoinette Gérin-Lajoie, thirty-four, who had secured an assignment from another Quebec City daily, *L'Événement*, a vibrant newspaper founded as a Conservative mouthpiece in 1867. The circulation of *L'Événement* hovered around seven thousand at the time of the trip.

Another fledgling journalist, Amintha Plouffe, thirty-four, represented *Le Journal*, a Montreal daily started in 1899 by politician Louis Beaubien and other prominent French-Canadian members of the Conservative Party but now in the hands of wealthy financier Rodolphe Forget, founder of the Banque Internationale du Canada.[10] *Le Journal* featured long articles and no illustrations, making it more like the political press of the nineteenth century than the consumer-oriented press of the early twentieth century embodied by *La Patrie* or *La Presse*.

Robertine Barry may have suspected that the fourth novice journalist in the French-Canadian contingent might never write a word about the trip. She recruited twenty-six-year-old Alice Asselin, the youngest among the Quebecers, because her husband, Olivar, was a rising star on the journalism scene and owned a weekly newspaper called *Le Nationaliste*, which he had founded three months before the trip was called.

The remaining four women in the French-speaking contingent, including Barry, had long-standing ties in the journalism field and were well known in Quebec. Léonise Valois, thirty-five, who used the pseudonym "Attala," (she later dropped one "t" from her penname), would file stories for *Le Canada*, a fledgling Montreal daily founded in 1903 as an organ of the Liberal Party. Though not as prominent as Barry, Valois was nevertheless an established pioneer. She had first published at the age of twenty-one, when Édouard-Zotique Massicotte, the young assistant editor of *Recueil littéraire*, opened the pages to women. Massicotte later hired Valois in 1900 to write and edit the Woman's Page at the prestigious weekly cultural magazine *Le Monde illustré*, and he presented her in strong terms to his readers. "We have entrusted this page to Mademoiselle Attala, whose knowledge and literary talent will be greatly appreciated by our readers," wrote Massicotte: "Her pseudonym hardly veils one of our more gracious feminine pens and we believe she will please our many readers."[11] Léo, as family members affectionately called Valois, made a place for stimulating ideas on her page, alongside traditional subjects like homemaking.[12] She lobbied for the rights of women in her "talks" with readers, advanced the notion of celibacy, and did not shy away from tackling thorny issues, including the "delicate subject" of family inheritance: "Is there any reason why a father and a mother, whose affection and solicitude seems evenly divided amongst all their children, act in a manner so biased and unfair to certain descendants? As usual, in the sharing of family assets, it is the sisters who are disadvantaged to the benefit of their brothers."[13]

Sent to a prestigious convent boarding school in Beauharnois due to the generosity of a wealthy cousin – where she learned English and started writing poetry – Léonise Valois may have been expected to make an impressive marriage with her fine education. But her relatives deemed a budding romance with a law student unacceptable, and her suitor, Rodolphe Lemieux, who would later become postmaster general under Prime Minister Sir Wilfrid Laurier, married someone else.[14] Valois firmly rejected subsequent family pressure to marry her off. "I made a vow to die an old maid rather than not be able to give all my soul to my husband, with confidence and happiness," she told her sister, who was encouraging a match with a widower around the same time that Valois began writing for *Le Monde illustré*: "How lucky I am! And how I bless my pen and my steps each day that assure my daily bread and make me proud of my own work."[15]

Léonise Valois oversaw the Woman's Page from 1900 to 1902 but lost her post when *Le Monde illustré* changed from a literary journal to a publication that emphasized illustration. She then wrote poetry and prose for *La Patrie* and *Le Journal de Françoise*, but occasional work did not provide a steady income. By taking an assignment to cover the St Louis World's Fair for the newspaper *Le Canada*, she probably hoped to secure a permanent position.

Léonise Valois bonded tightly in St Louis with Anne-Marie Gleason, twenty-nine, a rising star at *La Patrie* who was writing under the penname "Madeleine." Gleason's earliest journalistic work was published in the *Courrier de Rimouski*, a newspaper in her hometown. She then worked for *Le Temps*, a French newspaper in Ottawa, before replacing Robertine Barry in 1901 at *La Patrie*. Gleason and Barry were good friends, and they shared a similar heritage. They were both daughters of an Irish-born father and a French-Canadian mother. Like many female journalists at the time, Anne-Marie Gleason harboured loftier literary aspirations, and she had already written a play.[16]

The last member of the French-speaking contingent to arrive at Windsor Station could hardly catch her breath. Marie Beaupré represented *La Presse*, the undisputed circulation leader in French Canada. The newspaper built its readership under Trefflé Berthiaume, a former printer, who made wide use of sensational news and daring stunts, techniques popular in England and the United States. For example, *La Presse* set out to prove that the St Lawrence River was navigable all year round, and it did so by recruiting volunteers who successfully bashed through the ice in a boat they had re-christened *La Presse*.[17]

On first blush, Marie Beaupré seemed an unlikely choice to cover the World's Fair for a brash paper like *La Presse*. At age thirty-two, she was a poetic soul with a scholarly bent whose heartfelt prose read more like poetry. But *La Presse* also saw itself as the voice of the oppressed and the working person, and, under her nom-de-plume "Hélène Dumont," Beaupré had recently written an emotional article for a church-sponsored publication, *Le Foyer*, about the perils visited upon young women who were labouring in factories for too many hours at too little pay.

Marie Beaupré arrived at the train fresh from a whirlwind fiftieth anniversary celebration at Villa Maria Convent School, a private girls' school that still exists today on the western slope of Mount Royal. The school's festive Golden Jubilee had attracted hundreds of graduates from all over North America, and Beaupré remained deeply attached to the school more than a decade after graduating. Raised in rural Quebec, and the granddaughter (on her father's side) of the founder and first mayor of Sainte-Julienne de Rawdon, she had been sent to Villa Maria when her widowed mother remarried into a prosperous Montreal family.[18] She was fourteen years old at the time, shy, and unaccustomed to city life. "Raised in the countryside, I had taken on a few rough habits. Timid and proud by nature, I did not dare to step forward. In the middle of a large animated class, I found myself isolated," Beaupré confided in an autobiography that students were asked to write before graduation.[19] Her isolation was short-lived: she bloomed intellectually under the guidance of the Sisters, dedicating her autobiography "to all my wonderful teachers, a feeble tribute from a heart that remembers."[20] Fluent in French, English and Italian, she not only wrote for newspapers and magazines, but she translated documents for the federal government's department of public works, which paid handsomely at $1.50 a page.[21] At the Golden Jubilee celebrations the day before the women left for St Louis, Marie Beaupré had been recognized as a distinguished grad and asked to make a speech to dignitaries and invited guests.[22]

Marie Beaupré completed the French-speaking contingent, and, as she shared her reunion experience with her French colleagues, the last member of the travelling party from Montreal made her way onto the platform at Windsor Station. English-speaking journalist Katherine Angelina Hughes, twenty-seven, a lively conversationalist with a sprightly sense of humour, represented the largest circulating paper in Canada at the time, the *Montreal Daily Star*.[23] The paper was an imperialist organ owned and co-founded in 1869 by Hugh Graham, who relished fighting the establishment and cast his newspaper as the champion of the masses.[24] It was an approach that would have appealed to Katherine Hughes.

A native of Prince Edward Island, Katherine Hughes possessed a missionary zeal that infused all her work. Before becoming a journalist, she had spent several years teaching youngsters on the Mohawk reserve in St Regis,

Getting Acquainted

At the end of a few moments of lively conversation, we had already formed a family with one heartfelt desire: to be as agreeable with one another as possible, which led to the most perfect harmony throughout the voyage.

– Amintha Plouffe, *Le Journal*, 2 July 1904

Well into the night, as the train headed west through Quebec and into Ontario, the eleven women got to know one another. All the French-Canadian women understood English and most spoke it well, although a few were a bit embarrassed about their speaking skills. The three English-speaking women on the train, born and raised in the Maritimes, may not have been completely fluent in French. Nevertheless, conversation flowed freely between the Quebecers and the others.

A topic almost surely discussed was the grim news of the day. As the press party left Thursday night, Montreal newspapers were reporting that at least five hundred people had perished in a fire aboard the *General Slocum*, a steamboat carrying twelve hundred passengers on a pleasure trip along Manhattan's East River the day before. The *Montreal Daily Star* predicted that the grisly death count could double, and, indeed, the final tally exceeded one thousand.

For Cécile Laberge, assigned to cover the St Louis World's Fair for the newspaper *Le Soleil*, a discussion about accidents at sea likely triggered heart-breaking memories. Her younger brother Émile, a budding virtuoso

Quebec.[25] A devout Irish Catholic whose maternal uncle served as arch-bishop of Halifax for over two decades, Hughes attended Normal School in Charlottetown, graduated with a teacher's licence in 1892, and later plunged wholeheartedly into work on the reserve, at one point asking church fathers to help her form an association that would place Aboriginal graduates "out in the world, even for a few years ... in competition with the white race."[26] Hughes's mix of zeal and compassion for Aboriginal peoples would surface in the story she wrote about the fair for the *Montreal Daily Star.*

With the arrival of Katherine Hughes, the entire Montreal press party was now complete, and George Ham yelled, "All aboard!" Saying a final "bon voyage" and "au revoir," the eleven women took their places inside the train. The engine blew its loud good-bye, and friends and relatives waved from the platform as the train began to slowly fade from view. A photographer captured the departure with a flash-lit camera, and Ham beamed as the bulb popped.

From the start, Ham wanted to create a warm welcome for the journalists and impress them with the attributes of the CPR. He could see the women were pleased as they began to examine their new surroundings in detail. "The well lighted and luxurious sleeper," wrote Kate Simpson Hayes, "presented a sight of home-like comfort to those of us who had, that day, spent twenty-five hours of the twenty-four 'doing up' blouses, mending gloves, darning stockings, and trimming hats for the wonderful voyage of discovery."

The first sight that greeted their eyes was a daintily set table in the car laden with a tempting ladies' tea served on fine china. Sandwiches and cake surrounded a floral centrepiece. The women oohed and aahed, just as George Ham had intended. He jokingly told the women to call him "Papa Ham" and proceeded to make introductions all around as the women made themselves comfortable, pouring tea and cutting the cake, clearly thrilled to be the first female journalists to participate in "a race to the unknown," as Amintha Plouffe put it. Lively conversation ensued, and the hours between departure and dawn seemed to fly by.

who had been sent to Belgium to study music as a teenager, was never heard from again after a ship he boarded in Antwerp bound for Quebec City for a visit home apparently hit an iceberg in its second day at sea.[1]

As the women on the train became acquainted, the most notable difference between them concerned their professional status: four of the French-Canadian women were part of the artistic elite rather than journalists. Related to musicians and writers, these women were primarily supporters of culture, although in some cases they had sufficient talent to become practitioners themselves. For example, Cécile Laberge, like her late brother, was a musical prodigy, blessed with a beautiful voice and outstanding ability on the piano. Her Belgian-born father Jules Hone was a noted composer and professor of music but struggled to make a living in Quebec when the economy crashed in the late 1870s. With seven children to support, he feared he would lose the family home.[2] So Cécile taught piano lessons to augment the family income, and, in the midst of the financial crisis, at age eighteen, she married Napoléon Lefebvre, a wealthy jeweller and watchmaker many years her senior. The couple had two daughters before Napoléon died in the early 1890s.[3]

Cécile then decided to return to music, making it the central force in her life. In her words, the musical scene in Montreal at the end of the nineteenth century "was one of fiery enthusiasm and burning ardour among both musicians and audiences alike." She joined the fledgling Ladies' Morning Musical Club, a group of female classical music lovers, both French- and English-speaking, who met every Thursday morning. She wrote that the club "seem[ed] destined to be a patriotic organization fusing two races of Canadian women in their common love of music."[4]

In 1894, Cécile married Dr Jules Laberge, a surgeon and the love of her life, who died suddenly before the turn of the century.[5] At the time of the trip, she lived on St Denis Street close to Robertine Barry. It is unclear whether she hoped to become a regular contributor to *Le Soleil* after the trip to the World's Fair. Perhaps she toyed with the idea of becoming a music critic at some point and saw the St Louis assignment as a way to open the door to newspaper work.

Maybe Antoinette Gérin-Lajoie was also experimenting with journalism as a possible career when she accepted the invitation to go to St Louis and write for the Quebec daily *L'Événement*. Gérin-Lajoie shared strong ties with Cécile Laberge, although she was almost ten years younger. They were related through marriage, Gérin-Lajoie's sister having married Laberge's brother in 1898, thus merging two powerfully artistic Quebec families.

Antoinette Gérin-Lajoie seemed destined to write. Her maternal grandfather, Étienne Parent, served as the fearless editor of the newspaper *Le Canadien* in the early 1800s.[6] Her father, Antoine Gérin-Lajoie, also a journalist, left an enduring legacy with his classic novel *Jean Rivard*, which venerates the rural agrarian society in Quebec.[7] He was still regarded as a literary giant in 1904, more than two decades after his death.

As Antoinette Gérin-Lajoie enjoyed tea and sandwiches with the female journalists bound for St Louis, she seemed to be following a literary path. Born in Ottawa, where her talented father oversaw the Library of Parliament, she was educated in the capital city at a convent, where she won several academic prizes. She was a competent writer in French and English. The three articles she would write about the World's Fair were so greatly appreciated by *L'Événement* that assistant editor Jean-Baptiste Dumont told Gérin-Lajoie that he would welcome any future contribution.[8] She could have easily stepped into her father's shoes had she so desired. But, following the trip to St Louis, Gérin-Lajoie's life took a different turn.

The third novice journalist on the trip, Amintha Plouffe, also had a connection to the cultural elite. A dramatic photo of her sister, a celebrated pianist, had graced the cover of the Quebec cultural journal *Le Monde illustré*. Eva Plouffe was posed on a cane chair with a velvet cushion, wearing a low-cut ruffled gown, a hat with a plume, and multiple strands of pearls cascading from her neck. Older sister Amintha possessed no such glamorous profile. She was listed in the city directory as a stenographer – a job, interestingly enough, that many aspiring journalists, men and women alike, used at that time as a springboard into professional journalism.[9]

It is probable that Amintha Plouffe hoped to become a journalist, and it is also probable that Robertine Barry believed she could help her break into the field by granting her a place on the train. Plouffe would write a clear and well-organized narrative about the St Louis Fair for *Le Journal*, but there is no sign that her effort led to further employment. *Le Journal* folded in March of 1905, and Amintha Plouffe continued to be listed as a stenographer in the city directory for decades to come.

Oddly enough, the fourth novice journalist in the French-speaking contingent, Alice Le Boutillier Asselin, whose elder sister made a name for herself as a celebrated soprano in Quebec, could also claim a cultural connection. Asselin came from a family of wealth and influence. Her grandfather, John Le Boutillier, emigrated to Quebec from the Isle of Jersey to become a powerful economic and political force in the Gaspé, employing hundreds in his cod-fishing enterprise and serving three terms in the Quebec Legislative Assembly as a Conservative politician. Her father Charles had the opportunity to meet some of Canada's most illustrious political figures at the family manor in the 1860s, including George-Étienne Cartier, George Brown, and John A. Macdonald, as they debated the creation of Canada.[10]

But when the family fortune declined precipitously, Charles's children had to make their own way. Convent-educated Alice moved to Montreal, where she became one of the first female secretaries at city hall.[11] She married journalist Olivar Asselin in 1902, and the following year they had a son. Although the couple travelled in rarefied circles, consorting with the political and cultural elite, the family's financial stability would be thrown into a precarious state when, shortly before the trip to St Louis, Olivar started his own weekly newspaper. Published every Sunday, *Le Nationaliste* served as the mouthpiece for the Nationalist League, which promoted Canadian autonomy from Britain and an exclusively Canadian policy regarding economic and intellectual development. Olivar would become one of the most influential journalists in Quebec, and *Le Nationaliste* would serve as the template for *Le Devoir*, a newspaper that continues today.[12]

Although Alice Asselin had never written a word for a publication at the time of the St Louis excursion, she was surrounded by journalistic influences. Moreover, several women on the trip were nascent writers whose skills needed to be developed. Perhaps Asselin had that potential as well, given her family background, fine education, and journalistic connections.[13] But other issues made her inclusion in the trip to St Louis extremely surprising.

The couple's one-year-old son had Down Syndrome – then know as Mongolism – and Olivar, devoted to his newspaper work, kept irregular hours and was often absent. Travelling to St Louis to cover the World's Fair would seem a far-fetched venture for Asselin. In fact, her descendants never heard a word about the trip from family members and did not believe she had actually gone to St Louis until shown a photograph identifying her and fellow travellers.[14]

As Alice Asselin sipped tea in the sleeper car *Trudeau* and conversed with the other women, something else made her inclusion even more unusual. She was pregnant, although she may not have known it when she boarded the train in Montreal. Seven months after the trip, she would give birth to her second child. She would neither write about the fair nor be affiliated with presswomen in a professional capacity after the trip. But, in an interesting twist, she would pass the baton, in the form of a press credential, to her sister Eva Le Boutillier, who would join the women journalists on their next press trip in 1906.

Crossing the Border

It is an object lesson in every line of work in the world. It is a
European tour and sightseeing jaunt brought to your threshold.
Go and see it if you would know and learn what time has done
for us, and what we are doing for posterity.
– Kate Simpson Hayes, *Manitoba Free Press*, 2 July 1904

On 17 June 1904, shortly before half-past seven in the morning, the train
carrying eleven women journalists pulled into the old Union Station in Toronto. Just two months before, the Great Toronto Fire had shaken the city,
destroying more than one hundred buildings in the downtown commercial
and industrial district. Fire did not damage the train station, but flames
came very close. Traces of the destructive blaze were still evident as the
most famous female journalist in Canada, Kathleen Blake Coleman of the
Mail and Empire, stepped aboard the sleeper car *Trudeau* in Toronto and
joined the spirited group of travellers. Along with her came Mary Adelaide
Dawson, the attractive "Angel of the Telegram," as Kate Simpson Hayes
described the young woman (Kate would sometimes apply the term "angel"
to females in general).[1] The third woman to join the travelling party in Toronto was Grace Denison, long-time editorial staff member and columnist
for *Saturday Night*, then a weekly newspaper devoted to public affairs and
the arts. Along with the three women came CPR assistant passenger agent
A.H. Notman, who hoisted a large box onto the train.

Soon after the train pulled out of the station, Notman opened his giant parcel to reveal a mass of carnations and roses, dew still clinging to their petals and leaves. The passenger agent presented a floral bouquet to each woman. As George Ham anticipated, the women were charmed. Breakfast was readied in the dining car, and, while the women arranged themselves around a number of small tables adorned with glistening silver and cut glass, the new arrivals were introduced all around.[2]

Although she kept her age a mystery, Grace Elizabeth Denison was the oldest woman in the travelling party. She was fifty, but few would have guessed it from her infinite energy and ingrained work ethic.[3] Denison not only kept her age a secret but also other details of her life. In the circles in which she travelled as a society columnist it had been whispered that she and her husband were estranged, but few knew this with certainty. Although Denison continued to use her married name and the title of "Mrs," husband and wife had no contact.[4]

In her column for *Saturday Night,* Grace Denison wrote under the penname "Lady Gay," an incongruous pseudonym for a woman whom writer and colleague Hector Charlesworth described as seemingly "predestined to sorrow."[5] Yet even her co-workers could not agree on the origin of the penname. Charlesworth, a colleague for more than twenty years at *Saturday Night,* backed up the assertion of loyal readers, who believed the name derived from a fictional heroine in Dion Boucicault's comedy *London Assurance,* in which the heroine is a witty woman with the unlikely name of Lady Gay Spanker.[6] But another colleague insisted that Denison told her the name had been bestowed in childhood by a little brother, who could not pronounce the name "Grace."[7] Whichever way it came about, the name takes on a certain irony considering Lady Gay's life.

Daughter of Anglican archdeacon Francis William Sandys and the eldest of six children, Grace Elizabeth Sandys Denison was born and educated in Chatham, Ontario, and attended Hellmuth College in London, Ontario. A talented and versatile writer whose crisp prose reads well even today, Denison freelanced widely but did not become a full-time journalist until her late thirties, when she began an unbroken two-decade stint on *Saturday Night*, editing the society page and contributing a weekly column.

Grace Denison's most celebrated work before landing a job at *Saturday Night* recounts an audacious solo voyage to Europe, where she followed an unconventional route through the Netherlands, Austria, Germany, Hungary, and Switzerland. Canadian travellers to Europe at that time usually headed for Britain and France, with Italy and Palestine as secondary destinations, and, while Denison did visit France on the way home, she chose a vastly different path for most of her trip, travelling lightly, as a modern backpacker might see Europe today.[8] Her book, *A Happy Holiday*, published in 1890, starts with a sceptical friend questioning her decision to forego a trunk or valise and travel like a *voyageur* with a simple satchel she had fashioned herself. In her breezy prose, Denison describes the carryall upon which she was then sewing the finishing touches: "It was as elastic as a Congressman's conscience, and as neat as a Quaker's bonnet, and when the umbrella and parasol were slipped into their pockets, the carryall rolled and buttoned, and a handsome shawlstrap buckled securely round over all, I felt that my baggage would cause me not a fear nor a frown the long summer through" (n.p.).

As she joined the group bound for St Louis, Grace Denison was both a seasoned traveller and a reputed journalist. As a high-profile society columnist for the influential weekly *Saturday Night*, she mixed and mingled with the cream of Toronto's elite. The year before the trip, she had edited a book of recipes featuring contributions from Mrs Goldwin Smith and Mrs Timothy Eaton. Denison not only covered the social set, she appeared to be part of it, even throwing debutante parties.[9]

Yet she carried an underlying sadness that she shared sparingly and that countered the carefree image conveyed by her nom-de-plume. As a young woman, according to Hector Charlesworth, Grace Denison had been deeply in love with a man who died accidentally the day before they were to marry. To assuage her grief, she wrote a novel, which was accepted by a publishing firm. But a fire destroyed the sole copy of the manuscript and she had found it impossible to start anew and recreate what had disappeared. Later, she had made an unhappy marriage that, to her great regret, produced no children.[10] Harbouring a deep maternal instinct, she had become a mother figure to writers at *Saturday Night* and generously gave advice and money to young women who admired her position and wanted to follow in her path.

On the morning of 17 June, as George Ham introduced Grace Denison over the rattle of teacups in the dining car, she commanded attention, especially from the younger women on the train. She had travelled widely, been a journalist for decades, and already covered a world's fair. She would willingly share her wisdom later on the trip and would greatly enjoy St Louis, writing favourably about it for *Saturday Night*. But she would balk when it came to joining the women in a pivotal decision they would make later.

Much younger than Grace Denison, twenty-four-year-old Mary Adelaide Dawson represented the *Evening Telegram*, an arch-conservative newspaper whose political bent would later be reflected in her article about the fair. An odd-looking newspaper by today's standards, the first three pages contained only classified ads and no stories at all, except for an editorial cartoon that appeared above the fold on the front page. The classifieds were a huge attraction from the moment the paper was founded in 1876, and hundreds of men would gather outside the *Evening Telegram* office eagerly awaiting the paper each evening.[11] The *Evening Telegram* possessed a moralistic tone that made it "the stern maiden of Toronto's virtues."[12] But its most distinguishing characteristic, and a key to its success, was a relentless emphasis on local news. This was imposed by editor John Ross Robertson, a champion of civic parochialism. The paper consistently played down foreign or national news to focus on Toronto's backyard, including city council, the water commission, the hospital, local amusements, local sports, and local crime. It was a successful formula. Within a decade, it became the largest circulating paper in the city.[13] The St Louis World's Fair, while not in Toronto's backyard, was a chance to extol Canadian virtues, and when its female writer, Mary Adelaide Dawson, was offered the opportunity to go, the editors likely relished the chance to boost Canada's contribution to the exposition.

Mary Dawson joined the *Evening Telegram* in 1901. Born in Lambton, in southwestern Ontario, she was an Anglican by upbringing and the daughter of an excise inspector for the Canadian government. Like other reporters for the *Evening Telegram*, Dawson would not receive a byline for her story about the fair, a common practice at the time. Her article ran with the words "From Our Own Reporter" in parenthesis under the headline "Ripple from St Louis." A subhead hinted at the angle Dawson would take in the story and mirrored the insular tone of the paper in general: "Some Reflections by One Who Went the Rounds – Canadians Have No Need to Feel Small." In her coverage, Mary Dawson singled out all things Canadian for lavish praise and disdained anything that bore a foreign imprint.

Whether she agreed with the paper's parochial views or not, Mary Dawson would soon forge a life-long attachment to the *Evening Telegram* when, in 1908, she married its then city editor, C.H.J. Snider. As a journalist, her biggest scoop would come years after the trip, when she managed to gain exclusive interviews with survivors of the *Titanic*. In the years ahead, Dawson, who never had children and who worked as a journalist until she died, would become strongly invested in the advancement of women journalists and would twice serve as president of the Toronto branch of the Canadian Women's Press Club.

The leading lady in the entire cast of female characters on the train was clearly Irish native Kathleen Blake Coleman, born Catherine Ferguson but known to thousands of readers simply as "Kit." The most accomplished female journalist of her day, she carried considerable clout as a magnet for readers of the *Mail and Empire*, one of Canada's largest papers. Her columns and perceptive replies to readers seeking advice were avidly read by men as well as women, a fact noted in a publicity brochure prepared in 1896 by the *Mail and Empire*, which included Coleman's photo along with those of the paper's other prominent journalists, all male. Her column was, according to the brochure, "acknowledged to be unexcelled on this continent."

An avid reporter and an eloquent writer, Coleman was strikingly attractive, with chestnut gold hair and violet eyes. She was sometimes compared to actress Sarah Bernhardt,[14] whom she considered a friend. Whenever the French tragedienne visited Canada, according to Charlesworth, she would meet with Coleman.[15]

Married in Ireland at a young age to a wealthy older man, Coleman was left penniless when her husband died suddenly and his family disinherited her.[16] She went to work as a governess, spending some time in France before arriving in Canada in 1884, where she proceeded to reinvent herself in stages, changing her name from Catherine to Kathleen, slicing off eight years from her age, and ultimately creating an intriguing persona for herself in print.

A few years after landing in Toronto as an immigrant, Kit Coleman penned two articles for *Saturday Night* that drew the attention of Christopher W. Bunting, who ran the newsroom at Toronto's *Daily Mail*. He hired Coleman in 1890 to write "Woman's Kingdom," a page of lively editorial commentary paired with answers to questions from readers, which appeared in the Saturday paper. The advice column proved hugely popular, and Coleman received questions from correspondents around the world.

Kit Coleman married two more times in Canada, first to Englishman Edward J. Watkins, with whom she had two children, and who may have been a bigamist.[17] When that marriage ended, she dropped the name "Watkins" and again enhanced the reinvention process by adding the name "Blake."[18] She remarried in 1898 to medical doctor Theobald Coleman. Between marriages, making ends meet proved difficult. The top female journalist of her era, Kit Coleman likely earned no more than thirty-five dollars a week at her peak. At one point, she was forced to augment her income by doing light housekeeping in order to support herself and her children.[19] Like Grace Denison, with whom she had a friendship, Kit Coleman was coy about her age. She was really forty-eight when the train pulled out of the station in Toronto for St Louis, which made her a few months older than Kate Simpson Hayes and thus, behind Grace Denison, the second oldest woman on the train.[20]

Early in her newspaper career with the Toronto *Daily Mail* (which became the *Mail and Empire* when the papers merged in 1895), Kit Coleman conjured in print what proved to be an ingenious impression. She created an androgynous persona whose double-sided nature not only allowed her to keep readers of both sexes guessing but also permitted her to widen her range of topics.[21] And she wrote about everything. Coleman changed subjects frequently within the same column: she would make caustic remarks about inept politicians or the lack of ethics among Canadian businessmen, jump to a celebrity interview, include a fashion tip, and then suddenly make a trenchant observation, stating, for example, that husbands and wives dining out together rarely spoke to each other, brightening only when a third party joined them.[22]

Her readers, with good reason, puzzled over whether "Kit" was a man or a woman. At first she kept them keep guessing. Hired to lure female readers with tips on household matters and fashion, as were other women journalists of that era, Kathleen Blake Coleman transcended the confines of the Woman's Page, writing about subjects outside the domestic realm. Many women who entered journalism at the time were frustrated by the restrictions placed upon them by editors who believed that women were interested in reading only about lighter matters.[23] Kit Coleman was among a handful of female writers who, at the turn of the century, were able to overcome the restrictions on women and take on weightier subjects, probably because her colourful copy and pithy down-to-earth advice drew a vast audience.

Kit Coleman became internationally famous for covering the 1898 Spanish-American War from Cuba. She was the first woman in the world to be accredited as a war correspondent, although biographer Barbara Freeman notes that, in keeping with the lack of status women then had in the profession, her role in Cuba was secondary to those of male war correspondents.[24] Nevertheless, her daring persona made her an object of fascination to her devoted readers, who showed her such affection that, when she boldly published a reader's letter that criticized her, a barrage of loyal followers wrote laudatory letters in her defence.

Her presence on the trip to St Louis certainly conferred prestige on the venture as Kit Coleman was the celebrity journalist of her day. Writing for one of the top circulating newspapers in the country, Coleman drew legions of female readers. But she drew male readers as well, including Prime Minister Laurier, who invited her to be his guest at a ceremony at Buckingham Palace when she was in London to cover Queen Victoria's Diamond Jubilee celebration in 1897.[25] Men and women alike were eager to read her frank and insightful comments on subjects that ranged from personal hygiene to theology, from stain removal to spousal abuse. On that subject Kit strongly advised one reader, who had described her life with an violent husband, to leave immediately and move in with a relative. "No woman could live with such a fiend as you describe."[26]

When Kit Coleman stepped aboard the train to St Louis, her star power resonated. "Kit deserves a paragraph to her splendid self," Kate Simpson Hayes told readers of the *Manitoba Free Press*:

> When you read Kit's clever page you know you are listening to a woman of brains, but it is when you meet and know her you under-stand you are face to face with a Woman of Heart! Is she dark? Is she fair? She is most fair to see – a splendid type of the Irish gentlewoman of the Shamrock land, with the birr of the Kerry hills still clinging to her tongue. She is a linguist, a scholar, and a royal good fellow! She has the humor of her race and the dignity of her ancestors. She is a woman of genius, one of the most brilliant conversationalists of the day and as lovable as she is kind. That is a pen-picture of "Kit" as she appeared to us.

Kit Coleman certainly appeared differently to Gertrude Balmer Watt, who came aboard the sleeper car in Woodstock when the train arrived at 10:44 that morning. Age twenty-five, married, and the mother of a young child, Watt had just started writing for the *Woodstock Sentinel-Review* a few months before the excursion, adopting the pseudonym "Peggy," a name she would use inside and outside the journalism profession.

Peggy Watt was the product of a marriage gone awry. Her father, sheriff John "Wild Jock" Hogg, shocked the townspeople in Woodstock when he came home from a European holiday married to a Spanish flamenco dan-cer. The couple had two daughters, but the marriage ended badly when the dancer ran off with an army officer who was passing through town with his unit. An embittered Hogg sent young Peggy and her little sister to Loretto Abbey in Hamilton, a Catholic school that boarded girls until they were young women.[27]

Loretto Abbey was a beautiful and well-lit Gothic-style school set on a hill. Peggy received excellent training from the nuns in poetry, elocution, drawing, vocal music, harp, and piano.[28] She then attended Brantford Young Ladies' College, a finishing school that offered further instruction in music and the fine arts. She harboured a desire to become a concert pianist but, instead, at a tea given by a family member, was introduced to Arthur Balmer Watt, a recent graduate of the University of Toronto who had edited the university's paper, *The Varsity*. The two married in 1900.

In 1904, Arthur Balmer Watt was editor of the *Woodstock Sentinel-Review* and Peggy assisted him by writing a column called "The Mirror" for the Woman's Page. As she boarded the train to St Louis, the statuesque and normally confident young woman was riddled with doubt. Not only would she be writing about the fair for the *Woodstock Sentinel-Review*, but she had also been asked, as were others on the trip, to write for a string of American publications as well. She wondered if she was up to the challenge. Another factor troubled her even more: the immediate prospect of meeting Kathleen Blake Coleman face to face. Peggy Watt was still reeling from a threatened libel suit that Coleman had pressed against the *Woodstock Sentinel-Review* over remarks that she had made in her column of 18 February 1904.

Feisty and opinionated, a hot mix of Spanish and Scottish blood, Peggy Watt was not afraid to challenge or contradict anything or anyone. But she sometimes did so without considering the consequences. She had taken issue with Kit Coleman's claim, in a column for the *Mail and Empire*, that her stay in Sudbury, where her husband had a medical practice in a mining camp, produced no happy hours and constituted "the three meanest years" of her life. Peggy Watt flat out did not believe her. Calling Coleman "an irresistible writer if at times a woman lacking in the best of taste," Watt wondered how three whole years could be all that "mean" when Coleman lived under the same roof with her husband and child. "Three years without a happy hour," Watt wrote, "without happiness and yet with husband and child! What then does constitute happiness to such a one? The giddy whirl, the round of social duties, the trivial pleasures? ... Kit is an amazingly clever woman, but is she a happy one? Throughout her writing there is an air of discontent, an idea conveyed that Life has played her many underhand [sic] tricks, that Fate has bound her to a man she doesn't love." While not addressing Coleman directly, Watt admonished her readers: "Don't whine in public unless you wish to appear vulgar. A certain amount of pride is a very desirable thing. To strive to be good and to cease endeavoring to cut an interesting figure before the public would be a good axiom for most of us to follow. Don't let there be any mean years in our lives."[29]

Kit responded by threatening legal action. In a letter dated 2 March 1904, lawyer Edward Meek, writing on behalf of Kit, accused the *Sentinel-Review* of defaming Kit and charged Peggy with malice. "[Peggy] wrote with the deliberate intention of lowering, defaming and injuring the personal or moral standing, character and reputation of Kit or Mrs Coleman, both personally and as a writer," Meek stated in the letter. He added that Peggy distorted the meaning and intention of Kit's writing in such a way as: "to make the reader think that Kit has a false, unwholesome and immoral conception of the meaning of home – and is devoid of the natural affections of a wife and mother ... Those who enjoy the pleasure of Mrs Coleman's acquaintance know that she lives happily with her husband and that she is an affectionate wife and loving mother."[30]

The *Sentinel-Review*, a small publication, had no money to defend a charge of libel in the courts. Arthur Balmer Watt had to go on bended knee and plead with Coleman and the paper to rescind the threat to sue.[31] He agreed to publish Meek's letter decrying Peggy's column in the *Woodstock Sentinel-Review* and to issue the following statement: "We regret that in the article in question certain inferences were drawn in respect to Mrs. Coleman which we are informed and have every reason to believe are not justified by fact and cheerfully retract anything that has been published in these columns which would lead one to believe that Mrs. Coleman's marital, domestic and family relationships are other than they should be."[32]

Though the matter had been settled, the experience devastated Watt, particularly because Coleman was the role model she herself aspired to become. She tried to pattern her page in the *Woodstock Sentinel-Review* on Coleman's "Women's Kingdom." And, on the train, at that moment, Peggy Watt dreaded their impending encounter. In fact, she had agonized over her decision to go to St Louis at all, nearly turning down the assignment because she did not want to face the mighty writer. "What would she do to me, the small town writer unknown beyond my paper's circulating territory, who had dared to tilt words with her, the topmost top of Canadian women journalists?" she later wrote.[33]

Peggy Watt took her seat on the train and was trembling as Kit Coleman came down the aisle of the car and paused by her seat. "You must be Peggy," Kit said, as Watt braced for a torrent of abuse. "You're just like what I thought you would be, young, impulsive and daring. I imagine we two will be great friends." Completely disarmed, Peggy Balmer Watt was speechless and greatly relieved. Kit Coleman's prophecy would prove accurate in the coming years.[34]

The train picked up its last passenger at 11:35 that morning in London, Ontario. Positioned geographically midway between Niagara Falls and Detroit, London sits at the heart of the richest agricultural district in Canada. But the precocious young woman climbing on board was a city girl. Irene Currie Love, age twenty-three, was one of six children born to Jessie Currie and Francis Love, a lawyer who became London's police magistrate in 1899. As a teenager, Irene attended London Collegiate Institute and distinguished herself by winning the school's first Diamond Ring Competition. The competition began when a prominent London Collegiate alumnus noticed that girls were often slighted when it came to academic prizes awarded at the year-end ceremonies. Tom Gillean, a prosperous jeweller in London, offered a diamond ring to the girl who wrote the best original essay. Currie Love won the inaugural prize for exhibiting the writing prowess that would eventually lead to a long career in journalism.

In 1903, a year before the St Louis trip, Irene Currie Love's skill with a pen was again acknowledged when she was asked by her alma mater to contribute her reminiscences to a special school publication that would be distributed at a reunion of returning grads. In her article for *The Collegiate*, Currie Love joked: "I felt like a feminine Methuselah as I sat down and recalled some of the times I had had in those 'halls of learning.'" She noted that her first three years at London Collegiate "were remarkable for the amount of work I didn't do and for the number of good times I had." Only in her final two years, she stated, did she settle down and get serious: "I had always hitherto held quite a reputation for 'scrapping' with my teachers – quite undeserved, of course; but after this, I began to get quite good and industrious, save for an occasional spasm in the assembly-room where what is supposed to be a feminine propensity for talking used to get me into much trouble."[35] Irene Currie Love's hard work in those final two years at London Collegiate paid off. She won a scholarship to the University of Toronto and, upon graduation, joined the advertising staff of the *Toronto Star*, kicking off her affiliation with journalistic enterprises.[36]

In CWPC lore, Irene Currie Love is described as "a school girl" who won the trip to St Louis in a competition held by the *London Advertiser*. But Currie Love had already graduated from university at the time of the trip, and she was freelancing for the paper. More than likely, she got the opportunity to go to St Louis because her family had strong ties to Thomas Henry Purdom, a prominent London lawyer and financier who bought the *Advertiser* in 1902. Currie Love has also been described in club lore as "one person who may not have actually been on the news staff of any paper."[37] It is true that the *London Advertiser* had no women on staff at the time; however, several of the women on the trip were not permanent news staff members either.

Although the articles about the fair in the *London Advertiser* are signed with the pseudonym "Nan," there is little doubt they came from the pen of Currie Love. The writing style is comparable to the prose Irene penned for *The Collegiate* the previous year. Irene Currie Love's journalism career would bloom after the trip to St Louis and take her from Toronto to New York to Hamilton to Calgary and, finally, to Montreal, where she would become a famed writer and advice columnist for the Woman's Page of the *Montreal Daily Star*.[38]

With Irene Currie Love's arrival on the train, the party was complete. The train rolled on, arriving in Windsor in no time and crossing the Detroit River over to the American shore. At the border, a gallant customs officer took the women at their word when they attested that they carried no contraband wares. But one young woman warned the officer that, on the way back, they planned to stuff all the pretty blouses they could into their baggage and smuggle them over the border.[39]

In mid-afternoon, the party disembarked at Detroit, where, in a smooth hand off, their palatial *Trudeau* linked up with the Wabash train en route to St Louis. The women were surprised to see that, while their watches read 3:30 PM, in Detroit it was only 2:30 PM. They had gained an hour. "A day of twenty-five hours!" marvelled Amintha Plouffe, who was thrilled to tack an hour onto a dream trip she never wanted to end.

Once hooked up to the Wabash line, the train sped on, sweeping through Michigan in the afternoon, touching a corner of Ohio, crossing the vast corn belt of Indiana, speeding through Illinois, and finally entering Missouri itself. A porter waited on the women, polishing their high-button boots and serving tea. As evening fell, the group was served a lovely meal (and a glass of sauterne) in the palatial CPR dining car. According to Kate Simpson Hayes, they were made to feel that, in every way, "a pen-woman [was] just as good as a pen-man."

As anticipation of the destination built, the inexperienced journalists in the group grew increasingly anxious, and so the more experienced writers in the party convened a general session in which they offered words of advice and encouragement.

Kit Coleman, Robertine Barry, and Grace Denison had already covered at least one world's fair, and they passed on a few tips to the novices. George Ham also gave the women a little pep talk as they approached their destination, urging them, above all, not to be shy: "Now, girls, don't be afraid to talk too much. Just go down there and show them the beauty and brains of Canada."[40]

To further enliven the proceedings and perhaps alleviate the nervous tension, George Ham, in mock seriousness, warned that a party of such beautiful women absolutely needed a chaperone for protection. According to Kate Simpson Hayes, in hopes of finding a suitable chaperone Ham called upon each of the women to admit that she had reached the "age of discretion." None would own up. "All claimed to be sixteen, going on seventeen," Hayes declared. They had all sipped the elixir of youth from the dainty china placed before them when they had stepped aboard the train, she noted. But Ham persisted, egging them on and insisting that they had to have a chaperone. "A chaperone without the mildew of years was out of the question," Hayes wrote, "so what was to be done?"

Ham suddenly announced that his grandfather had gone to school with Mary Markwell – Hayes's pseudonym. "There being no one to challenge the dreadful statement," wrote Hayes, "poor Mary Markwell was therefore appointed." Having had the position of chaperone thrust upon her, Kate Simpson Hayes reported to her readers that, by the time Mary Markwell returned to Canada, her hair had turned snow white.

Meet Me in St Louis

It is here that the entire world has set up an appointment.
– Amintha Plouffe, on first viewing the fairgrounds,
Le Journal, 2 July 1904

Early Saturday morning on 18 June 1904 in St Louis, Missouri, rain fell in torrents as the sleeper car *Trudeau* pulled into the railway station built especially for the World's Fair and located at the main entrance to the fairgrounds. The sunshine that accompanied the presswomen all the way from Montreal had temporarily deserted them. But grey skies and a teeming downpour did not prevent the group from experiencing the grandeur of the exposition as they debarked from the train and scanned the horizon. Before them lay a breathtaking city of ivory, streaked with azure waterways, a human-made wonder that seemed like it had been conjured by a genie.[1]

City fathers had chosen Forest Park as the fair site, at the extreme western end of the city, veering away from the congested downtown area near the Mississippi River, which was heavily industrial, and opting instead for rolling and wooded terrain on the city's outskirts. They wanted the Louisiana Purchase Exposition to eclipse all previous exhibitions in beauty, size, and grandeur, thus the bucolic locale, where they could build a showcase of astounding dimensions. The Paris Exposition in 1900 covered 549 acres and included 125 buildings. The fair in St Louis doubled the acreage and the number of buildings.

But transforming a sylvan forest into a fantasyland proved a monumental effort, and, by late 1902, it became clear the work would not be done in time to mark the actual date upon which Thomas Jefferson completed the Louisiana Purchase with his French counterpart Napoleon Bonaparte in 1803. Opening day had to be postponed by one year.

Early in the planning process, architects struggled to create a unique design for the exposition. They had no natural wonder to serve as a backdrop. The 1893 Chicago World's Fair had Lake Michigan; the 1901 Pan-American Exposition in Buffalo had Niagara Falls. Planners in St Louis felt pressured to come up with an original layout. They finally decided to position eight neo-classical buildings in a fan shape radiating from the highest point in Forest Park, a sixty-foot elevation they called Art Hill. Lagoons and terraced gardens would flow from Art Hill, and so would the Cascades, a series of tumbling waterfalls and fountains illuminated at night by electricity – Thomas Edison himself supervised the lighting. A spectacular music auditorium called Festival Hall, with a gold-leaf dome larger than the one at St Peter's in Rome, would be placed atop Art Hill.[2] (See illustration 4.)

On the morning of 18 June 1904, as the presswomen exited the train, they saw the fan-shaped plan come to life. Where three years ago there had been shaded woodland and a slow purling stream, wrote Grace Denison, the presswomen now saw the "first great wonder of the new century."[3] They were speechless – deeply moved and inspired. Under tightly packed umbrellas, the Canadians left the train and dashed to the intramural railway circumventing the grounds. In the mad rush, the women had their first encounter with a new innovation: turnstiles. Peggy Watt called them the greatest nuisance on the face of the earth, telling her readers that she was nearly cross-eyed as she attempted to wedge her way through them while struggling with her baggage in the rain, only to miss the tram.

The women did not have far to ride. They headed to the Inside Inn, a temporary structure designed to hold up to 4,500 guests in 2,357 rooms. Reservations were made in advance for their party of nineteen, a number that included the three railway men. George Ham approached the reception desk while the women waited with their baggage in the lobby. Suddenly, the party faced its first crisis. The Canadians were stunned to learn that only eleven rooms were available for a party numbering nineteen. No cajoling on the part of Ham and the railway could pry loose additional accommodations. They were stuck.

"Where to stay and find shelter while in the city of St Louis is the greatest puzzle the visitor will run up against," Kate Simpson Hayes wrote of the dilemma: "It is needless to wire ahead for rooms. You spend telegraph money on impossibility. The Canadian press party, nineteen strong, wired ahead for nineteen rooms. The wire was acknowledged [but] wet, weary, wicked news-women arriving at the boasted refuge to demand their due, discovered that eleven rooms were at the disposal of the entire party. No matter what argument we offered, we were met with one answer 'Full up.'"[4]

Although none of the women wrote about the lively discussion that surely ensued upon discovering that eight in the party were suddenly without lodging, two of the presswomen did record the resolution. It was decided that the sleeper car *Trudeau*, that palace on wheels, would remain at the railway station on the fairgrounds and offer shelter for part of the group.

At that point, a split of convenience divided the party. The eight French-Canadian women agreed to make *Trudeau* their residence for the duration; the remaining eleven members of the travelling party would stay at the Inside Inn. A touchy dilemma had been solved, but the separation – unintentional – made the experience in St Louis different for the women on either side of the language divide. The French women would choose different activities; they would also tightly bond in a way that, at the outset, not even they had expected. The split would perhaps also augur the direction that French-speaking journalists took in the years ahead when it came to forging stronger ties with their English-speaking colleagues.

As the party divided, those staying in the hotel may have been more aggravated than those who returned to the train. As Kate Simpson Hayes wrote: "To distract distractions, we learned that our rooms would be ready for occupancy 'in a few hours,' and we were obliged to hang on to valise, umbrellas, checks, veils and gigantic appetites until certain sight-seers had turned out to allow us to turn in! That is why we dubbed our domicile 'The Inside Out.'"

Upon settling or resettling into their quarters, the next order of business was finding breakfast. The Quebecers, having deposited their valises back in the train, went in quest of toast and coffee. The English-speaking women did the same at the inn, where the busy restaurant routinely served as many as fifteen hundred patrons at once. By the time the women finished their meal, the sky cleared, the sun emerged, and spirits soared. As they walked the grounds, the French-speaking presswomen noticed the fleur-de-lys, which is part of the city's coat of arms, reproduced everywhere.[5] The French influence seemed pervasive, particularly in statuary scattered around the fairgrounds.

No one could miss "The Apotheosis of Saint-Louis," the central ornament on the spacious plaza inside the main gate. Rising fifty feet in the air, the majestic statue of King Louis IX, canonized by the Roman Catholic Church and thus known historically as "Saint Louis," would be cast in bronze following the fair and remains outside the St Louis Art Museum to this day.[6] The statue symbolized the City of St Louis until the Gateway Arch was built in the 1960s.

The Quebecers also pointed out statues of René Robert Cavelier (Sieur de La Salle), the first European to explore the Mississippi Valley and claim it for France; Père Jacques Marquette, the Jesuit priest who first navigated the Mississippi River; explorer Louis Jolliet, who set out from Quebec to explore the Mississippi and met up with Père Marquette along the way; Jean-Baptiste Le Moyne de Bienville, founder of New Orleans; and, of course, Napoleon Bonaparte, who held the position of first consul of France in 1802–03 when the negotiations for the Louisiana Purchase took place.

They finally found the Administration Building (today Brookings Hall on the campus of Washington University), where they were greeted by the president of the local journalism association and each was given a press pass – a precious "Sésame, ouvre-toi" as Anne-Marie Gleason called it – entitling them to free admission to the fairgrounds and to all midway exhibits that charged an entrance fee.[7] Most of the women had not anticipated the rousing welcome accorded them. It was different from anything they had experienced as female journalists. "From the first morning," wrote Marie Beaupré, "we appreciated the advantage of belonging to the press: all barriers and all doors opened before us with a facility heretofore unsuspected."[8] Once they obtained their press passes, they went directly to the Canadian Pavilion, using a guide map provided by George Ham, and were reunited with their English-speaking companions, with whom they shared first impressions.

Some of the women were overwhelmed by the grandeur and scope of the exposition. "When you are taken from the quiet of Woodstock life," wrote Peggy Watt, "rushed here and there amid a thousand strange things, brought to view colossal structures scattered over twelve hundred acres of ground, filled, many of them, with marvels which the mind has never conceived of, you are apt to rub your eyes and ask if it isn't after all a wonderful dream through which you have been passing."[9]

Peggy Watt levelled with her readers, cautioning that she was no authority on expositions and could not make instructive comparisons with other fairs, having never visited any. Her education at Loretto Abbey and Brantford Ladies' College had certainly given her a deep appreciation of the fine arts, which she would build upon in the years ahead; however, in 1904, she felt like a greenhorn. "All that I have seen this time has been with the eyes of a child," she wrote, "looking out upon new wonders that have ceased to be wonders to many others."

The Canadian Pavilion, where the entire party met up, was rendered fondly in the dispatches the women later filed for their respective publications. "Our small French-Canadian hearts trembled and a cry of joy escaped our chests," wrote Amintha Plouffe, describing the scene as the French-speaking women caught a glimpse of the Canadian Pavilion: "Our home. And to bid us welcome, each letter of CANADA seemed to come to life and smile at us."[10] Patriotism reached tidal wave proportions as the women approached the building. "All that we had dreamed of," wrote Marie Beaupré, "we found it – and something better: elegance added to comfort, cordiality to politeness." Cheerful in its simplicity and a welcoming contrast to the

grandiose neo-classical structures that surrounded it, the Canadian Pavilion captivated the women. "This pretty corner brightened the smile," wrote
Anne-Marie Gleason.

Kate Simpson Hayes admitted that she had had her doubts about the
Canadian Pavilion before she set foot in it. She had read an article in the
Toronto Star referring to the pavilion as an "ugly and common building."
Undoubtedly exaggerating for dramatic effect, Hayes said she had all but
decided to bypass the place, until she sat down to breakfast in the Inside
Inn that morning and overheard a man at a neighbouring table discussing
the Canadian contribution. She turned to him and asked whether the Canadians had made a good showing. "Made a showing?" replied the man, an
American with a heavy southern accent. "I should say so; we're losin' from 30
to 60 good American settlers every day in the week, countin' Sundays." He
told Hayes that, because land was so much cheaper in Canada, Americans
were buying property north of the border to ensure prosperity for their sons
and daughters. He then volunteered to escort Hayes right up to the entrance
of the Canadian Pavilion, displaying "that rare courtesy which you find in
the well-bred southerner, who is ever a gentleman from his hat to his heels."

Indeed, in the eyes of many observers, Canada's overall strategy in St
Louis had more to do with recruitment than with display. Over the years,
thousands of settlers from the United States had been lured across the border to the far northwest by the promise of cheap land and free transport.
Estimates put the number of newcomers from the States at between twenty
thousand to forty thousand per year. According to a July 1904 article in the
National Monthly of Canada magazine, all the Canadian exhibits at the fair
were "really of small moment in comparison with the frank appeal [Canada
made] to the prospective settler: It is men, above all things, that Canada
craves, and it is to the winning of men that she has wisely directed her special effort."[11]

George Ham and Kate Simpson Hayes, of course, were keenly aware of
the recruitment movement in their daily work for the CPR. Ham also wisely
deduced that, in order to lure men to Canada, the women in their lives had
to be convinced; and he had no doubt concluded that, in their dispatches

from the fair, the presswomen were in an ideal position to help make the case for Canada.

Centrally located and featuring a welcoming verandah, Canada's pavilion offered a hospitable place to recuperate from the rigours of sightseeing. Visitors were invited to eat a picnic lunch on the porticos surrounding the building or simply to settle into easy chairs. A glass of fresh water was offered at no cost when other places charged a penny. But the Canadian Pavilion provided far more than rest and refreshment for the weary: it was meant to expose the visitor to the "magnitude and possibilities" of the Dominion.[12] In the main hall, Canadian newspapers were artfully spread on a massive table. The walls held a series of five paintings by Ontario artist Paul Wickson, known for his renderings of horses and cattle, and commissioned by the government to depict life in the Canadian west. Skilful taxidermy work was evident in the heads of moose and bison on display. An exquisitely detailed map of Canada illustrated the country's immense acreage, vast mineral resources, and rich agrarian possibilities. (See illustration 5.)

On the top floor of the Canadian Pavilion, a private lounge had been reserved for the female journalists, who found paper and pen waiting. The superintendent of the McKay Telegraph Service, an Irishman who spoke French "like one of us," according to Robertine Barry, and whose wife had been educated by the Ursuline nuns in Quebec City, graciously offered to send dispatches to family and friends in Canada at no cost. "The ink began to flow and the Dominion was inundated with affectionate messages," wrote Barry in *Le Journal de Françoise*. She told her readers that one particular message caused great consternation when it arrived in Montreal in the middle of the night, jolting the occupants awake when the delivery boy adamantly rang the doorbell and the residents responded: "What's happening? What's the noise? What do you want?" Upon hearing it was a telegram from St Louis, the immediate thought in the household was bad news. "Hearts were broken, tears were forming," Robertine Barry relayed. "'Let's have courage,' said the mother, as she took the sealed message and prepared for a variant of 'She is dead, pray for her!' In lieu of these words, she read: 'Je suis bien et je m'amuse beaucoup.'"

As word of their arrival circulated, the presswomen were visited by an assortment of countrymen, everyone from the mayor of Vancouver to an employee at the Inside Inn who lived in Canada. Robertine Barry wrote: "M. Louis Larivée, a Canadian's Canadian, who occupied an important position in the Associated Press bureau of St Louis, presented us his respects and rendered himself so generally useful that our memory of him remains inseparable from the favorable impression we had of the Canadian pavilion." Anne-Marie Gleason also made it a point to single out the French connection at the Canadian Pavilion, where, she wrote, "we shook the hand of our benevolent colleague, M. Louis Larivée, who didn't hide his satisfaction at finding natives from the same village."

And it was likely at the Canadian Pavilion that the Sweet Sixteen linked up with two more Canadian presswomen who, probably together, had made the trip to St Louis from the west coast. They were Sara Jennie Crowe Atkins of the *Vancouver Province* and Sara Ann McLagan, who, with her husband, had founded the *Vancouver World* in 1888. After her husband's death in 1901, McLagan became the only woman publisher of an urban daily in Canada. The two Saras may have been involved in early discussions about the formation of a women's press club while still in St Louis. Indeed, their presence as journalists in St Louis came back to torment club historian Kay Mathers when she painstakingly attempted to assemble a faithful rendition of the club's beginnings for the fiftieth anniversary celebration in 1954. Poring over meeting minutes and a triennial report prepared by Katherine Hughes and covering the years from 1910 to 1913, Mathers was confounded by a statement that listed McLagan and Atkins as two of "eight charter members" of the club. Writing to Mae Clendenan, national corresponding secretary of the club in 1954, an exasperated Mathers asked: "Do you know, Mae, that neither Mrs Atkins nor Mrs McLagan were on that trip!? ... So how did Mrs McLagan and Mrs Atkins become Charter Members??"[13] Thanks to a photograph of the group supplied by Peggy Watt, Mathers was able to determine that the two Saras joined the club early on but were not part of the Sweet Sixteen.

Cordial greetings having been made at the Canadian Pavilion and final pleasantries exchanged, the women readied themselves to leave a little piece of home in order to explore the world around them. Just steps away from the Canadian Pavilion stood the largest exhibition hall at the fair. A monumental structure spread over twenty acres, the Agricultural Building, like all the grand palaces except for the Fine Arts Building, was meant to be a temporary installation that would be dismantled at the conclusion of the exposition. While they conjured visions of antiquity, the palaces were actually built of humble yellow pine. They achieved their palatial grandeur through the clever use of an ivory-tinted material called "staff" to construct the exterior walls. A mix of plaster of Paris, water, and fibre that included linen, cotton, and horsehair, "staff" was lightweight, pliable, and easily cut so that it could be shaped and hoisted into place to create the fabulous faux facades that distinguished the palaces and made the Ivory City look like a cross between ancient Greece and Rome.[14]

Before stepping inside the Agricultural Building, the presswomen were mesmerized by a breathtaking floral clock, said to be the largest timepiece in the world, set on a gentle slope so it could be seen from a distance. Rows of tightly planted verbenas formed the dial, while coleus formed each numeral. Lights concealed in the flowerbed provided illumination at night. The women watched the minute hand travel five feet in sixty seconds. A bell chimed the hour as they entered the Agricultural Building, where farm products from fifteen countries and forty-two states were displayed, some in extremely imaginative fashion. The *Toronto Telegram*'s Mary Dawson noted that children relentlessly dragged their weary parents from one end of the Agricultural Building to the other to see such innovative exhibits as a life-sized black bear made of prunes, a fleecy "King Cotton" from Mississippi whose head rose forty feet above his legs, and an elephant made entirely of almonds.[15]

The women naturally gravitated to Canada's contribution to the Agricultural Building, described by Mary Dawson as "by far the finest exhibit." No doubt it caught the eye of less partisan observers as well. The Library of Parliament in Ottawa, one of Canada's most famous public structures, had been replicated in St Louis using sheaves of wheat, oats, clover, brome, and blue grass as construction material. The women had an opportunity to meet the chief decorator and superintendent of installation, whose inventive display featured buttresses made of millet and a spire sixty feet high that almost reached the girders of the building. At each corner of the structure, they found bronzed maple leaves set in pillars of glass that, marvelled Marie Beaupré, "seem[ed] to have been sculpted in ice from the Saint Lawrence." (See illustration 6.)

"We have only 144 square feet to show our agricultural exhibits in," wrote Kate Simpson Hayes, "but we do it … A tower-like structure composed of all our grains and grasses, 300 varieties, taken from all parts of the Dominion, are there. 'Grown two thousand miles north of St Louis,' is the sign that attracts the eye of the passing visitor here. Paneled paintings, showing scenes in Canadian farm life, are neatly inserted here, and an object lesson in grain growing, from seed to the flour stages, is arranged with both taste and skill."

Courtesy of their hosts, the presswomen sampled golden sugar buns, buckwheat pancakes soaked in maple syrup, and Canadian-grown apples. In their dispatches, a few women noted that the tempting fruits grown on Canadian soil were as flavourful as were the apples, peaches, plums, and cherries from California,[16] although at least one woman had a different view. Amintha Plouffe wrote, perhaps with clearer vision, that while Canada deserves special mention when it comes to horticulture, "Canada cedes its place to California, whose exhibit is of undeniable superiority."

Not far from the Agricultural Building, the women paused for refreshment at the Ceylon Pavilion, where they sipped "the most delicious tea in the world," according to Anne-Marie Gleason, served by male waiters who wore long skirts and tucked their hair into place with tortoise-shell combs (see illustration 7). Finally, the women headed for the Fine Arts Building atop Art Hill.

The only palace intended to be a permanent fixture, the Fine Arts Building would become the art museum of St Louis after the fair. It took the women only a few minutes once they stepped inside the majestic hallway filled with statuary to draw the same conclusion: there was simply too much to see and not enough time. They felt overwhelmed by the artistic genius that surrounded them and keenly regretted that time did not allow them to visit thirty-two galleries filled with priceless paintings, exquisite sculpture, ivory carvings, rare tapestry, and finely crafted pottery. "It is almost tragic the little one can take away from such a magnificent exhibit," Peggy Watt lamented. For young Watt, who had already admitted to her readers that she lacked the sophistication and experience to make sweeping judgments, the Fine Arts Building represented a dream come true. Surrounded by precious works she had only read about or seen in photographs, her sense of awe blended with pangs of disappointment. She wondered if the opportunity to see so many art treasures under one roof would ever present itself again. Anne-Marie Gleason felt similarly humbled by all the beauty displayed throughout the fair. Collapsing on a bench that afternoon along with Léonise Valois and Marie Beaupré, she felt deeply discouraged.

"Think about it," wrote Anne-Marie Gleason, addressing her readers directly as if conversing with them, a method used by women writers of the day: "We had to visit many worlds in four days. We were therefore condemned to look superficially, and for us, it was often painful." Contemplating the splendid paintings in the Fine Arts Building, Gleason actually felt tormented. So did Marie Beaupré, fresh off her reunion at Villa Maria, where she had mingled with a sophisticated group of women from every corner of North America. She shared Gleason's dismay at the unhappy realization that no one could possibly comprehend so much artistic merit in so short a span. Like Peggy Watt, Beaupré felt that the great opportunity the women had been given to visit the fair had a bittersweet consequence. "It will take years to see and understand it all," Marie Beaupré told her French-speaking colleagues. "And we have only hours."

In their communal frustration, Anne-Marie Gleason, Léonise Valois, Marie Beaupré, and others in the French-speaking contingent, made a strategic decision. In the Fine Arts Building, they would narrow their focus. They would see only a little, but they would see it well. They decided to target the paintings from France, spending time with these masterpieces in order to imprint key details in their minds. They were moved beyond words. As Amintha Plouffe wrote: "Before these living canvasses, silence is still the most expressive language." The women made another decision in the Fine Arts Building, one that all journalists make when considering the likely trajectory of a story they will ultimately write. They thought about their readership.

According to Anne-Marie Gleason, the French-speaking journalists made sure to "salute" the work of contemporary Quebec artists, including that of landscape painter and portrait artist to the wealthy Edmond Dyonnet, who, with Alfred Laliberté and Marc-Aurèle de Foy Suzor-Coté, would later found the School of Fine Arts in Montreal. They also admired the work of local Joseph-Charles Franchère, a church decorator who had painted three murals in Notre-Dame du Sacre Coeur chapel in Paris. Last, they viewed the work of painter-poet Charles Gill, who married a Quebec journalist known by the pseudonym Gaëtane de Montreuil.[17]

While the Quebecers engaged with paintings from France and Quebec, the English-speaking presswomen admired art that resonated with their distinct readership. Peggy Watt made certain to see paintings by those whom she deemed the greatest artists of all time – Rembrandt, Hals, Gainsborough, and Turner. She then singled out the work of English painters famous in the late 1800s – John Everett Millais, Frederic Leighton, and Edward Burne-Jones. As a loyal resident of Woodstock, Watt also made it her mission to find the work of local artist Florence Carlyle. Peggy Watt told her readers that the search was well worth the effort. The subject of Carlyle's painting was a lovers' quarrel, and Watt felt it was a keen depiction. "I wish you all could see it as I saw it," she wrote. "If you did, you would realize what a God-given gift reposes in one of our own Woodstock girls. Nothing that Florence Carlyle may accomplish will astonish me. I am only waiting to see her treasure-laden ship come in."

Leaving the Fine Arts Building regretfully, and feeling overwhelmed by the magnitude of the grand palaces, the Quebec contingent sought out smaller pavilions on the exposition grounds. They were deeply impressed with a display of finely crafted lace in the Belgium Pavilion. To their dismay, a visit to the Italian Pavilion proved disappointing. An enticing exterior, featuring white marble colonnades and guardian golden eagles, led to an empty space inside. Italy had not yet received its precious treasure. Aware that Italian objects of arts were scattered around the grounds in other pavilions, the scholarly Marie Beaupré retained as a guide a certain Signor Nelli, once a professor of Italian in Montreal and now a journalist in St Louis. "With her esteemed professor," Beaupré wrote, "the representative of *La Presse* had the pleasure of hearing the Tuscan dialect as well as classical Italian while admiring the Florentine mosaics … [and] the gold and silver filigrees from the Genoese merchants." The incomplete state of several pavilions and exhibits prompted Kate Simpson Hayes to advise her readers to wait a few weeks before venturing to the fair: "There are unfinished corners, adjustments to be made and added sights still to be revealed."

At the end of a long day, the Quebecers were drawn to the French Pavilion, a stunning replica of Le Grand Trianon at Versailles built by King Louis XIV for Madame de Maintenon. "We are always hungry for France," wrote poetic Marie Beaupré, who in her dispatches refers to France as *la Chérie*: "We will devour her with our eyes, we thirst to understand her thought, to assimilate into her, to lose ourselves in her, as is lost the feeble light of the candle in the brilliance of the electric lamp." The chief landscape architect for the City of Paris designed the outdoor gardens at the French Pavilion using the espalier method, through which he created a variety of shapes by training the branches of fruit trees to lie flat like vines along the pavilion wall. The populace of St Louis had never seen anything like it.[18]

After admiring the gardens, the Quebecers stepped behind a tall decorative wrought-iron fence and respectfully entered a pink interior filled with priceless paintings, life-sized statues, fine French furniture, and original tapestries valued at millions of dollars. Once inside the pavilion, Anne-Marie Gleason felt the shadow of Marie Antoinette following the women as they explored. She sensed that the beautiful queen, both loved and reviled by her subjects, smiled upon her visitors.

Again, the women regretted they did not have more time to admire the visual bounty. "When the time came to wean ourselves from the harmonies of incomparable colours marrying the paintings to the brocades with which the walls are laden," wrote Marie Beaupré, "we grew sad." According to Anne-Marie Gleason, the Quebecers felt they were leaving behind a piece of their soul. No wonder she was not amused at the scene that ensued when they exited the premises.

"Vive la France," cried Léonise Valois as the party walked out the door. "And the French fries," quipped a young man holding the door for the women. Although Gleason steamed over the comment, deeming it rude and impertinent, she must have temporarily tucked away her annoyance since the entire press party was about to link up for a nighttime adventure. The women had been advised not to see certain portions of the exposition until evening. As twilight fell, they prepared to explore that territory. They could see that the fairgrounds took on a different aspect at night. In the glow of thousands of electric lights, the palatial buildings looked even more magnificent than they did in the glare of daylight.

Down the Pike

The Pike is a marvel of what man and faker can do to amuse a world
that is forever demanding the startling and surprising.
– Kit Coleman, *Mail and Empire*, 25 June 1904

As evening fell Saturday, the journalists left the grand palaces that astounded
them in daylight and flocked to the sites best viewed at night. "The moving
world was pouring towards the Pike, with its atrocious attractions and its
vulgar displays," wrote Kate Simpson Hayes. "Naturally we joined in the
human swirl and an hour later were giggling over the antics of the clown in
'comic opery.'"[1] The Pike, as the joke went, was not a freshwater fish; rather,
the Pike was a mile-long amusement park in which over six thousand en-
tertainers took part in forty shows and in which rides, games, and fortune-
tellers co-existed with zebras, polar bears, and camels.

From its inception, the Louisiana Purchase Exposition had been designed
as an educational enterprise, its grand palaces touting humanity's achievements in the fields of art, transportation, electricity, education, mines, and
metallurgy.[2] But the lighter fare to be sampled on the Pike – the fare that
made the presswomen giggle – was not without its educational aspects. The
women learned about other cultures in ways that moved and inspired them.
Historical events were recreated through displays they found both kitschy
and marvelous.

The evening began with a cruise on an authentic gondola brought to St Louis from Venice. Irene Currie Love painted a word portrait of the picturesque gondolier, who lazily propelled the boat across the lagoon while crooning an Italian love song. Bubbling fountains sent up jets of silvery spray while electric lights created a rainbow on the water, turning the rippling surface from gold to ruby to emerald. Amintha Plouffe described a scene "full of soft emotion carrying us into the realm of the stars." That may have been true, but once the women debarked and joined the hurly-burly on the Pike, they descended rapidly from heaven to earth, plunging, as Plouffe noted, into "the domain of laughter and even insanity."[3]

They laughed until they cried when three members of the press party took a camel ride and clung to each other for dear life as the animal slowly collapsed in stages, jolting back and forth. "Riding the camel costs you twenty-five cents," observed Kate Simpson Hayes, "but seeing another ride him gives you the same laugh for nothing."

The most popular feature on the Pike was a replica of an Alpine village. Spread over nine acres, it included a faux mountain range topped by snow-covered peaks. Completing the powerful illusion were German restaurants and beer gardens, where pretty young women in velour vests and white shirts circulated with tankards. The press party paused for refreshment at a Bavarian café, where a splendid orchestra captivated Cécile Laberge, who was always on the lookout for talented musicians. She routinely recruited performers for the Ladies' Morning Musical Club, a task that sometimes proved a hard sell. Male performers were especially sceptical that a group of women could pay their fee.[4]

Now, listening to an orchestra in St Louis, Cécile Laberge was gently reminded by her colleagues that they could linger no longer. They felt badly about disturbing her musical communion but were eager to move along to a more pious corner of the Pike to view a faithful rendition of the Passion Play of Oberammergau, named for a town in Bavaria where the play originated. George Ham also attended the performance, accompanied by Kit Coleman. As, years later, Ham related in his memoirs, during one scene Kit suddenly began sobbing. "What's the matter with you, Kit?" Ham whispered sympathetically. "Oh, see our blessed Saviour; they're crucifying him," she replied. "Well," Ham insisted, "let's get out of here."[5]

Kit Coleman later told her readers about the "heartbreaking story" she had viewed through tears. In 1633, she told them, a plague raged in the region around Oberammergau. Village fathers, desperate and afraid, vowed that if God would spare the town, they would stage a play to commemorate the life and death of Jesus. "It is terrible," wrote Coleman:

It is heartbreaking. It wakens all that is loveliest, simplest, most divine in the human breast. All the poor, futile passions and aspirations sink before it, are absorbed in it. You are your own Ego, lonely, abstracted, apart from all other human beings – just you and the God that knows you. It is the Pike, and foolish and a place of laughter, but for you, in one of those inexpressibly lonely and beautiful moments, it is yourself and the grieving human heart in sympathy and suffering with a beloved and noble figure … One sees the Crucifixion; one almost hears the dull thuds of the hammers piercing flesh and muscle; there comes the Centurion with his bitter draught. Then the 'father forgive them – they know not what they do' – and you find yourself crying feebly, humanly, under your veil.

Ham hustled Coleman out of the theatre and over to a jollier performance at the nearby Irish Village, where a songstress was energetically crooning "The Wearing of the Green." Kit Coleman, her face now wreathed in smiles, vigorously kept time with the tune by patting the floor with her foot. "What a difference a few minutes makes," Ham remarked with relief.[6] The picturesque Irish Village served as an exposition within the exposition, given its location directly on the Pike. The Irish Village architects worked diligently to achieve realism. Visitors entered through a replica of St Lawrence's Gate at Drogheda, other landmarks dotted the landscape, and even the soil in the village had been imported from Ireland.[7]

The Irish exhibit stayed open until midnight, and the Canadian women took full advantage of the late closing time, deeming the Irish Village far more convincing than exhibits that depicted the North Pole and Creation. Those exhibits, Robertine Barry wrote, seemed deceptive, with their "shifting canvases, artificial wind and tons of tin plating."[8] The Irish Village, on the other hand, felt authentic to this French-Canadian of Irish extraction as well as to Anne-Marie Gleason, whose own background likewise embraced a dual heritage. They both delighted in an Irish jig danced by colleens – real colleens. "If you are in doubt," Robertine Barry wrote, "you will quickly be persuaded by watching their bright eyes."

Kate Simpson Hayes wrote about the village at length and with passion, first in a folksy way, using her keen ear for dialect to describe her quest to find "some of the foine ould Irish blood of the Markwells." But she may have been remembering her Irish-born father, whose sympathy for an independent Ireland ran deep, when she abruptly turned serious in her column. Perhaps she was recalling the morning, when she was seven or eight years old and living in New Brunswick, that she awoke to find her father arguing with D'Arcy McGee at the kitchen table and defending the Irish cause for independence. He had met McGee after a speech the fiery orator had given in St John advocating a United Canada aligned with Britain.[9]

Kate Simpson Hayes wrote that it troubled her deeply that the fine examples of Irish workmanship she saw at the fair – lace, tapestry, and hand-loomed cloth – went unappreciated by consumers in North America. Using uncharacteristically strong language, she expressed sadness and disgust that trade policies and buying habits in North America were harmful to Ireland:

It makes one sick at heart to know and remember how the industries of Ireland have been squelched and ground under foot by the light-minded people of our day, who buy and barter with foreign nations; 'thumb-sucking,' as you might say, for 'the policy of the things,' while the little children of Erin go hungry for lack of the food their fathers cannot earn by honest toil! Oh, the nation that has no recognition for its own worth within lacks the highest thing the world wants! 'Made in Ireland' should be the cry in trade lanes; but it isn't. It's the shoddy of the Bowery shops we want!

It was not the only exhibit that aroused ire, challenged preconceptions, and encouraged bursts of emotion. The women marvelled at one of the most arresting attractions on the Pike, the "Baby Incubator" exhibit, which offered state-of-the-art nursing care to premature infants as the public watched the tiny babies grow day by day through glass windows. Kit Coleman found the exhibit "somehow foolish," although she failed to explain why. Perhaps she felt the juxtaposition of the baby incubators next to an exhibit on ancient Rome made the former seem trivial. But, given the dire situation in Quebec, where the infant and maternal mortality rate was among the highest in the world,[10] the exhibit was particularly poignant for the French-Canadian women, who were deeply touched by the invention that saved so many lives.[11] In Quebec City and Montreal at the turn of the century, one infant in four did not reach its first birthday. Léonise Valois knew the situation well, given that her mother, who had fifteen children, lost six at birth or in infancy. Valois routinely wrote odes for relatives and friends who had lost a child. Anne-Marie Gleason, too, had been forever marked by the perils of childbirth: her mother died at age twenty-six shortly after giving birth to her sister. (See illustration 8.)

Amid the celebration of innovation and scientific progress, there were freak shows that exhibited the basest displays. Ironically, one such exhibit featured Marie Beaupré's first cousin, Édouard Beaupré, better known as Beaupré the Giant. He was the eldest of twenty children born to Marie's uncle Gaspard Beaupré, who had moved from Quebec to Saskatchewan in the 1870s and married a Métis woman named Florestine Piché. Their son became a mythic figure in Canada, ultimately reaching eight feet, three inches and weighing nearly four hundred pounds before joining the circus at age sixteen. He supported his family as a freak show performer strong enough to lift a horse.

It is uncertain if Marie Beaupré knew her cousin Édouard other than by reputation. In 1901, he had fought a well-publicized wrestling match sponsored by La Presse against renowned strongman Louis Cyr in Sohmer Park, then a popular amusement park along the St Lawrence River east of Old Montreal. The match turned out to be a sham. Beaupré the Giant was not trained to be a professional wrestler and did not know how to approach the formidable Louis Cyr. Despite his size, Beaupré was thrown four times, hurt his elbow on the first tumble, and lost the match in just over three minutes.[12]

Beaupré the Giant would begin his stint on the Pike a few days after the Canadian women left, so Marie Beaupré never got to see her cousin in St Louis. However, she most likely read about his tragic demise: he died two days after arriving in St Louis, at age twenty-three, succumbing to a high fever brought on by tuberculosis. His family could not afford to bring his body home to Saskatchewan, so a local promoter exhibited it instead, and, in a macabre twist, Beaupré the Giant became a bigger attraction in death than in life. While Marie Beaupré may not have seen him in St Louis, she certainly heard about his arrival in Montreal, where, in 1905, his body ended up on display at the Musée Eden, where wax sculptures of historical figures and other curiosities were exhibited in the basement of the Monument National on St Laurent Boulevard.[13] The body of the world's tallest man drew huge crowds, overwhelming the museum, which had to send the corpse elsewhere. Ultimately abandoned in a warehouse, the body was later claimed by the University of Montreal for research purposes. Not until 1989 did family members finally surmount bureaucratic obstacles in order to bring his remains back to Saskatchewan.[14]

It was on the Pike that the presswomen confronted every form of humanity – and inhumanity – and where they stretched and tested their own biases and preconceptions. What we would consider blatant racism was commonplace at that time in North America. Fair organizers barred an all-black military regiment from staying on the fairgrounds, and ragtime musician Scott Joplin, a black Missouri resident, could not perform on the main stage – only on the Pike.[15] Racist ideas permeated the economics, politics, and social policy of early twentieth-century Canada as well. The *Canadian Magazine*, analyzing the 1901 census and other government documents in an attempt to assess Canada's progress, found it reassuring that the foreign-born population had not increased enough to jeopardize the country's advancement: "There is little probability that Canada will soon have to deal with those evils which flow from the presence of an 'ignorant, foreign' element. In this regard, her position is superior to that of the United States."[16]

Many English Canadians felt that British values formed the basis of civilized society, and they viewed white people of British descent as superior to Aboriginal peoples, blacks, Jews, or Asians.[17] Editors reflected that viewpoint, deeming it sound policy to preserve the nation's purity by restricting the type of newcomer arriving in Canada.[18] There was tremendous fear, in particular, that Canada would be inundated with Asians. In the 1880s, fifteen thousand Chinese men were brought to Canada to work on the transcontinental railway, and Asians were still being treated with open hostility and denied rights accorded to other Canadians.[19]

The preferred immigrant was white – either British, French, or American – in that order. But since Canadian immigration authorities were eager to settle the west and develop farms on Prairie land, they also accepted large numbers of what they deemed to be hardy immigrants from Eastern Europe, all of them white.[20]

Few citizens were as enlightened and as tolerant of difference as Kit Coleman, who, in 1895, consoled a black Canadian who had written to her for advice. "You must not call the race that has produced a Fred Douglass 'low' or even 'downtrodden,'" she advised: "There are black and coloured men holding high positions in the West Indies. It is all a matter of education. I hold that the black man is as good as his white brother, both being given the same chances. We are all – no matter what colour – of God's making, and made in His image."[21]

And when it came to religion, Kit Coleman again stood out for her openmindedness. At the turn of the century, Canada was overwhelmingly a Christian country: 97 percent of the population was either Catholic or Protestant.[22] Although Coleman described herself as "a reverent believer in Jesus Christ and His exquisite teaching," she showed disdain for those who would impose religious dogma on others instead of simply preaching the doctrine of brotherly love. She told one correspondent that, as a rule, there's "too much mind and too little heart in religion nowadays."[20] By pointing out the gap between Christian teaching and Christian practice, Kit Coleman raised an issue that eventually led, in the late nineteenth century, to a revision of Christian thought and forced churches to focus more on social questions and less on theological argument.[24]

At the World's Fair, racial and religious stereotypes were severely challenged. Several of the presswomen had a startling awakening as they beheld wonders produced by people of different ethnic origin. "You view with amazement the work of nations which you have hitherto regarded as inferior in brain and culture," stated Irene Currie Love, "and you silently learn."[25] As an example, Currie Love cited the contribution made by the Japanese. At every pavilion she visited at the fair, no matter what the theme, the display by the Japanese went far beyond anything she could have imagined. "I could not help but think," she wrote, "as I looked at their wonderful art, simply beautiful productions, of how arrogant and conceited we are in our attempts to introduce western civilization and western ideas in Japan. It is a wonder they do not retaliate by sending missionaries to us!"

St Louis revealed a confusing dichotomy with regard to race. While fair organizers denied blacks full rights, they proudly showcased a wide range of Aboriginal cultures. Patagonians from South America, Ainu from Japan, Pygmies from Africa, Cocopa Indians from northern Mexico, Kwakiutl Indians from the Northwest Coast of British Columbia, and a large group of Aboriginal peoples from the Philippines lived along the Pike. Indeed, Apache warrior Geronimo was among the Pike's biggest draws, sitting on a platform and charging ten cents for an autograph. Presumably organizers hoped to broaden the horizons of visitors and open hearts and minds. But some detected an underlying discourse behind the importation of "primitive" cultures, believing that organizers wanted to demonstrate how "civilized" the visitors could become with American influence and education.[26]

To that end, model schools in the Palace of Education used English as the language of instruction for children from visiting cultures, not their native language. Several Aboriginal groups, including the largest delegation from the Philippines, lived in dwellings they built themselves with materials imported from their homeland. These people suffered hardships as they struggled to keep warm and preserve their way of life when the weather grew colder.[27]

Perhaps no presswoman better personified the contradictory impulses that seized well-meaning Canadians than did Katherine Hughes, who had once taught Aboriginal children on a Mohawk reserve. The Indian Act of 1876, which sought both to protect and to assimilate Canada's First Nations population, established residential boarding schools funded by the government and run by missionaries, with the goal of introducing Aboriginal children to European culture, traditions, and religion. Hughes believed in the system. She urged the Roman Catholic hierarchy to support an association that would send gifted First Nations graduates of the Catholic Indian Industrial Schools to work in the community at large. And, while it is clear that Hughes sincerely sought to better the living situation of her pupils, particularly young women (whom she believed should be trained as nurses and not employed as domestics), she also advocated their assimilation. In letters to Bishop Émile Legal, she writes that the great majority of the Canadian population is "pitifully ignorant of the Indian of today – of the new Indian who is ready now to benefit materially by the years of [our] devoted work in missions and schools."[28] Little did she envision the disastrous consequences that would later result for Aboriginal people who were educated at mission schools, where they would suffer much abuse.

At the time of the World's Fair, Katherine Hughes was certainly more progressive and enlightened than were many Canadians. She exemplified, like the fair itself, both a generosity of spirit and the impulse of a kind-hearted reformer seeking to civilize the foreigner in the belief it would better their lot. Hughes's preoccupation with Aboriginal peoples and their welfare would likely explain why she began her coverage of the World's Fair for the *Montreal Daily Star* in a most unusual way: "There is not much analogy between an Apache babe and the average Montrealer, yet the brown toddler finally released from the strappings of his cradle-board and the Montrealer set down for the first time at the gates of the World's Fair must feel something of the same wild gladness."[29]

In her story, Katherine Hughes continually returned to one theme: the chance the fair offered one to mingle with other cultures. "When the black and the brown and the yellow man sit down together in amity with the white," she wrote, "when they bring with them the oddest and most beautiful products of their hands and mind, and best of all when they bring themselves open-minded and full of responsive good-nature – then you have a motley world-assemblage to delight the soul." She recounted a chance meeting with a group of blanketed Pueblo Indians from New Mexico, who crossed her path while she left the Pike to return to the Inside Inn:

> A display of the real friendliness you feel thaws out their self-contained reserve. One of them speaks a little English and small Picardo, round and brown, tells you his Indian name Opaman, then gives you his wee brown fist to shake. A promise to visit their camp on the hill, a caressing hand on the small baby's cheek and lo, the little dark woman with touched mother-pride, puts out her hand with hasty impulse to clasp yours in the pale face's salute. To one who knows the Indian this little action is so significant that it spells the whole motif and spirit of the Fair.

In writing about the Pike, Katherine Hughes showed a deep appreciation of the richness arising from the multicultural mix. She noted that, under all its "patchwork garments and fools bells," the Pike was permeated with the real spirit of the fair, which she described as "the kinship of man." She concluded her story for the *Montreal Daily Star* with this line: "The great Fair gives you pleasure and new ideas in art, industry and commerce, but most of all it gives you sympathy with your neighbour."

Katherine Hughes's sincere sentiment was also felt by several women in the French-speaking contingent, who were moved by the fraternity that seemed to be evident everywhere. "Since our arrival in St Louis," wrote Antoinette Gérin-Lajoie, "we've met with such perfect concord and beheld with such a tender eye all the nations openly shaking hands, that we've assimilated that beautiful phrase from the Gospel: 'Love one another.'"[30]

Léonise Valois chimed in with identical observations, almost thinking out loud in print as she considered matters of race relations from a different perspective:

Of all the impressions gathered at the St Louis Exposition, one stands out for me and floats above all others. I was greatly struck by this very great harmony, this perfect order, which, I was told, never ceases to reign between representatives of different countries, who temporarily cohabitate in voluntary exile, and those cosmopolitans who cross this universe in miniature. Might the humanitarian dream of all the great philanthropists come to life? Could making people know each other better, even in an ephemeral manner, bring them to better appreciate each other, to love one another more?[31]

Cécile Laberge drew similar conclusions at the close of her only article for *Le Soleil*. The fair, she wrote, demonstrated "that there are people who, without having our ways of dressing, housing or eating, can create forms of art that are not ours, but which are not unworthy for all their difference. The representatives of various races display ingenuity." Laberge told readers she was convinced that, in the contemporary world, a world's fair carried a high moral value: "This way of extending hospitality … shows to men that they are not made to hate, but rather to understand one another."[32]

Pondering the displays of human kindness they had witnessed at night and marvelling at the displays of human creativity they had seen during the day, the women gratefully returned for some much-needed rest to their respective residences – the English-speaking women to the Inside Inn, the Quebecers to the train. "Had not more graphic pens than mine already done the trick," wrote Grace Denison, "I should wallow in superlatives about the 'Inside Inn,' which is perhaps the most wonderful of its class on earth." The rooms provided a cozy nesting place, she wrote, wall-papered in cool deep green, topped with a canvas ceiling and shaded by boughs of live oak foliage. "If you want sweet sleep," she advised, "commend me to the pine needle mattress which upheld my weary frame each all-too-short night."[33]

The French-speaking women retired to their "dear Wabash," as they called it, a "good companion" that welcomed them warmly. It was on the train, wrote Anne-Marie Gleason, that the French-Canadians passed their most joyous moments at the fair, where they chatted and laughed in what they mockingly called their living room. In those hours of calm and quiet, they bonded. Their unusual accommodations proved to be the source of deepening friendships and moments that they believed they would always remember. But the separate quarters for the English-speaking women and their French-speaking colleagues did have repercussions as the two groups would go their separate ways the next day – and for the rest of their stay in St Louis.

1 (*facing page, above*)   Office of the Regina *Leader* in the late 1880s when Kate Simpson Hayes began writing for the paper. Settlers were beginning to transform the former no-man's land into a vibrant town after the arrival of the Canadian Pacific Railway. Courtesy of the Saskatchewan Archives Board.

2 (*facing page, below*)   From an office in Old Montreal, Robertine Barry, the first female journalist hired by a newspaper in Quebec, later published a newspaper of her own. Courtesy of the Bibliothèque et Archives nationales du Québec.

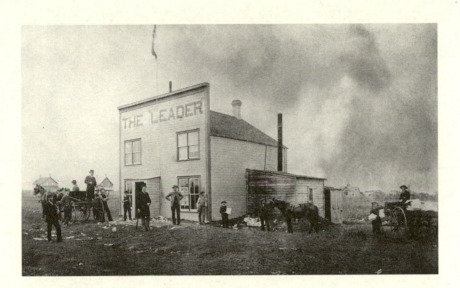

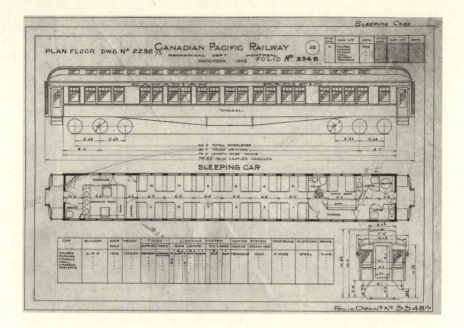

3 *Trudeau*, the plush CPR sleeping car that carried the "Sweet Sixteen" to St Louis. Floor plan courtesy of the CPR Archives.

4 (*facing page, above*) Festival Hall, a music auditorium at the St Louis World's Fair, served as the centrepiece for the entire exposition. From *The Greatest of Expositions Completely Illustrated* (St Louis: Samuel Myerson Printing Co., 1904). Courtesy of the Bibliothèque et Archives nationales du Québec.

5 (*facing page, below*) The Canadian Pavilion at the fair was purposely designed to entice visitors to move to western Canada. From *The Greatest of Expositions Completely Illustrated* (St Louis: Samuel Myerson Printing Co., 1904). Courtesy of the Bibliothèque et Archives nationales du Québec.

6　A replica of the Library of Parliament in Ottawa, fashioned
from grains and grasses, was Canada's contribution to the
Agricultural Building at the World's Fair. From *The Forest City: A
Portfolio of Official Photographic Views of the Universal Exposition,
St Louis, 1904* (St Louis: N.D. Thompson Publishing Co., 1903).
Courtesy of the Bibliothèque et Archives nationales du Québec.

7   The Sweet Sixteen savoured tea served by Cingalese waiters at the Ceylon
. Pavilion in the midst of a frenzied day of sight-seeing. From *The Greatest of
Expositions Completely Illustrated (St Louis: Official Photographic Co., 1904).
Courtesy of the Bibliothèque et Archives nationales du Québec.

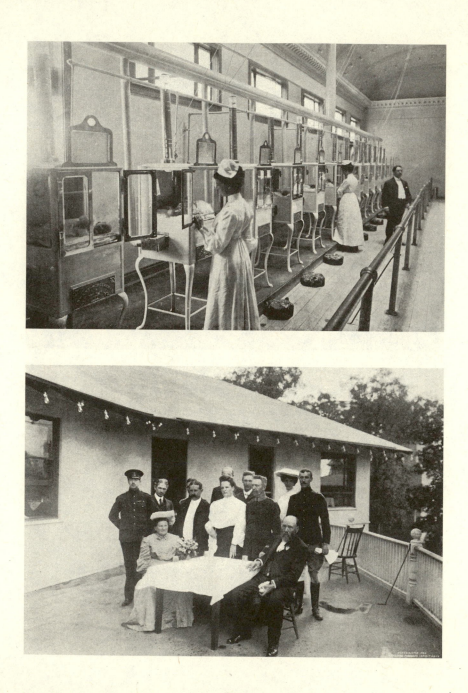

8 (*facing page, above*)   Baby incubators were a huge attraction at the St Louis World's Fair as visitors could watch nurses attend to the premature infants through a glass window. From *The Greatest of Expositions Completely Illustrated* (St Louis: Samuel Myerson Printing Co., 1904). Courtesy of the Bibliothèque et Archives nationales du Québec.

9 (*facing page, below*)   Defeated Boer War general Piet Cronje announced that he would marry Johanna Sterzel, the widow of a fallen comrade, on the fairgrounds in St Louis. From *The Greatest of Expositions Completely Illustrated* (St Louis: Samuel Myerson Printing Co., 1904). Courtesy of the Bibliothèque et Archives nationales du Québec.

10   The humanitarian work conducted by Jane Addams at Hull House in Chicago inspired the presswomen when they stopped there on the way home from the fair. Postcard obtained from the Hull House Museum.

11 (*overleaf*)   The travelling party in Detroit: Standing in the back row from left to right are: Katherine Hughes, A.H. Notman, Mary Adelaide Dawson, Antoinette Gérin-Lajoie, Alice Asselin, Cécile Laberge, Robertine Barry, Marie Beaupré, George Ham, Gertrude Balmer Watt and C.E.E. Ussher. In front from left are: Anne-Marie Gleason, Amintha Plouffe, Léonise Valois, Margaret Graham, Irene Currie Love, and Kate Simpson Hayes. Missing from the photo: Kathleen (Kit) Coleman and Grace Denison. Photo courtesy of Margalo Grant Whyte.

12 (*above*)   A postcard sent by Robertine Barry while travelling west during the Canadian Women's Press Club excursion in 1906. Barry expressed great admiration for western Canada in her dispatches. Courtesy of the Bibliothèque et Archives nationales du Québec.

13 (*facing page*)   The *Edmonton Journal* welcomed one hundred female journalists when the Canadian Women's Press Club held its first triennial meeting in the city in 1913. Courtesy of Tony Cashman, Edmonton historian.

A Day of Rest

In this city, formerly so French, we seldom heard
the language dear to our hearts.
– Léonise Valois, *Le Canada*, 9 July 1904

Sundays were deemed sacrosanct at the St Louis World's Fair. The exposition was closed, pronounced shut by an act of Congress. A staid Victorian ethic still governed entertainment on the Sabbath at the turn of the twentieth century; thus, when the Canadian presswomen awoke on Sunday, 19 June 1904, all activity at the fair had ceased.

It was a stark contrast to the party atmosphere that reigned on weekdays. Almost daily, celebrations were held for the grand opening of a pavilion, the commemoration of a thematic day, or the arrival of a dignitary such as President Porfirio Díaz of Mexico, who welcomed twenty-five hundred guests, including President Theodore Roosevelt's daughter Alice, to a lush garden filled with banana trees at the Mexican Pavilion. Sunday was meant to be a day of rest. Some of the women treated it as such, while others took advantage of the lull to explore the City of St Louis.

The French-Canadian women, good Catholics all, first attended to their devotions, as Léonise Valois attested with a wink, then made a beeline for downtown, drawn to the city because of its French origin.[1] This Sunday they could not wait to discover more of the French heritage of St Louis, a city founded by French fur trader Pierre Laclède in 1764. They were also eager to find descendants of those long-ago residents who, according to Robertine Barry, did not celebrate the historic Louisiana Purchase in 1803 but, instead, sat stoically silent when the American flag replaced the Tri-Colour.[2]

What they found, however, took them by surprise. St Louis was a booming city in 1904, heavily industrial and the world's largest producer of beer, shoes, stoves, and wagons. With a population of 600,000 – nearly double the population of the city today – St Louis was then the fourth largest city in the United States, behind New York, Chicago, and Philadelphia. As the Quebec women took in the sights from a tramway that followed a sinuous path around the city, they could not hide their displeasure. The city was flat. The streets offered only dreary factories and commercial enterprises; the only bright spot on the tour was a glimpse of the Mississippi River. And while the fair venerated the city's French roots, the women were shocked to find no vestige of that same French heritage downtown. Instead, they saw a multitude of commercial signs in English and, even more surprising, in German. They were stunned.

By the turn of the century, immigration had radically transformed the cultural face of St Louis. The women had not realized that now the city's largest ethnic group was German. They were unprepared to hear so much German spoken on the street. "German is a priority in the popular neighborhoods, and aboard the tram, the German dialect holds court," observed Léonise Valois. The discovery was disturbing. "It is hardly a reassuring prospect, it seems to me," wrote Valois, "for the most elegant nation of all." She also wondered if the female elite of French descent were "puritanical to a fault" and stayed inside observing the Sabbath since the only faces on the streets, she noted, were "round and attached to corpulent frames." In other words, they were German.

Only one French-Canadian woman experienced a different view of St Louis that Sunday. Robertine Barry, the consummate journalist, had pre-arranged to meet up with two well-to-do women living in St Louis who had family ties to Montreal. Barry told her readers that the cream of the aristocracy in St Louis was still of French heritage. Her two escorts showed her the city's most elegant parks, avenues, and residences. They also explained how the citizens of St Louis helped to underwrite the exposition, contributing through individual donations to the $50 million total cost. Barry was extremely impressed by the generosity of taxpayers like her guides, who did not hesitate "to pay at the door," as she put it, and happily bought tickets to the fair even though they had already helped finance it with their donations. "It would be very easy to obtain my entry free," one of her escorts told Barry, "but is it not better to add as much as one can to the national success, and to give a part of ones fortune to the country to which you owe everything?" Barry was moved by these patriotic sentiments, which "[gave] more strength to the Republic than an army ready for battle."

In contrast to Robertine Barry's guided tour, the rest of the Quebec press group wandered the streets of St Louis in a muddle. From the German neighbourhood where they had accidentally drifted, they somehow made their way to the city centre, stomachs rumbling as, well past lunchtime, they sought a place to dine. A sympathetic woman directed them to a restaurant on Pine Avenue, where they found what seemed to be the highlight of their day: a delicious meal at bargain prices.

Several members of the English-Canadian contingent used the enforced Sunday respite to discover a completely different part of the city. They took a morning sightseeing tour of St Louis by automobile, probably arranged by George Ham. Irene Currie Love and Kate Simpson Hayes told their readers that they had seen palatial homes at each turn, parks almost beyond description, and boulevards shaded with trees. In the afternoon, the English women were admitted, through the largess of the mayor and as a special favour to Canada, to the Missouri Botanical Gardens, which were normally closed on Sunday.

British immigrant Henry Shaw founded the gardens. He came to St Louis in 1819 and made a fortune selling hardware. Retiring as a wealthy man in 1840, Shaw devoted himself to beautifying the grounds around his home. Over the years, this monumental effort made Shaw's property one of the city's main attractions. When he died in 1889, Shaw willed the gardens to the City of St Louis, on the condition that they not be open on Sundays, except twice a year: the first Sunday in June and the first Sunday in September.[3]

Irene Currie Love thought the stipulation a great pity. It made no sense to her that the gardens would normally be shuttered on Sundays when there were "so many poor people" in the city for whom a cool garden on a hot summer's day would have provided a "glimpse of Paradise." Kate Simpson Hayes told her readers the public gardens were the most beautiful she had ever seen. As the English-speaking women meandered through the beds of rare plants, they stopped to pick ripe berries from a mulberry tree and savoured the fruit. Currie Love, the youngest in the group, suggested that they form a circle and sing the childhood ditty "Here We Go Round the Mulberry Bush." Some members of the party frowned upon the suggestion.[4]

Peggy Watt may have been among those who did not appreciate Currie Love's humour. Watt seemed lost in reflection that Sunday. She would later write that her visit to the gardens was among her best memories of the trip. That day, she wandered over to a mausoleum located on the gardens' grounds, where she was startled to find a life-size statue in repose. It was Henry Shaw, asleep and holding a single flower in his hand. Legend had it, Peggy Watt told her readers, that Shaw had been "crossed in love" as a young man and, as a result, plunged into a life of dissipation until his retirement, after which he lived alone with only a few servants and his adored plants and flowers. Standing at the mausoleum and observing Shaw's statue, Watt was prompted "to ponder on human life, its ups and downs, its strange multitudinous forms of expression, its loveliness and its finality." Before the women left the gardens, the German groundskeeper, who lived on the premises in a little vine-covered lodge, emerged to greet them. He indulged their attempts to use their limited German vocabulary and afterwards presented each woman with a souvenir book of photographic views of the garden.

On Sunday evening, several in the English-speaking group returned to the fairgrounds for supper and opted to dine at the Inside Inn. "Ah! That dining room," Grace Denison enthused. "There was the perfection of system, the plethora of good, wholesome food, and considering the usual exhibition tariff, the modesty of charges!" She asked her readers to imagine the relays that transpired in the dining room as five thousand people tried to eat around the same time on Sunday evening and two thousand servers waited on customers. "The system seemed as near perfection as one can get," she marvelled: "I am not under the smallest obligation to tell of the merits of the place, but as one who has often suffered from want of them, I gladly note what pleased me. When dinner was over it was a sight to see the whole community empty the rotunda, and dragging rockers and rush chairs group themselves on the enormous boarded plateau before the deep verandah."[5]

The French-speaking women, having enjoyed a plentiful meal in the late afternoon, had no need for dinner. They returned to their "home" on the train and plotted their next move. Four in the party preferred to stay put and rest. The others decided to head to a theatre called Delmar Garden. They wanted to see a play entitled *Louisiana* that had been strongly recommended. The play captured the essence of the spirited negotiations that took place between Napoleon Bonaparte and Thomas Jefferson as the two haggled over the Louisiana Purchase.

The amiable theatre manager at Delmar Garden gave the presswomen the best seats in the house, close to the stage. They were not disappointed. "I wish that all efforts could be rewarded like ours were that evening," Léonise Valois wrote. They loved the artistic set décor, the splendid costumes, and the theatrical performances. But they were particularly moved by the delirious reaction from the audience as visitors to the fair from all over the world cheered and applauded their respective national anthems, which were played during a portion of the show called "The Dance of Nations."

Listening to the fervent display of patriotism all around them, the Quebec women's moods turned suddenly gloomy when the band struck up Canada's anthem. They regretted that they could not share the same loyal enthusiasm for "God Save the King" as did other patrons for their respective anthems, and they returned to the train in a pensive frame of mind. Readers of Léonise Valois would have readily understood why. It was not Quebec's independence from Canada that the French-speaking women sought but, rather, Canada's independence from Britain. "[The] Independence – of Canada!" Valois wrote: "How much we desire it in this hour, and back from our agreeable evening, we had but one regret, that of having been able to acclaim our country only through the veils of the British Empire – and the lone strain of *God Save the King*."

The Boer War

The best thing at the Exhibition, even apart from its interest for
Canadians, is the Boer war spectacle.
– Grace Denison, *Saturday Night*, 2 July 1904

Time was running out and there was still so much to see. On their last full
day at the fair, the women packed in as much sightseeing and socializing as
possible. The French-speaking women flew through some of the major palaces. They examined the mineral riches of Canada in the building devoted
to mines and metallurgy, where they were drawn to beautiful pieces of gold,
silver, and copper from the mines in Matane, Quebec. They traced humanity's progression from the ox-driven cart to the modern automobile in the
Transportation Building. They saw such remarkable marvels of ingenuity in
a palace devoted to machinery and electricity that they wondered, according
to Amintha Plouffe, "whether the next electrical invention will not carry us
from the clouds to the dwelling place of our Supreme Master."[1]

They lingered a little longer in the Manufacturing Building, admiring
eye-catching dresses in velvet and silk made in France and England. A superb collection of lace from Ireland drew sighs, and, in the same building,
the exquisite marbles and bronzes from Italy left a deep impression. But the
Japanese corner of the exhibition hall stole the show, with a superb array of
porcelains and papier-mâché crafts unlike anything they had ever seen. "I

would have liked another twenty-five-hour-day to admire at my leisure those works of art that seemed to have come from heaven above rather than from the earth," Plouffe wrote. Marie Beaupré echoed the sentiment: "Japanese embroideries kept us for one hour. Embroideries where the needle, without exaggeration, competes with the paintbrush for the exactness of line, the subtle gradation of colour and the intensity of expression. There … as with its war machine, the Country of the Rising Sun ranks with the greatest nations in the world."[2]

While the Quebecers visited the palaces, the English-speaking women were drawn to a popular military exhibit on the Pike known as the Boer War, in which contingents of British and Dutch South African (Boer) troops recreated battles from the Three Years' War of 1899–1902. Grace Denison concluded that the Boer War spectacle was the best exhibit at the fair. Many observers agreed. However, at the time, the Boer War and Canada's participation in it (on Britain's side) was a hotly debated topic. It divided the Canadian public, particularly in Quebec, and set the stage for spirited arguments over Canada's place within the Empire – a debate that still resonates today. In 1899, Hugh Graham's *Montreal Daily Star* had denounced the reluctance of Prime Minister Laurier's Liberal government to enter the conflict. Indignant that New Zealand promised troops while Canada debated its commitment, Graham cabled every mayor in Canada, asking if they thought Canada should follow New Zealand's path. The resulting outcry put pressure on Laurier, pushing the government into action.[3] Troops were soon being readied for embarkation,[4] but not before Laurier reached a fiscal arrangement meant to appease French Canada whereby the country would send troops to South Africa at its own expense, but once there, Britain would support the troops financially.[5]

In St Louis, the Boer War re-creation took place on twelve acres of land designed to replicate the African veldt. More than five hundred veterans of the British and Boer conflict participated, simulating the Battle of Paardeberg in February 1900, when fifteen thousand soldiers fighting for Britain – including those from Canada – overwhelmed the Boer contingent of seven thousand. In the re-creation, ammunition roared, a Red Cross ambulance careened down the field, and Kaffir servants solemnly bore away the dead and dying.

According to Grace Denison, when the siege of famed Boer general Piet Cronje finally unfolded, the audience members grew more animated, not only because the scene was so realistic but also because they knew that the general, who was about to surrender, was no understudy for the part but the genuine item. Cronje appeared "ramping across the veldt, between long lines of khaki troops, among whom were originally our own boys of Toronto," Denison wrote. When Cronje pulled off his old straw hat to surrender, some audience members yelled and cheered as if the battle had just taken place.[6]

Interestingly, none of the French-speaking journalists wrote about the Boer War spectacle. This absence no doubt reflected a reluctance to introduce a hotly contested political issue into their coverage. In the early 1900s, at the mid-point of the Boer War, a young Quebec politician named Henri Bourassa founded the Nationalist League, which called for Canada's political autonomy from England. The league preached Pan-Canadian nationalism – a very different concept from contemporary Quebec nationalism – calling for the creation of a national spirit that would distinguish Canadians as a people.[7] *Le Nationaliste*, the newspaper founded by Alice Asselin's husband Olivar and the league's editorial voice, expressed the view that Canada should never be required to send troops to fight a war waged by Britain.

Politics aside, all the women were intrigued by an announcement made by General Piet Cronje at the fair. He told the press corps that he would marry Johanna Sterzel, the widow of a comrade killed at Paardeberg, in a wedding ceremony on the fairgrounds on 5 July. Several of the presswomen noted the impending marriage in their dispatches. In fact, Kate Simpson Hayes got the thrill of her journalistic career when she was granted an interview with the general and met his fiancé during the session. "I had the distinction of being presented to General Cronje this afternoon in the military lines of the Boer war encampment," she wrote. "This was really the most agreeable surprise of my newspaper life."[8] (See illustration 9.)

Hayes described the meeting and the events leading up to it in detail. First, she saw the re-enactment, which she found "realistic to a painful degree" and "very terrible to see." She was greatly moved by General Cronje's appearance on the veldt:

> He rode ahead of his shattered army down the double line of British troops just as he did, poor fellow, on the day his flag went down, and the depressed look of dogged despair on the faces of the men, women and children following after, lent all the sadness and much of the horror of what such a scene must have been in reality … It was a saddening scene, and it required more than an ordinary amount of nerve to witness it, even in play!

At the end of the reenactment, a young soldier clad in khaki presented Kate Simpson Hayes to several officers of the British regiment, and the next thing she knew, she was invited to take afternoon tea in the camp. "A very delightful 'tea' it was," she told her readers,

> served with true soldierly style, a small table set in the middle of a tent, milk and sugar accompaniments, and the tent flap thrown back to show us the "Kaffir Village" outside. The black man was there just as nature made him; the camp fire, the passing soldiers; the Boer women, who "followed after," so nobly in the real fight, and a Madame Botha was introduced to our small circle to give the finishing touch to the scene. Mme Botha rode the same little spirited horse she did during the war, and the affection of the dumb brute was very nice to see. The lady, I may add, participates with the other Boer women, in the battle scene of each day.

As Kate Simpson Hayes absorbed the scene around her, the general suddenly appeared.

> Here comes General Cronje! At the whispered word we all crowded to the tent door. Up came the grizzled old soldier, somewhat bowed by the weight of years … but there is a sort of subdued light in the

eye – it is a sort of flickering flame, I might say – which might mean:
"Ah, yes, I was General Cronje, of the Boers once" – Here the flame
says – "I am he still!" Dear, quiet-voiced old man! He gave me a
hard-veined, sinewy set of fingers as my name was mentioned, and he
very gravely and with great dignity, greeted me in Dutch. He sat in
his own headquarters, a soldier's tent, and received his visitors with a
gentle humility that it hurt one to see. Poor old man! Failure in such a
cause is a bitter dose at seventy! He looks a broken "soldier of fortune,"
but as I said before, he is Cronje still!

A few moments later, a short and amply proportioned Dutch-speaking
woman with a pleasing smile entered the tent. "My lady," said the general,
greeting her with the only English words Kate Simpson Hayes heard him
speak during the interview. Sure enough, it was Johanna Sterzel, age fifty,
who was to become Madame Cronje in a few days' time, "the widow of a
Boer soldier who fell fighting, and – oh, sentiment, sentiment! – now the
widow becomes the bride!" Hayes was able to ask the general a few questions through Sterzel, who spoke English extremely well. "General Cronje,
[Hayes asked,] do you think the Transvaal difficulty is settled now?" The
question was translated by Johanna Sterzel. "Yes – for now! (It was then
the flame leaped from cavernous depths). But perhaps – in twenty or more
years – ?" "Silence said the rest," concluded Hayes: "Cronje is Cronje still!"

Kit Coleman, too, had a chance to meet General Cronje, and though she
agreed with Kate Simpson Hayes that "he is simply force personified," and
concurred with Grace Denison that the dramatic re-enactment of the Boer
War was a brilliant spectacle, she had harsh words for the staged play and
for what she termed the general's "tawdry" performance. Coleman's sentiments could have easily been applied to Apache warrior Geronimo. The
one-time symbol of fearless resistance to encroachment on Aboriginal lands
had simply become a carnival attraction on the Pike.

"Jove!" Coleman exclaimed when writing about the Boer War. "When you
come to think of it, how would England look, how would glorious Scotia,
or my own loved Ireland look 'demonstrating' a defeat! Piet Cronje, great as

he undoubtedly is, is somehow a petty man ... Maybe he did not realize that he was exploiting the defeat of himself and his gallant countrymen ... One cannot forgive Cronje for so belittling himself and his truly great and brave people."[9] Kit Coleman admitted the play provided great drama. But for her, routinely ahead of her time on a range of issues, there was something wrong with hailing a dramatic re-enactment of war. It prompted her to make a trenchant comment – a comment perhaps forged by the sights she had witnessed in Cuba during the Spanish-American War in 1898. Or maybe it simply expressed her own deeply felt views. "The Boer fight drama," she acknowledged, "is perhaps the greatest thing on the St Louis Fair Grounds. That is, if one views war as a 'great' thing. But through the battle of the years, one comes to think of Peace as the only good."

About Cronje's impending marriage, however, Kit Coleman was much more sanguine. She didn't get a chance to meet the future Mrs Cronje, she wrote, but a colleague had described her. "His wife is not a Cleopatra," Coleman noted: "She is better. She is a human being with a noble soul, which is better than one with a merely handsome body. And she loves him. One can love at even the eleventh hour, and mayhap, the love brews the more ardent for the keeping."

Farewell to the Fair

Personally, our short stay simply whetted my appetite. Like
Oliver Twist, I cry for "more" and should like to spend a month in
observation of the fair and its many wonders.
– Irene Currie Love, *London Advertiser*, 9 July 1904

As the women wrapped up their exploration of the World's Fair on Tuesday, they began to think about the stories they would compose upon their return to Canada. One woman did not wait until she returned home to write a story. On her last day in St Louis, Kit Coleman wrote the first of three columns she would devote to the fair. Seated in the vast hallway of the Inside Inn and hunched over her notes, she composed a three-thousand-word article in longhand. By preparing what she described as a "more or less impressionistic" piece for her readers while she was still at the fair, and transmitting it by telegraph, Coleman was able to get a jump on her fellow travellers and have a story published in Toronto's *Mail and Empire* a week before any of the other journalists. Her story appeared the very day the journalists returned to Canada, while the other women had to wait until the following Saturday – the day usually reserved for the Woman's Page – to see their stories in print.

Also thinking ahead and organizing her ideas was Antoinette Gérin-Lajoie, who had already decided which part of the fair mattered most to her. "The Exposition comprises over a hundred buildings," she would tell readers of the Quebec City daily newspaper *L'Événement*: "We will cast a furtive glance at some, and dwell somewhat on those where the heart speaks strongly."[1] Gérin-Lajoie's heart spoke most strongly when she toured the Palace of Education and Social Economics. According to her, a visit to the Palace of Education was "of heart-stopping interest to all, but especially parents and schoolteachers." She wrote about the Education Building at length, devoting far more words to it than to any other exhibition and making it the focus of her coverage.

A potent family connection to the science of education likely led Antoinette Gérin-Lajoie to take that particular path. Her older brother, Léon Gérin (he dropped "Lajoie" from his name) was a pioneer social scientist in Canada and is sometimes referred to as the country's first sociologist of education.[2] Interestingly, during the 1960s, decades after Antoinette Gérin-Lajoie's trip to St Louis, her nephew Paul Gérin-Lajoie, a Rhodes scholar, would usher in revolutionary changes as Quebec's provincial education minister, wresting control of schooling from the Roman Catholic Church. Antoinette Gérin-Lajoie signalled her fascination with the process of education to her readers: "I would have seen little and would not have been satisfied if I had left unmentioned the building dedicated to Education. Education is the basis of everything: if education is properly given, do we not owe it our happiness? Does it not dictate our future?"

In her articles for *L'Événement*, Antoinette Gérin-Lajoie rhapsodized about a large display in the Palace of Education that showcased the "Sloyd" system developed in Scandinavia, a method stressing the importance of incorporating handicrafts and technical training into a general education. The Cleveland public school system, she noted, gave the system "a place of honour." Educators inserted into the regular curriculum classes in music, sewing, culinary arts, hygiene, physiology, photography, and gardening. "By experience, we all know how much a child likes to 'do' something," Gérin-Lajoie wrote: "How great is his joy, when with tools in his possession, he succeeds in creating the product he had first imagined?" By building skill upon skill, starting with the simplest and moving to the most complex, Gérin-Lajoie believed a student could acquire qualities essential in life: agility, confidence, precision, and perseverance. "In days of yore," she wrote, "education had an abstract character. The educated man was isolated from his peers and only had influence on a narrow circle. Today the aim is to give instruction of a practical character."

Antoinette Gérin-Lajoie believed that a practical education had more to offer a student, but her views were not widely shared, even by her peers – a fact she tacitly acknowledged. She rued that the Sloyd system was misunderstood: "The goal of the Sloyd system is not to create tradesmen – contrary to what is believed by some lady visitors to St Louis, who would ignore it, scorning these superb displays. No, as much as the Sloyd develops simple manual ability, the Sloyd is above all a process of education, a means of developing the intellectual faculty of precision – the exactness of the eye – as well as the moral faculty of execution." Gérin-Lajoie's keen interest in education and her familiarity with current methods and practice not only spoke to her concerns at that time but also foreshadowed her future endeavours.

For her part, Kate Simpson Hayes showed a strong interest in the role that women played at the exposition. At receptions given for the Canadians by the women journalists of St Louis and the general Missouri press, Hayes quizzed her confreres about the role of the Board of Lady Managers. In the early 1890s, an act of Congress officially formalized the role of women at a world's fair by establishing a "ladies branch" for the Chicago World's Fair and funding a building at that exposition that was strictly devoted to women and that served as a central location for highlighting a range of women's achievements, from art to education to engineering.

The same Congressional act funded a ladies branch in St Louis, but that group of women put a new twist on female contributions. In St Louis, women's work was blended with that of men, a truly revolutionary step and one that raised great debate. It is not clear whether the presswomen from Canada knew that there was a heated controversy surrounding the role of women at the fair. Some prominent members of the women's movement in the United States felt that blending the work of men and women in St Louis represented a great leap forward for women, putting them on par with men. Others vehemently disagreed, feeling that the St Louis framework failed to raise the awareness and visibility of women's accomplishments. They argued that combining women's work with men's work actually meant that the former received less notice.[3]

In St Louis, the Board of Lady Managers consisted of twenty-three women. They were socialites and philanthropists connected to wealth and prestige through their fathers or husbands. Ostensibly, the women were allowed to operate the government-funded Women's Building without interference from the all-male National World's Fair Commission and to express their opinions about other aspects of the fair as well. In reality, their clout was limited, although they did decide that the Women's Building in St Louis would not showcase women's work as did the Women's Building in Chicago but, rather, serve a purely administrative and social role.

For Kate Simpson Hayes, the purpose of the Women's Building in St Louis accorded with her own view of the womanly function. "The Board of Lady Managers stands in the position of hostesses of the American nation," Hayes informed her readers in the *Manitoba Free Press*. "It is a happy thought, and one that might well be copied by our own Winnipeg exhibition male management," she noted: "A building has been set apart for these Lady Managers, where they are 'at home' to all women from all parts of the world."[4]

The Winnipeg exhibition to which Kate Simpson Hayes referred was the largest agricultural and stock show held in western Canada at the time. By recommending that its organizers provide women with a place to hold their social functions, Hayes reflected the views of many of her readers and certainly of her editors, who thought the role of hostess was a fitting one for women. Hayes saw women as protectors of the sanctity of the home. She believed their behind-the-scenes role as keepers of the hearth was indispensable to Canada's growth and stability as a nation and did not feel women had a place in the public sphere.

As a fervent and "determined anti-suffragist," Kate Simpson Hayes ardently believed, and often told her readers in Winnipeg, that it was the duty of wives and mothers to influence their husbands and sons when it came to casting a ballot but that a woman had no business openly participating in the political process.[5] Hayes was, nevertheless, acutely aware of the debates surrounding the "new" woman. Shortly before the St Louis trip, she held an essay contest on the question of whether Canadian women should have the vote. On 9 July 1904, in one of her *Manitoba Free Press* columns about the World's Fair, she mentions the competition and notes that the contest had elicited a deluge of mail from as far south as California and as far east as New Brunswick.[6] She had been a little frightened, she wrote, "by the deadly earnestness" with which readers handled the question. She also expressed surprise that "so many women in remote districts have so keen a scent for what is going on in the outer world." She wrote: "Indeed, the editor of this page, always a most determined anti-suffragist, has almost 'keeled over' to the arguments of the ballot-believers, so strong, so convincing, so sensible, and so tolerant have they been in placing their opinions."

But a few years later, while working for the Canadian Pacific Railway in England on behalf of immigration to western Canada, Kate Simpson Hayes's views would actually harden against suffrage for women when she witnessed British suffragettes demonstrate in the street and go on a hunger strike. She strongly opposed their strident tone and denounced women who created a spectacle. She would proudly boast that no female in Canada had yet been connected with politics; she would praise the wives of Canadian politicians for using their influence wisely and discreetly in the social realm.[7]

Other women on the trip shared Kate Simpson Hayes's anti-suffrage stance. Grace Denison of Toronto's *Saturday Night*, a daring traveller who supported herself as a journalist all her life, did not favour the vote for women. Nor did Katherine Hughes, who would eventually cover the Alberta Legislature as a reporter for the *Edmonton Bulletin* and take on journalistic work as rugged as that taken on by men. A devout Catholic, Hughes's position on suffrage may have been influenced by the Roman Catholic Church, which did not support it.

But even staunchly independent Kit Coleman, who opened doors for female journalists by transcending the limitations of the Woman's Page, and who believed women deserved the same opportunities as men when it came to education and salary, did not support the vote for women. Coleman's non-support was likely both a reflection of her personal views and the views of her newspaper.[8] Women journalists could only push conventional bound-aries so far and still hold a job, and most female journalists shied away from endorsing the franchise for women.

Interestingly, there were outspoken men at the time who wanted women to have the vote, among them journalist and politician Nicholas Flood Davin, Kate Simpson Hayes's lover and the father of her two illegitimate children. Davin lobbied Parliament to give the federal franchise to women, but his plea had little traction. The inspiration for his request apparently did not come from Hayes, although she is sometimes mistakenly credited for it.[9]

As the Canadian women prepared to leave St Louis for the trip home, they realized that the most crucial information they could impart to their readers would deal with practical considerations. What would it cost to see the fair? What items should a traveller pack? What was it like to spend a few nights on the train? Mary Dawson tackled the question of cost, telling her *Toronto Telegram* readers that a week's visit to the St Louis exposition could be made for between fifty and fifty-five dollars, including train fare, room, meals, admission to the grounds, and fees to some exhibits on the Pike. The presswomen had not expended money for transport, but a stay in the Inside Inn, where the English-speaking contingent resided, cost two dollars per night at a time when salaries for journalists were roughly twenty-five dollars per month (although it is likely the CPR picked up the bill).

"Of course you must leave a margin of, say, at least $5," Dawson cautioned: "All manner of things may happen. You might forget or lose your rubbers or umbrella, or be caught in one of the many violent thunderstorms that break over St Louis and spoil part of your finery. You'll certainly need a shine or two and maybe a few headache powders. The hotel drug clerk told us he sold more of these powders and 'foot rest' preparations than any other three articles."[10]

Irene Currie Love warned her readers not to be seduced by the Pike, where vendors were selling everything from exquisite amber necklaces to a kimono made in Japan. "These are the places where you can waste the most money," she cautioned: "In almost every case the vendors will 'do' you if they get the chance, and it behooves you to be very wide-awake."[11] Before leaving

St Louis, Irene Currie Love interviewed a railway official from the United States who enumerated a number of blunders overnight travellers make; for instance, he related, they don't realize they are allowed to summon the porter with the touch of an electric button, even in the middle of the night. Should the sleeping car become too stuffy, the railway official noted, the porter could open the ventilator. If the traveller needed to use the bathroom, the porter could bring portable steps to the sleeping berth for the descent and ascent. "You'd be surprised if you knew how many people there are who have never traveled on a sleeping car, and the funny mistakes they make on their first trip," the railway man told Currie Love: "I often wonder why some of you newspaper women don't write up a little schedule of what to do in a Pullman. It would save us a lot of trouble."

Irene Currie Love took his advice and coached her readers on everything from proper bathroom etiquette to tipping the porter ("from 50 cents to $1, according to the amount of attention you demand"). She urged women to choose wisely when they picked a berth in the sleeping car. "It is better for a woman to take the lower berth," she wrote, "as it is rather difficult to climb in and out of an upper one, though if I were a man, I should much prefer an upper berth, as it is really more comfortable."

Kate Simpson Hayes cautioned her readers to pack lightly. "In dress, take only what is absolutely necessary for comfort," she advised, providing a succinct checklist to simplify the process. It included a dozen shirtwaists, or what we today call blouses; a tweed skirt, light in texture; a straw hat with as little trimming as possible; ties, stockings, and underwear to last through the stay; plus rubbers and an umbrella.

Boarding the train for the overnight trip that would put them in Chicago by morning, the women found tasty gifts in the sleeper car: two immense baskets of apples and a plate loaded with sugar buns, courtesy of one of the welcoming hosts whom they had met at the exposition's Agricultural Building. "We savoured the treats," related Amintha Plouffe, "and wished him good health."[12]

A Presidential Convention

It is as hard for a woman to gain admittance as for a camel
to go through the eye of a needle.
– Irene Currie Love, *London Advertiser*, 16 July 1904

An animated group of women representing the Illinois Woman's Press Association gathered at the train station in Chicago early Wednesday morning to welcome the Canadian presswomen. Marguerite Springer, wife of millionaire real-estate mogul Warren Springer and an extraordinary beauty, led the Chicago contingent. Many of the Canadians later mentioned her good looks in their dispatches. Léonise Valois wrote that Marguerite Springer's striking face and upswept hairdo were engraved in her memory, much like the cameos that featured Marie Antoinette and other women of nobility during the revolutionary epoch. Little did the visitors realize how apt the comparison would be. Like Marie Antoinette, Marguerite Springer had a reputation as distinctive as her appearance.

There is no record that Marguerite Springer ever worked as a journalist. A one-time salesgirl who married into wealth, she had been the subject of newspaper articles in the Chicago press rather than their writer. In 1894, she had been indicted for offering bribes to jurors who were hearing a case against her husband that involved the condemnation of properties on land that he owned.[1] Warren Springer regularly attempted to evade ordinances governing Chicago buildings. In 1892, after a boiler in one of his buildings exploded, killing five people, he was indicted but never punished.

Controversy seemed to follow Marguerite Springer. A few weeks before the Canadians came to town, a group of prominent clubwomen in Chicago announced publicly that they planned to socially ostracize her for trying to disbar a local lawyer who was pressing an action against her husband. The clubwomen claimed that Springer deliberately set out to destroy the lawyer by digging up incriminating information from his past. Club members rallied to the side of the lawyer's wife and vowed to make Springer pay for her spiteful behaviour.[2]

Despite her notoriety, Marguerite Springer was a woman of influence, active in women's organizations and devoted to the cause of suffrage. Since the Illinois Woman's Press Association was firmly embedded in the women's club movement, as were other regional women's press organizations in the United States,[3] Springer would have known journalists such as Jennie Van Allen of the *Chicago Daily Tribune*, who was by her side at the train station on Wednesday morning, 22 June 1904, and who watched as she charmed the Canadians with her beauty and graciousness.

A large contingent of Chicago women joined Springer in greeting the Canadians, perhaps some of them taking her side in a brewing feud pitting the Daughters of the American Revolution, the group to which the lawyer's wife belonged, against the rival Daughters of the Revolution, which was led by Springer. And although some of the women meeting the train were active journalists, there was another potent bond that drew them together: they all belonged to the Chicago Cat Club. The care and breeding of pedigreed cats was a preoccupation among well-to-do Chicago females, including those waiting at the train station. Animal lover Kit Coleman shared a passion with these women, although hers was focused on dogs. The previous year, Coleman's Bedlington terriers had won every award for the breed at the American Bench Show in New York.[4]

The Chicagoans quickly ushered the Canadians to a hurried breakfast in a restaurant near the train station and were so bent on giving the visitors the best time possible that several of the latter felt that the hours spent in

Chicago were the most enjoyable of their entire trip. Indeed, the Chicago women were so generous and kind, that, according Léonise Valois, those Quebecers whose English lacked polish "spoke their gibberish better" in order to respond to the amiability of their hosts.[5]

In short order, Marguerite Springer and her colleagues whisked the Canadian women to the Coliseum on South Wabash Street to attend the Republican National Convention then being held to nominate the presidential candidate for the party. Fortunately for the women, they paid a visit to Chicago on the most stirring day of the convention and were doubly fortunate to have Marguerite Springer as a guide. Simply to be visiting the City of Chicago hardly entitled one to gain access to a presidential convention, as Peggy Watt told her readers, and it was only through the good offices of Marguerite Springer, whose influence in political and social circles was substantial, that entrance was secured to the vast building in which thousands of delegates and spectators gathered.

The presswomen were acutely aware that they were a distinct minority. Women had yet to gain the right to vote on the national level in the United States, although they had been granted limited voting rights in towns, counties, and some states. That year, four women delegates were designated to sit as alternates at the Republican convention, a minuscule female presence in a hall filled with more than eight thousand men. Three sons of former US presidents were in the crowd (Garfield, Grant, and Hayes), and Marguerite Springer arranged for the Canadians to meet Illinois governor Richard Yates before the names of President Theodore Roosevelt and Senator Charles Fairbanks of Indiana were placed in nomination as candidates for president and vice-president, respectively. "I understand that [Yates] has always been a popular candidate with Canadians resident in Chicago," wrote Peggy Watt: "From what we saw of him, I do not wonder at this. In the most cordial terms he bade us welcome to the State."[6]

As the woman entered the convention hall, the divide that until now had only been an undercurrent between the French- and English-speaking journalists surfaced. The band acknowledged the presence of Canadians in the hall by breaking into a rendition of "God Save the King." Everyone stood, and, as Kit Coleman rose to her feet, she dramatically flung her handkerchief to the breeze. "Perhaps you know what our feelings were when we heard *God Save Our King* played under the Stars and Stripes?" Kate Simpson Hayes asked her readers. Such exultation was not recorded by the French-speaking contingent. No mention of "God Save the King" appears in any dispatch, although there is mention of an orchestra in the convention hall that played charming melodies for an hour, to which Cécile Laberge exulted while others in the party shared her joy and savoured the lovely sounds themselves.[7]

Once the business of the convention began, the women, seated a distance back in the hall, thought the speakers looked like pygmies gesticulating wildly. They were unable to hear what was being said. "It seems to require almost superhuman powers to score a great oratorical success in such a gathering," wrote Peggy Watt, whose budding interest in politics shines through her dispatches and who writes in greater detail about the convention than any woman on the trip. Among the speakers who scored an oratorical victory, Peggy Watt singled out Senator Chauncey M. Depew of New York, a railroad industrialist who had written a book entitled *Orations and After-Dinner Speakers*. Another who drew praise from Watt was convention chair Joseph Cannon, the speaker of the House of Representatives, a man Canadians had heard much about due to his pugnacious style. "It was not difficult to recognize him," wrote Peggy Watt. Hearing him speak even briefly, she contended, made one "realize how winning are his ways and what the force of his character is."

But the featured speaker of the day really seized Peggy Watt's attention. Lawyer Elihu Root, secretary of war under President William McKinley and soon to be secretary of state under Teddy Roosevelt, would go on to win the Nobel Peace Prize in 1912. "He seems to be regarded as the man of foremost ability in his party," Peggy Watt wrote. Years later, in awarding the Nobel Prize to Root, the Nobel Committee singled out his work in "bringing about better understanding between the countries of North and South America."[8]

Peggy Watt was also struck by something odd in the assembly hall: the spirit of a dead man haunted the gathering. Senator Mark Hanna, industrialist and crack fundraiser for William McKinley's 1896 presidential campaign, had died suddenly five months before the convention. Hanna might have posed a challenge to Roosevelt's candidacy in 1904, but, now in his grave, he no longer loomed as a threat. A large draped picture displayed on the convention floor, along with frequent references to Hanna on the part of various speakers, almost brought him to life. "The casual visitor came away with the impression that if Hanna had lived, the President would not have been the candidate," wrote Watt: "During our stay we saw no evidence of any great love for Roosevelt." The president, who had been McKinley's running mate during the latter's second campaign in 1900, was elevated to the presidency in a flash when McKinley was assassinated while attending the Pan-American Exposition in Buffalo in 1901. Roosevelt would go on to win the party nomination in Chicago and the general election in 1904.

Given that the presswomen had limited time to spend in the city, Marguerite Springer herded the group out of the convention hall and off on a whirlwind excursion through Chicago's big department stores on State Street in the Loop. They visited Siegel, Cooper & Co., located in a landmark building designed by William Le Baron Jenney, and the Fair, a discount department store whose marketing slogan promised "everything for everybody under one roof at a cheap price."

But the high point of the shopping trip for everyone was a visit to iconic Marshall Field & Co., established in 1852. In addition to the glistening displays of merchandise that captivated the group, the women could not conceal their extreme satisfaction at the way the employees were treated by their bosses. Robertine Barry often wrote about labour conditions for women and would later be appointed by the Quebec government as inspector of women's work in industrial establishments. She and the other presswomen marvelled at the spacious rooms set aside for Marshall Field employees during their lunch hour, remarking that the workers enjoyed a level of comfort unknown in Canada. "The generosity of the big American merchants is something we'd like to see here," wrote Léonise Valois: "There is an affinity there between bosses and employees and everyone is happier for it."

The women were invited to inspect the cold storage department of Marshall Field, where furs were kept throughout the summer. Donning heavy winter coats for the inspection on that warm June day, the women felt like they had travelled from the tropics to the North Pole. They were amazed at the ingenuity of the cold storage room, and the French-Canadian women, especially, thought the innovation could be applied back home in Montreal, a city known for its furriers. Shedding the coats after the tour, they left the store and exited into Chicago's busy downtown core. Several intrepid members of the party took up an invitation to climb to the roof of one of the city's tallest buildings, where they had a superb view of Lake Michigan. They were deeply impressed by the size of the lake, which seemed as large as an ocean, as it disappeared into the horizon.

Having eaten only a light breakfast that morning, the Canadian women were famished. Their hosts had prearranged a luncheon at Hull House, a settlement refuge founded by Jane Addams at the western end of Chicago's downtown Loop. Daughter of a prominent Illinois banker and politician, Addams was a pioneer in the settlement movement that had started in London, England. She and fellow reformers believed not only that the poor had to participate in their own betterment but also that men and women of all classes must contribute to the public good. To that end, Addams established Hull House in the middle of Chicago's slums as a community where social reformers, including idealistic doctors, lawyers, and academics, could live among the poor while they campaigned for better housing, cleaner water, and basic health services. (See illustration 10.)

Hull House benefited from the philanthropic patronage of Marguerite Springer and her friends, including Annie Meyers Sergel, wife of the wealthy publisher Charles Sergel, president of the Chicago Women's Press League, and a serious social reformer who would soon make waves by founding the Anti-Smoke League. Annie Meyers Sergel and her female supporters would take on big business by vowing to halt their domestic routines unless the trains of the Illinois Central Railroad stopped emitting smoke and polluting Chicago's Southside with soot and noise.[9] Through Annie Sergel's intervention, the Canadians were shepherded through Hull House. Unfortunately, Jane Addams was absent the day of their visit, and, thus, the presswomen were denied the privilege of meeting the most famous woman in the United States at that time.

No one regretted Addams's absence more keenly than Marie Beaupré, who had eagerly followed her work and shown great interest, through her own writing, in the social reform Addams had undertaken. A few months before the trip to St Louis, Beaupré had published an article in a magazine called *Le Foyer* decrying the sorry state of the working girl in Quebec. According to Beaulieu and Hamelin in *La presse québécoise, 1886–1910*, the title of the publication was somewhat misleading. While the word "foyer" refers to the hearth, the magazine itself held that women should also partake in the intellectual and cultural life of the era. The content of *Le Foyer* was divided into two parts: (1) articles useful to women in everyday life and (2) essays and short stories written under pennames.

Marie Beaupré, who used the penname "Hélène Dumont," told readers she was haunted by recurrent images of a lonely, isolated girl who worked long hours in a factory or an office in Montreal and lived a friendless existence away from her family in squalid quarters for which she paid a good portion of her meagre wages as, day by day, her spirit drained away. In an article entitled "Ma Hantise," Beaupré describes the young girl who disturbed her dreams at night and troubled her thoughts during the day:

> Evening comes, her little forehead will be tightened in a band of iron. Shoulders curved, she leaves and returns very weary, all alone in the dark. Where? Towards which threshold? Towards a threshold where she will be awaited without anticipation, without affectionate worry? Where she will be received without tenderness and without joy? A banal meal and then a room, cold and bare. There's nothing for the mind. No mouth to say a word to light an avid spirit, to warm a heart. No hand to guide her efforts or lift her courage. She is alone, alone![10]

Marie Beaupré suggested that the solution for the young girl, and others like her, would be to engage in church work to break the isolation and to provide spiritual nourishment. "Here there will be real friends," she wrote: "Practical lessons will instruct and open the spirit to abundant ideas that are sane and useful. The noblest movements of the heart will be encouraged and enlivened. Legitimate hopes will grow daily."

Others in the press group aside from Marie Beaupré also knew about the work of Jane Addams, and they knew, too, that there was a potent Canadian connection to Hull House. Future prime minister William Lyon Mackenzie King (then deputy labour minister) lived at Hull House briefly while attending the University of Chicago in the mid-1890s. Peggy Watt had heard King speak about Jane Addams when he'd addressed a crowd at Woodstock's city hall. After hearing King's description of the work being done by Hull House, she was thrilled to be able to see it for herself. "There is no doubt about the great work which it is doing for the poor, in the midst of whose dwellings it is situated," she wrote:

> Thousands of young men and young women arise today to call it blessed. From a life that means darkness and disgrace, they have been rescued and led to the path that means self-respecting manhood and womanhood. Educational classes of all kinds are carried on within its walls. Into many a cheerless existence it carries brightness. I had a chance myself of seeing an example of its work for children when at the entrance gate a girl of six or seven years asked me if this was the place where you put your name down to get some fresh air. To get "fresh air," think of it!

After lunch, Marguerite Springer had more plans for the press party. She took everyone for an automobile ride along Lake Shore Drive north to Lincoln Park. A number of cars were provided, and the Canadian flag flew from one side of the leading auto, with Old Glory on the other – a gesture that was greatly appreciated by the Canadians. Enchanted by the splendid mansions of the city's millionaires and by the verdant land in sprawling Lincoln Park, the women were caught off guard when police stopped their entourage for speeding. Silently thrilled as they watched the action unfold, the Canadian women reported that police captain Busch and a brawny officer called Murphy all but dragged one poor chauffeur from his seat. Told that the women were Canadians, the gallant captain let them go. Kit Coleman reported that Captain Busch told Marguerite Springer that she had a fine Canadian face. "I can tell you," Kit wrote, "Canada appreciated the compliment."[11]

After the excursion it was time for an early dinner, and the three men from the CPR graciously invited the Chicago women to join the Canadian women at a fine meal in an elegant Swiss restaurant. Since there still remained a few hours until departure following their dinner, the entire party visited one of the most beautiful hotels in Chicago, and although none of the dispatches name the hotel, it was almost certainly the lavish Palmer House, built by Potter Palmer for his wife Bertha and featuring a separate "Ladies Entrance." The women had already visited the Marquette Building earlier in the day and admired the superb mosaic that traced the path of Father Marquette's effort to evangelize the Aboriginal peoples living along the Mississippi River, and now they were left breathless as they viewed the exquisite marble and granite interior of the hotel where the Republican politicians they'd seen earlier were likely staying. As day turned to night, it was time to return to the train. "The dear ladies accompanied us and it was with emotion that we said goodbye in all hope that we could soon return their cordial welcome," wrote Léonise Valois.

A Club Is Born

There seemed to exist between us a communion of ideas, of tastes,
I dare say, of sentiments, which lasted until the end, and which,
it seemed to me, embellished the beautiful days
we spent on the trip even more.
– Léonise Valois, *Le Canada*, 9 July 1904

At seven o'clock the next morning, another joyous group of female journalists awaited the arrival of the Canadians as their train pulled into Detroit. Despite the early hour, almost the entire membership of the Detroit Women's Press Club assembled at the station to greet the Canadians. Representatives of the city's four leading newspapers – the *Detroit News*, the *Detroit Free Press*, the *Detroit Journal*, and the *Detroit Tribune* – were included in the entourage. Even though they would spend only a short time in Detroit that Thursday, the women from Canada would strike up friendships that, in some cases, would endure for years.

Founded by thirteen female journalists and literary writers in 1901, and simply called the Detroit Press Club at that time, the organization was now in the process of amending its name. In the spring of 1904, the women learned, much to their dismay, that their club name had been summarily hijacked by a newly formed group of 125 male journalists. In order to avoid confusion, they had inserted the word "Women's" in their title.

Led by Pruella Jane Sherman, women's editor for the *Detroit Sunday News-Tribune* and a founding member of the club, the contingent on hand to greet the Canadians also included Alice E. Bartlett, the club's first president, a journalist for the *Detroit Journal*, and a celebrated novelist and poet who used the pseudonym "Birch Arnold."[1] A dozen or so other presswomen met the train as well, and the entire group piled into automobiles for a tour through the city streets and, ultimately, to Belle Isle, where they were transported by carriage around the largest island park in the United States, a recreational paradise bigger than New York's Central Park and designed by the same man, Frederick Law Olmsted, who also designed Mount Royal Park in Montreal.

"Nature seemed to have taken particular favour to this small corner of our world," wrote Amintha Plouffe, "and our crossing the immense park has charmed me so much that if Montreal did not exist, it is there that I would want to live."[2] Belle Isle captivated the other presswomen as well. "It is a kind of Eden where the roses blossom in marvelous fashion," Léonise Valois wrote.[3] The city's commissioner of parks showered the Canadians with as many roses as they could carry (plucked from forbidden fields in the botanical garden, according to Kate Simpson Hayes) and showed off a newly built conservatory patterned on Thomas Jefferson's home in Monticello.

The group then left Belle Isle by boat for the return trip to Detroit. More roses awaited on banquet tables in the Wayne Hotel, where the Sun Parlor dining room sat at the very edge of the St Clair River, a tributary of Lake Huron. Unfortunately, the Canadians had to eat their meal in haste as they were running late for the train. "How little importance it had to eat lightly or a lot!" remarked Amintha Plouffe: "We had already tasted so much of the Ideal."

Before the women climbed aboard the train, they posed for a group photograph in Detroit that has now become an iconic image. Taken by a professional photographer, the photo shows them dressed in their best and looking surprisingly fresh, given their travels, probably due to the purchase of crisp new blouses and other items of clothing in Chicago. All are wearing smart elaborate hats, except for Margaret Graham, ever the maverick, who is positioned smack in the centre of the photo, hatless, head turned sideways to the camera. The three men in the party – Ham, Notman, and Ussher – wear dark suits and bowler hats. (See illustration 11.)

Missing from the photo are Grace Denison and Kit Coleman. Coleman's reputation as the first woman war correspondent and Canada's most prominent female journalist drew an interview request from members of the Detroit press corps. The interview took place while the group photo was being taken, and since a posed photograph of the entire group had not been taken in St Louis or Chicago, there is no permanent record of Coleman's place in the party. The reason for Grace Denison's absence from the photo remains a mystery and is elaborated upon further in the text.

At what precise point in their journey the women formed the Canadian Women's Press Club is not clear. It is certain that the club was founded on the train, but the timing is in dispute. Peggy Watt recalls the club's being formed right before the train reached St Louis. Other accounts, written years after the founding, state that the club was formed when the women crossed the border into Canada on their return trip. Kate Simpson Hayes, in her stories about the excursion, gives weight to Watt's recollection that the club was formed early in the trip, long before the women reached the Canadian border. "It was our good luck to meet representatives of the leading city dailies," Hayes wrote of the group's visit to Detroit, "and they showed a very great interest in us and our newly formed club."[4]

No matter when it was established, the formation of a press club for Canadian women had actually been discussed before the trip, but in different realms. Margaret Graham may have been the driving force behind the trip to St Louis as she was the one who asked Ham to offer women the same travelling privileges as men, but others had commented on the inequity between presswomen and pressmen before the excursion. As Barbara Freeman points out in *Kit's Kingdom*, in May 1904 Kit Coleman raised the issue of a club to guard women's interests, perhaps planting the seeds that would sprout soon after. Three weeks before the St Louis excursion, Coleman responded to a young reader interested in becoming a journalist by saying: "I think we press women ought to get up a club or an association of some kind and try to meet once a year. I don't suppose we would claw each other too awfully and a little fun might be got out of our speech-making. Why should Canadian men journalists have all the trips and banquets?"[5]

Kit Coleman may not have known that, in 1903, Anne-Marie Gleason had been a founding member of the Association des journalistes canadiens-français (AJCF). The organization, composed of men and women, sought to raise the prestige and dignity of the journalism profession in Quebec, to provide mutual support to fellow members, and to ensure that publishers relied on Quebec authors instead of poaching the work of writers from France or Switzerland. The AJCF proposed the creation of ethics tribunals, identity cards for journalists, and a retirement residence for those who had served the profession. But its main battle revolved around the issue of copyright. Members were angry that Canada was only paying lip service to the Berne Convention, an international pact governing copyright, which meant that, according to the AJCF, the country was flooded with unauthorized cheap versions of foreign books.[6] In early 1904, perhaps in recognition of her rising status as a journalist, Anne-Marie Gleason had been made a member of the executive board guiding the AJCF. It seems likely that the fledgling Canadian Women's Press Club borrowed some of the AJCF's founding principles when a rough draft of the club's first constitution was hammered out on the train.

No doubt the women's knowledge that they would be meeting up with members of women's press clubs in Chicago and Detroit also spurred the club's formation. A slate of officers was quickly drawn up aboard the train. In a perfect French-English divide that also reflected, to a great degree, journalism experience and professional status, Kit Coleman was elected president, Robertine Barry was elected vice-president, Kate Simpson Hayes was elected secretary, and Anne-Marie Gleason was elected treasurer. Acknowledging that the club could not possibly have come into existence without the support of George Ham, the women named him honorary president, a title he apparently cherished all his life and one that would prove exceedingly helpful to the Canadian Women's Press Club in years to come.

Some suggest Ham may have been the real force behind the club's formation. Once he realized how impressive and powerful they were as a group,
Ham, it is said, urged the women to unite.[7] Through the years, Ham would
joke about his status in the club, stating in his memoir that "somehow or
other – guess for lack of better material – I was made honorary president,
and have been the only male member of a female press club in the world ever
since. Some are born great, you know, others achieve greatness, and others
still have greatness thrust upon them. You can readily see to which class I
belong, can't you?"[8]

Grace Denison mentioned the formation of the club in her column for
Saturday Night while shrouding in mystery her own lack of participation.
She failed to say why she refused to join her fellow journalists in the endeavour, offering faint praise and, at the same time, teasingly raising questions
about the group's aims:

> The private car which took the women guests of the CPR to St. Louis
> on the sixteenth was the scene of the formation of the first Canadian
> Women's Press Club, of which Mrs Blake Coleman ("Kit" of the
> "Mail and Empire") was elected president. As I did not enroll my-
> self among its members, I know little of what its aims are, but fancy
> it should be a useful and enjoyable institution for the women of the
> Canadian press. Certainly, if it fosters a study of journalistic ethics
> and eliminates the possibility of certain happenings of which I have
> heard, its advent comes none too soon.[9]

Denison did not elaborate on the "happenings" to which she alludes, but
she did go on to say that she advocated, among presswomen, loyalty and
consideration. "And with such women as the gifted president, the brilliant
vice-president, one of the finest types of French women, and a loyal rank
and file, the Women's Press Club is bound to be a power in journalism,"
she stated. "My non-membership is not at all due to lack of interest or non-
assurance of worth but from purely personal reasons which have nothing to

do with the club and which for the present influence me. My best wishes are respectfully offered to my dear friend 'Kit' in her new dignity, and as for Mlle Barry, she is already queen of my heart in its French quarter section, and has my joyous congratulations." With this opaque endorsement, Grace Denison raised more questions about her motivation for opting out of the club than she answered.

For her part, Kit Coleman seemed extremely pleased that the women had decided to band together. "It has been my hope for years that the press women of the Dominion of Canada would combine and form a club," she stated in her first column on the St Louis trip: "That hope is at last realized."[10] She predicted that the organization would become an important one in the years ahead. She noted that admission was restricted to working journalists only. "This is not to be merely a society of authors, although distinguished Canadian women authors will be always welcome and honored," she told her readers.

Kit Coleman revealed that the group planned to hold yearly meetings at which members would present scholarly papers pertaining to the profession. It was an early sign of the educational component the club members felt crucial to the group's purpose. In the absence of journalism schools in Canada and certainly in the absence of mentors in the newsroom, the women were eager to learn anything they could about their craft. Coleman also told her readers that the club would hold receptions at the annual meetings, which would openly welcome members of the various women's press leagues in the United States. Finally, she informed readers that "camaraderie" had been adopted as the club motto, which might also have been a code name for unity as members hailed from Ontario, Quebec, and Manitoba, and they sought in their constitution to promote a common vision of a strong and united Canada no matter where they resided. Reflecting on the shared aims of the club women, Coleman wrote: "À bas les politiques. The so-called 'racial' cry does not touch our clever French-Canadian women journalists. Such dear women! Polite –'to make us ashamed'— gentle, capable and very sweet companions. Whatever you gentlemen politicians may have to grumble about, let me assure you that the Press Women of Canada … are in unity, and will, I hope, remain so, no matter what political storms – Conservative, Liberal, and other – disturb the Canadian atmosphere."[11]

Heading home from their great adventure, the women had mixed emotions. They were eager to regain their routines, but they found it hard to let go of the experience they had shared. They had cherished the opportunity to travel to another country, to absorb the remarkable sights at an astounding world's fair, to meet fellow female journalists in Chicago and Detroit, and to be treated like professionals every step of their journey. But they were also thinking, during the last stretch of the trip, about the dispatches they would begin filing within hours and the pressure to churn out copy for their editors. Some of the women would be writing multiple articles containing as many as seven thousand words apiece. For the novices in the crowd, that responsibility weighed heavily.

As their minds filled with practical considerations and looming deadlines, there were also tender thoughts of the journey that was rapidly coming to an end. Kate Simpson Hayes reflected on the bonding experience among the Canadian journalists. "Contrary to expectations," she stated, "the ladies started out in brave, good humor and returned friends. This knocks the bottom out of an old belief." She went on to affirm that: "The sixteen ladies behaved with rare good sense. Not one of them referred to her 'rich relations' once! Not one referred to the others in terms of 'rebuke.' Not one said she 'was ashamed to be seen with the others'; and not one held feminine spite nor said unkind things of her sisters there. In short, we almost realized 'canonization,' so perfect was the circle of pen-women on that never-to-be-forgotten trip."

Unlike the light-hearted Hayes, Léonise Valois used a serious tone to describe their homecoming and offered a typically poetic expression of profound gratitude. As the women boarded the train for the final leg of the journey, she described her feelings to her readers: "Then we take the train again, leading us once and for all to Canadian soil en route towards our joyous home, where dear arms embrace us upon our return. How the air of our country is good! Pitch our tent here! Let us live, love and die at home, in our beautiful Canada, which is worth all the countries in the world. This is our last impression and we summarize it in these words: Long live our beloved country!"

Winnipeg and Alberta, 1906

The outcome of the trip was that the Canadian Women's
Press Club has arrived.
– Kit Coleman, *Mail and Empire*, 25 June 1904

Kit Coleman trumpeted the new club in her first column about the fair. "The heart and object of the club," she wrote, "is to bring together and make known to each other the women who are working on various newspapers in the Dominion, that we may be friendly and helpful to one another in the work."[1] Kate Simpson Hayes also wasted no time advertising the formation of the Canadian Women's Press Club when she returned to Montreal. The newly elected club secretary announced in her 9 July 1904 column for the *Manitoba Free Press* that the club was soliciting membership. "The rules are 'emergency' ones, pending the building of our constitution, and are liable to change," she wrote:

> Applications will be received until further notice under the following conditions: Any Canadian newspaper woman having had one full year's (salaried) experience on a paper in good standing. Her name, with an admittance fee of $2, must be submitted for the ballot acceptance. Money returned if the applicant is not accepted. For

further information apply (postage enclosed), Mrs K.S. Hayes, secretary CWPC, 80 "C" Crescent street [sic] Montréal.[2]

Eager to keep the momentum going, Hayes wrote to club vice-president Robertine Barry in July of 1904 proposing a meeting in September between herself, Barry, and honorary president George Ham. Spending the summer in the Charlevoix area in Murray Bay (today called La Malbaie), Barry missed Hayes's letter because she dropped by the summer post office in Pointe-aux-Pic only once. Weeks passed before the letter finally caught up with her in Montreal. In an apologetic note written in English and dated 3 September 1904, Robertine Barry told Kate Simpson Hayes she would be happy to meet for club business. Writing under her pseudonym "Françoise," which she now used exclusively in both her journalism and her personal life, Barry ended the letter by "wishing our club all kinds of prosperity, I remain your friend and unworthy vice president, Françoise." She then added a postscript. "Please if you see Mr Ham and Mr Ussher, tell them something nice for me. F."[3]

Club members originally hoped to assemble in 1905, to adhere to an annual schedule. But it is likely that the death that year of George Ham's wife Martha, with whom he had five children, meant the meeting could not take place. Ham was the journalists' patron, mentor, and godfather rolled into one. He had persuaded the Canadian Pacific Railway it would be advantageous to underwrite train travel and hotel accommodation for the women journalists beyond the St Louis venture. The fledging CWPC, which by this time had sparked interest from women journalists around the country, could not assemble a far-flung group without his involvement, and so a 1905 meeting was out of the question.

Instead, a decision was made to hold the next club meeting in Winnipeg in June of 1906, two years after the club's formation. Ham offered free passage on the railway to any credentialled female journalist interested in attending, and he promised an excursion further west into territory that most of the women had never seen. Westward expansion was in its infancy, and so, in 1906, the meeting in Winnipeg would present a new experience even for those journalists like Robertine Barry and Kit Coleman who had travelled widely in Europe and other parts of North America but not in their own country.

One hundred women received invitations to the Winnipeg meeting: forty-four registered for it. Only six had been on the trip to St Louis: Kit Coleman, Kate Simpson Hayes, Robertine Barry, Peggy Watt, Mary Adelaide Dawson, and Katherine Hughes. Three of these women were officers of the club; the only officer who did not come to Winnipeg was treasurer Anne-Marie Gleason, who was still writing for *La Patrie*. In fact, other than Robertine Barry, none of the French-speaking women on the St Louis trip came to Winnipeg in 1906. Part of the reason may have been the explosive Manitoba Schools Question, which left many Quebecers embittered. In the 1890s, Manitoba's provincial government had abolished public funding to Catholic schools – schools that served a largely French-speaking population. In Quebec, the action was considered a severe encroachment on the rights of French speakers and Catholics.

A more pragmatic explanation probably accounts for the absence of Anne-Marie Gleason. Her life had radically changed since St Louis as she had become a wife and mother. In October of 1904, Anne-Marie Gleason married Dr Wilfrid Huguenin, and the couple had a daughter in 1905. It is likely she was caring for a baby and unavailable to venture out west.

Most startling of all, however, was the absence of groundbreaker Margaret Graham, who was responsible for convincing Ham to sponsor the trip to St Louis in the first place. By not coming to Winnipeg, the so-called mother of the club once again proved a maverick – or demonstrated that she no longer wished to be one. In response to a journalist from the *Manitoba Free Press* who asked if she would be coming to the meeting, Graham wrote a light-hearted letter that seemed to contradict her strong feelings about equality for women professionals. She hinted that a trip out west might promote domestic discord and implied that a journalism career could not possibly be fulfilling for a woman, particularly for a married woman.

"You women can pretend you're happy talking press matters if you like," she wrote: "I'm going to stay home and do 'me duty!'"[4]

"Coming to the Winnipeg convention? Not me – not Miggsy," she continued. "I went to your cold land once, just once. I haven't eaten, slept, or been happy since! It caused the first row between me and my other half. I wanted to stay there – to become 'wild and woolly' – to buy land – to start a farm – to run a ranch – oh, I wanted to stay west and it almost broke up a happy home, seeing that West of yours! No, I am not going. I am twirling the biscuit rolling pin just now and reading up soup and pie recipes for a husband."[5]

Margaret Graham had married Albert Horton in 1905, a year after the trip to St Louis. Perhaps the couple had then taken a trip out west on their honeymoon. At fifty-one, Albert was sixteen years older than Graham and worked on the staff of Hansard in Ottawa, which published the official record of parliamentary speeches and debates. After they married, Graham apparently settled into a domestic routine and only wrote sporadically for newspapers.

Journalists and other professional women certainly faced societal pressure to quit working once they married, and that pressure continued for decades. As late as 1941, less than 4 percent of married women in Canada were employed.[6] The image of a woman at home, caring for her children and husband became "the measure of respectability, and unmarried women or women who worked were to be pitied or criticized."[7] If women engaged in work outside the home, they were accused of supporting a women's rights movement that sought the destruction of the family.

In fact, early suffragettes nearly always framed their arguments in a way that held the role of wife and mother sacrosanct. Nellie McClung was not only a celebrated suffragette and a member of the CWPC but also a mother of five children, and, in her speeches, she routinely emphasized that women had no intention of neglecting the home fires once they gained the vote. The prejudice against women working essentially pertained only to married women; it was permissible for single women to work.[8] Many of the women attending the general meeting in Winnipeg in 1906 were unmarried.

Some, like Peggy Watt, were married to journalists with whom they worked. Peggy and her husband Arthur had made a life-changing move in 1905. Packing up Peggy's precious piano, and with only five dollars in Arthur's pocket, the couple boldly left Woodstock and ventured to Edmonton, where Arthur started the *Edmonton Saturday News* and Peggy edited its Woman's Page.[9] They embraced the frontier mentality in Alberta with zeal, setting up a printing press in a trapper's cabin and publishing their own paper.

Another soon-to-be Edmonton transplant was PEI native Katherine Hughes, who had represented the *Montreal Daily Star* in St Louis and not long after began writing for the *Montreal Standard*, a Saturday weekly newspaper launched in 1905 that attempted to pair serious issues with lively writing and photographs. But the sudden death of her uncle, Cornelius O'Brien, archbishop of Halifax, appears to have abruptly prompted Hughes to move west and join members of her immediate family in Alberta. In June 1906, as the CWPC women gathered in Winnipeg, Hughes was in the process of moving to Edmonton to take a job with the *Edmonton Bulletin* covering women's issues and, eventually, the provincial Legislature.

The 1906 meeting in Winnipeg brought together that city's journalists along with others from Halifax, Montreal, Toronto, Kingston, Ottawa, Vancouver, and Edmonton, courtesy of the Canadian Pacific Railway, which offered free passage. Journalists from the United States also attended the meeting, fulfilling the wish of Kit Coleman, who, in 1904, expressed the hope that Canadian women would one day welcome sister journalists from south of the border.

Robertine Barry travelled to Winnipeg from Montreal with Eva Le Boutillier, Alice Asselin's older unmarried sister. Asselin herself had given birth to her third son in 1906 and now had three boys under the age of five. Robertine Barry and Eva Le Boutillier previously travelled together to the Paris Exposition in 1900, where the former represented the Canadian government and the latter served as a hostess. A noted beauty, Le Boutillier, thirty-one, was listed on the train roster in 1906 as a journalist who was representing her brother in law Olivar Asselin's publication *Le Nationaliste*. Le Boutillier's daughter, Raymonde Marchand Paré, who lives in Montreal, remembers her mother speaking about the trip out west, but there is no evidence that Le Boutillier ever wrote a story about it.[10]

The train trip to Winnipeg took two days from Montreal, providing much time for reflection. Robertine Barry pondered a question that she later posed to her readers: "Why, instead of traveling to major American cities or overseas, don't we think about exploring our own territory about which we know so little?"[11] On the train Barry witnessed unforgettable beauty and serenity, particularly watching the full moon rise over Lake Superior, and she told her readers that knowledge of the under-explored west could only come from experiencing it. (See illustration 12.)

An enthusiastic welcome awaited the women at the imposing train station in Winnipeg – a Beaux-Arts style building designed by the Maxwell Brothers of Montreal and completed just two years before. "I'd never seen anything like it elsewhere in Canada," Robertine Barry wrote.[12] Today, the building on Higgins Avenue is a heritage site owned by the Aboriginal Centre of Winnipeg. The grandiose structure, with huge columns at the entryway, reflected the CPR's great expectations for the west.[13]

Indeed, Winnipeg was a booming city in 1906. No city in North America had seen such rapid growth in the previous three decades, and it been helped immensely by the arrival of the railway in 1881. In 1876, the population of Winnipeg stood at six thousand. By 1906, it had reached 150,000. Nearly three hundred people a day crossed the border from the United States into Canada's west, many settling in Winnipeg, then the biggest grain market in the British Empire. The city had slowly become a mosaic of different cultures: the Bible Society of Winnipeg boasted that it printed books in fifty-one different languages, including Armenian, Arabic, Cree, Korean, Urdu, and Yiddish.[14] A row of architecturally impressive bank buildings lined Main Street, and, according to Robertine Barry, at the intersection of Portage and Main, the city's principal streets: "Everything breathes animation and life."[15]

The two-day visit to Winnipeg on 8 and 9 June 1906 was punctuated with non-stop receptions and sightseeing excursions, although limits were imposed by the city's notoriously unpredictable weather and a heavy downpour that washed out some plans. The rain started the morning of their arrival. Umbrellas were raised the moment the women debarked from the train. They were whisked off immediately to a meeting at Elks Hall, home of an exclusive men's fraternal organization lent to the women for the occasion. Its well-appointed interior and cushy leather chairs caused Robertine Barry to coyly remark that any woman who still believed men's clubs were sober places of reflection was under a grave misconception.

At the business session, Kate Simpson Hayes received the endorsement of the membership to replace Kit Coleman as president. The women discussed the club's constitution. Early meeting minutes set down several goals for the club: to promote camaraderie among presswomen; to maintain and improve the status of journalism as a profession; to promote Canadian national sentiment in all the newspapers or magazines for which members were connected; and, last, to push for a high standard of literary excellence in newspaper writing.

After the meeting, the women were transported on a special streetcar chartered by Winnipeg mayor Thomas Sharpe to a civic luncheon at Deer Lodge Hotel. Originally a private home, Deer Lodge later became a hospitality centre for railway pioneers and, in 1892, was rebuilt as a villa for tourists. The women were seated at long tables decorated with lilacs. Town officials, including a number of aldermen and their wives, keenly understood the value of the pen-power now in their midst from both sides of the border. In his welcoming speech, Mayor Sharpe first toasted the king, then the president, then the American presswomen, and, finally, the members of the CWPC, speaking about the importance of the press in general and the welcome contribution of women working in that realm.[16]

The women also benefited from George Ham's connections to a city in which he had gained prominence as a journalist and local politician. His links to the powerful served the women well at Government House, where Lady Mary McMillan, wife of Manitoba's lieutenant-governor, offered a tea in their honour, heightened by the arrival of Sir Daniel Hunter McMillan, who, like George Ham, came from Whitby, Ontario, and who offered the women his good wishes.

On their first night in Winnipeg, members of the party visited Happyland, a new amusement park that had just opened to huge crowds over the Victoria Day weekend. Park officials gave the journalists free admission and an escort around the grounds, which, besides rides, included a baseball field that served as the home of the Winnipeg Maroons. The next day, a planned luncheon in the country was cancelled due to roads having been rendered impassable by heavy rain, but a motorcade led by Robert Rogers, the province's minister of public works, took the women on a tour of Winnipeg in order to convey the dimensions of the city and the beauty of its buildings. The city tour ended at the minister's residence on Assiniboine Avenue with a tea hosted by his wife.

On the second night in Winnipeg, a singer, a poet, and a musician entertained at a dinner thrown by the Western Press Association, a male preserve. Outgoing club president Kit Coleman spoke to the gathering about her personal experiences in journalism. The content of her speech is not recorded, but it likely included the prized scoop she had earned the previous year, when she talked her way into a Cleveland jail and became the only journalist to interview famed swindler Cassie Chadwick, the Ontario-born con artist who defrauded banks of millions by claiming to be the illegitimate daughter of Andrew Carnegie.

The Winnipeg meeting also set the precedent for future club gatherings: there would always be business sessions, intensive discussions about the craft of journalism, entertainment on a royal scale, and a fact-finding tour of the surrounding area that would provide the women with first-hand knowledge of their own country and ample material to write several articles. In 1906, the fact-finding tour in Winnipeg was extended with a special excursion to Banff.

Before Robertine Barry could leave Winnipeg, she felt compelled to visit the gravesite of Louis Riel. In Winnipeg, she had been introduced to Judge Joseph Dubuc, chief justice of Manitoba and a former Quebecer who had gone to school with Riel. After regaling her with anecdotes associated with the Métis hero, Dubuc quickly arranged for Barry to visit Saint-Boniface (a Winnipeg ward), where Riel was buried, guided by Henri Royal, a young lawyer from the ward and the son of the former lieutenant-governor of the Northwest Territories. Robertine Barry visited Saint-Boniface's cathedral and saw the steel and granite burial monument on which was simply written: "LOUIS RIEL 16 Novembre 1885." According to Barry, a plain iron fence around the grave somberly summoned up "the days of torment, acts of injustice and fanaticism."[17] She told her readers that work on a new cathedral and a new monument would begin soon, tapping the talent of two young Montreal architects, Samuel Stevens Haskel and Jean-Omer Marchand. Interestingly, Barry's travelling partner on the Winnipeg trip, Eva Le Boutillier, would later marry Jean-Omer Marchand in 1912.

For the excursion to Banff, the women divided into two railway cars, one operated by the CPR and the other by the Manitoba-based Canadian Northern Railway. The rail lines had united for the occasion to transport the women as guests of the Western Canadian Immigration Association (WCIA). The cars would travel different routes to Alberta and eventually meet up in Banff. The guide for the group on the Canadian Northern Pullman car was Herbert Vanderhoof, once a journalist in Chicago and now a railway employee and representative of the WCIA, which was formed in 1904 in the United States with the goal of attracting people and investment capital to western Canada.

Vanderhoof was convinced that the thousands of words the women would write on the journey would do as much for the cause of western immigration as would any promotional venture undertaken by the WCIA.[18] His enthusiasm was not misplaced. According to Kate Simpson Hayes, an article written after the 1904 trip to the St Louis World's Fair entitled "The Kind of Women Canada Wants" brought thousands of women to Canada from the United States. Unfortunately, Hayes did not mention who wrote the article or where it appeared. The women on the 1904 trip represented more than thirty newspapers and magazines, and, despite an extensive search, the article could not be located. Undoubtedly, however, the CPR hoped that the 1906 trip west would have an even greater impact on immigration than did the trip in 1904.

Aboard the Canadian Northern car were a group of distinguished Canadian and American journalists and freelancers who wrote for publications all over the globe. Best known among the Canadians were Robertine Barry and Kit Coleman, accompanied by her daughter Patsy, who was listed as a writer for the *Hamilton Herald*. Also aboard was Agnes Deans Cameron, the first female school principal in Victoria, British Columbia.

For Cameron, 1906 was a life-changing year. Her teaching certificate had been suspended for three years after she had been accused of permitting students to cheat on an exam by allowing them to use a straight-edge in a freehand drawing exercise. At age forty-three, her teaching career was effectively over. She turned to writing for her livelihood, moving to Chicago for more opportunity. On the 1906 trip to Winnipeg, she represented both *Century* magazine and the *Atlantic Monthly*. That trip likely sparked the idea for a monumental excursion she would make two years later. Accompanied by her niece, she journeyed from Chicago to Winnipeg and then to the farthest reaches of the Canadian northwest across the "belt of wheat" and the "belt of fur." Cameron and her niece were the first white women to travel overland to the Arctic Ocean.[19] She later published a lively account of the trip in a book entitled *The New North*, in which she explains that her motivation for the venture stemmed from a desire "to call attention to the great unoccupied lands of Canada, to induce people from the crowded centres of the Old World to use the fresh air of the New."[20]

The "great unoccupied lands of Canada" were also of keen interest to Americans aboard the Canadian Northern car, including Iowa-born New York City resident Cynthia Westover Alden, who wrote for several publications, including the *Ladies Home Journal* and the *Brooklyn Eagle*; and Ohio-born Annie Howells, sister of celebrated writer William Dean Howells and wife of Achille Fréchette (interpreter for the House of Commons in Ottawa), who represented *Harper's* magazine. The group aboard the Canadian Northern made the nine-hundred-mile journey to Edmonton with several stops. They paused in Dauphin, Manitoba, which owed its existence to the Canadian Northern station and whose grain elevators bordered the railway tracks; in Warman, Saskatchewan, just north of Saskatoon; and in Lloyd-minster, hard on the border of Saskatchewan and Alberta, provinces formally carved from the Northwest Territories in 1905.

The rich wheat fields and abundant pastures along the route amazed Robertine Barry. "Nothing arid or desolate," she wrote, "rather life and the beauty of large open spaces."[21] The train travelled near an Aboriginal encampment, where the inhabitants, looking stoic and grave, according to Barry, moved away and disappeared without acknowledging the waves from the women on the train. In her narrative, Robertine Barry wondered why the Aboriginal people refused to acknowledge them, but she did not dwell on the answer. Instead, she focused on the villages sprouting from the land and expressed a hope that Quebec farmers could enjoy the same bounty even if they had to leave Quebec: "How much I would like to see those farmers from Lower Quebec, laboring futilely against the aridity of their rocky terrain, discouraged by their lack of success, take the road to exile!"

Once in Edmonton, cars ordered by the Chamber of Commerce took the women on a drive around town accompanied by members of the Royal Daughters of the Empire, a philanthropic group formed in 1900 during the Boer War. The journalists saw the proposed site of the new Parliament buildings and a beautiful park carved out of a forest. They counted eleven banks, a number of hotels, churches, a hospital, lovely homes, stores, and a theatre where internationally celebrated soprano Emma Albani, born Emma Lajeunesse in Chambly, Quebec, and the pride of that province, had performed the previous winter. Robertine Barry, who was completely captivated by Edmonton, made sure to visit the offices of the *Courrier de l'Ouest*, a French-language weekly newspaper where she met the ex-Quebecers who directed the publication. She regretted, however, that she was unable to meet Magali, director of the "Page des Femmes," whose articles she read regularly.

The CPR Pullman guided by George Ham had taken a different route from Winnipeg, stopping at Brandon, Indian Head, and Calgary. Aboard were five women who had covered the fair in St Louis: Kate Simpson Hayes, who still represented the *Manitoba Free Press* and now also the *Dublin Freeman's Journal*; Mary Adelaide Dawson, still with the *Toronto Telegram*; Katherine Hughes, now representing the *Ottawa Citizen*; Sara Ann McLagan, owner of the *Vancouver World*; and Sara Jennie Atkins of the *Vancouver Daily Province*. Also travelling in the CPR car were journalists from Woodstock and Kingston as well as Robertine Barry's travelling companion Eva Le Boutillier. According to one account, at Indian Head, Saskatchewan, the women in Ham's car dropped in without any warning at the home of a settler in order to view a real-life success story. An article on the first page of the *Evening Times* in St John, New Brunswick – written, it would appear, by Mary Dawson (it was signed M.A.D.) – details "another graphic story of a wonderful country" by relating a tale of "successful settlers who soon progressed from penury to opulence in the new land."[22] Without notifying the occupants of their intended invasion, fifteen members of the CWPC stopped by the farm home of Mrs W.M. Douglas near the experimental farm at Indian Head, and were received with true western hospitality. Their surprise at the comforts and luxuries of that Prairie home, according to Dawson, was even greater than the astonishment their visit caused their hostess.

The journalists were amazed to see fancy polished tables, cushioned window seats, an upright piano, well-curtained windows, and a cabinet of fine china; they had expected to find "a shack with a lean-to, deal furniture and a stove with a smoking chimney." Their hostess modestly commented, "Oh, this isn't anything," as she passed around the buttermilk the women wanted to sample. Mary Dawson quoted Mrs Douglas as saying: "Lots of farm houses out here are very much finer than mine. We women in the west are comfortable. We don't work anything like as hard as we did down home. None of us ever do the milking and we've far more time and opportunities to play the piano or go to church and parties than we had when east."[23] Dawson then told readers that all along the Indian Head stretch of the CPR farmers had the same story of prosperity to tell and that their beautiful homes, good barns, and superb horses substantiated their statements.

All members of the travelling party were finally reunited for a two-day visit in Banff, where they were given the option of staying at the majestic Banff Springs Hotel, built to resemble a Scottish baronial castle, or remaining on the railway car and sleeping there, just as the French-speaking women had done in St Louis two years before. Wherever they chose to rest, Banff's astounding natural setting mesmerized everyone.

Most of the women had never seen the Rocky Mountains. Snow-covered in places even in June, splashed with fir trees, and presenting a kaleidoscope of colour depending on the vantage point, the Rockies were an ever-changing palette of red, pink, violet, and mauve. Robertine Barry called it "un spectacle intraduisible" – a spectacle that could not be translated. "Words could only render imperfectly impressions of the soul," she wrote.[24] Touring Canada's first national park, the women pulled out Kodak cameras from their pocketbooks when they spotted buffalo. They thought the waters of Lake Minnewanka were as blue as those of the Mediterranean Sea. They visited a nearby grotto, where, eerily, stalactites seemed to evoke figures resembling humans and animals.

One evening, the women were dinner guests of the CPR in the Banff Springs Hotel, located in the heart of Banff National Park. Mackenzie King, then minister of labour under Sir Wilfrid Laurier, happened to be in Banff at that time and joined the women for dinner. One of Ottawa's most eligible bachelors sat next to Robertine Barry. "I remember he was the partner of Françoise and Dame Gossip thought what a dignified couple they made," recalled CWPC member Effie Laurie Storer years later. On the trip, Storer represented the *Saskatchewan Herald*, a Battleford paper founded by her father.[25]

Given that Mackenzie King and Robertine Barry had many points of connection and that both were credited with being artful conversationalists, one imagines they must have talked easily. King had briefly worked as a reporter, covering police and courts for the *Globe* and, in 1897, writing a series for the *Mail and Empire* on sweat shops and the working poor. Could he and Robertine Barry have discussed her visit to Hull House in 1904 and King's admiration for reformer Jane Addams? Or perhaps the conversation centred on Sir Wilfrid Laurier, King's mentor and a Barry family friend?[26] Robertine Barry kept a hand-written letter from the prime minister in her files.

She had written him to argue that the government should underwrite her trip to the Paris Exposition as a representative of Canadian women. Laurier had answered that he would be pleased to plead her case, coyly adding that he would have to advocate on her behalf before Agricultural Minister Sydney Fisher, who just happened to be an eligible bachelor.[27]

Perhaps King and Barry touched on another subject then in vogue: spiritualism. Examples of spirit return and existence after death were seriously contemplated in both religious and secular circles at the turn of the century.[28] Although it would be years before King took an active interest in spiritualism, he had already sought the advice of a fortuneteller,[29] and Robertine Barry herself wrote openly about inexplicable phenomena. While denouncing charlatans who exploited the sick and vulnerable, Barry nevertheless consulted clairvoyants and believed in premonitions, telepathy, spirit communication, and the power of certain objects to bring good luck.[30] Whatever the two discussed, their meeting marked the end of the journalists' stay in Banff.

The women left Banff with deep regret, making silent vows to return some day. Everyone headed home via Calgary, three hours away by train, where the first question they were asked when they got into town still resonates a century later: which town do you prefer – Edmonton or Calgary? Robertine Barry compared the rivalry to the age-old battle for supremacy between Montreal and Quebec City. She diplomatically declined to make a choice but told readers that her guide in Calgary was unequivocal: "This is the most important place, as well as the handsomest, between Winnipeg and Vancouver," he assured her, ticking off what he saw as Calgary's obvious advantages: an irrigation system that was the biggest in North America, a climate that was a known cure for chest maladies, and cowboys who were more than picturesque.[31]

Lady Belle Lougheed, wife of lawyer and politician Sir James Lougheed and Calgary's principal hostess, entertained the presswomen with a musicale at Beaulieu, the grand sandstone mansion the couple built in southwest Calgary where they would later greet royalty. But what made Calgary most memorable for Robertine Barry was the presence of an uncle with whom she toured the town.

Leaving Calgary, the women were given a guided tour of southern Alberta. They stopped for a short time in Fort Macleod, made another stop in Raymond (famous for beet sugar), and then a longer stop in Cardston (a Mormon stronghold), where town officials and a brass band joyfully received them at the train station. The ebullient greeting could perhaps be credited to a prank supposedly pulled by a CPR employee, who wired ahead from Raymond to say that George Ham, a wealthy Mormon, would soon be arriving in Cardston with a number of his wives and other female friends.

But the alleged prank could not be the only reason the women were made so welcome in a town that condoned polygamy. The visit had apparently been well planned before their arrival. The women witnessed a bronco-bucking contest at a local corral and were later treated to a banquet. After lunch, they reboarded the train heading for Lethbridge but were forced to stop beforehand at the station serving Magrath, a tiny village where school children serenaded them. The president of the Chamber of Commerce addressed the women and handed each a small silk banner which read:

> Sorry you haven't time to stay
> But mighty glad you came our way.
> – Magrath, June 16, 1906

When they finally reached Lethbridge, where the women spent a full day, Robertine Barry was surprised to meet people of English heritage who spoke French as well as did Quebecers. Jobs were plentiful in Lethbridge and, she was told, the pay was good. Bricklayers and masons were earning six dollars a day, painters and carpenters four dollars a day, journeymen $2.50 a day, and miners twenty-five dollars per week. In describing these alluring possibilities, the women journalists were fulfilling the role that the railway ardently hoped they would. Readers in the east might have heard rumours about the bounty that awaited in the west, but now they had it confirmed by reliable witnesses.

In Lethbridge, the women journalists realized their importance not only to the railway but also to the townspeople, particularly the women. They were entertained at a grand gala at the Club Chinook, marking the first time the club opened its doors to females. The women who lived in the town had never before been allowed on the premises. The female journalists saw that, by their very presence, they were literally opening the doors for other women. "We began to realize our importance," wrote Robertine Barry about the Lethbridge visit: "What a triumph for the good of feminism."[32]

The Rise and Fall

The club has prospered amazingly,
notwithstanding my association with it.
– George Ham, 1921[1]

The seeds planted on the St Louis trip sprouted more rapidly than anyone could have dreamed. The Canadian Women's Press Club grew quickly and attracted the leading female journalists in the country. Year after year, decade after decade, membership rose until it peaked at almost seven hundred. In the field of journalism, the club had become a powerful entity and its members were among the most influential women in the country. But by the start of the 1970s, membership in the oldest national women's press club in the world began to decline precipitously. Here is the story not only of its rapid expansion and accomplishments but also of its downward turn as the status of women improved and as women journalists sought parity with men.

The club's roots were solid, with a strong foundation having been built in its earliest years. Robertine Barry, editor of *Le Journal de Françoise* and still the leading female journalist in Quebec, was elected president at the club's general meeting in 1907, held once again in Winnipeg. She replaced Kate Simpson Hayes but was travelling overseas at the time and unable to preside. In 1906, Robertine Barry had been named a Canadian government delegate to the International Exposition in Milan, and she followed her Italian journey with an extended stay in France in 1907. Her travels and her responsibilities as editor of *Le Journal de Françoise* prevented Barry from actually serving her term.

Nevertheless, her elevation to president of the CWPC did not go unnoticed by Anne-Marie Gleason Huguenin, who mentioned it in her September 1907 column for *La Patrie*. "The Association founded on the return from that beautiful excursion to the St Louis Exposition includes very few French Canadians," wrote the woman now known simply as "Madeleine," "but they will be grateful to their English Canadian colleagues for according them a courteous gesture by electing the First Lady of women's journalism in French Canada to head the Association." With this statement, Gleason identified a trend that would only intensify in the next few years.[2]

A club whose initial membership came mostly from eastern Canada began to shift strongly to the west. In the process, the French-Canadian presence diminished significantly. Driven by a desire on the part of George Ham and the CPR to promote immigration and recruit settlers to the west, the CWPC held its first three meetings in Winnipeg in 1906, 1907, and 1908. Because of the westward tilt, many of the original travellers on the 1904 trip to St Louis drifted away from active participation, and the French-Canadian membership dwindled.

In addition, regional branches established so that presswomen could create that sense of camaraderie envisioned in the club constitution sprang up first in the west, where they took strong root. Winnipeg was the first regional branch, formed in 1907, then Edmonton in 1908, Vancouver in 1909, and Calgary in 1912. Although a Toronto branch opened in 1909, a Montreal branch did not formally organize until 1915, followed by Ottawa in 1916. Branches in New Brunswick and Nova Scotia did not form until the 1920s.

The CWPC branches in the west were particularly robust. The Winnipeg branch, for example, initially coalesced around only six presswomen, but these journalists avidly backed the enterprise and sent invitations encouraging others to join them. Within three years, membership tripled, and by 1912, the club had permanent quarters and held regular meetings every

Thursday. Along the same lines, members of the Calgary branch, which briefly included St Louis veteran and newlywed Irene Currie Love, were activists from the start. For their respective publications they wrote a series of human-interest stories about rampant unemployment among women who had lost their jobs in the market crash that had followed the oil boom in 1912. Their stories helped more than one hundred unemployed women secure jobs on farms.[3]

As early as 1910, at their annual general meeting at the King Edward Hotel in Toronto, members recognized it was becoming impractical and expensive to meet on a yearly basis. A decision was made to meet every three years instead. At the same session the governor general, Earl (Albert) Grey, made an appearance, signalling the club's growing importance. One of the keynote speakers at the meeting, the *Globe*'s former editor-in-chief John Willison, now writing for the *London Times*, elicited "disdainful sniffs and emphatic shakings of ... heads" when he suggested that Canadian women, like their European sisters, would soon be adopting cigarette smoking as a general habit. Also notable at the session was the election of Lucy Maud Montgomery as a regional vice-president.[4] She had recently published what would become the bestselling Canadian book of all time, *Anne of Green Gables*.

The decision to meet every three years did not deter the CWPC's growth, although it did continue its westward bent when the first triennial, convened in June 1913, was held in Edmonton. Membership now stood at 219. More than one hundred members came to Edmonton, where original club members from the St Louis trip, Katherine Hughes and Peggy Watt, had been instrumental in setting up the local branch. (See illustration 13.)

By 1913, though, founding club members had a limited role in leading the CWPC on a national basis. In fact, by that time, neither Katherine Hughes nor Peggy Watt wrote regularly for newspapers. Hughes had become Alberta's first provincial archivist in 1908 and then secretary to the provincial premier. She had also published a book in 1911 – a biography of Father Albert Lacombe, a missionary priest known as the Black-Robe Voyageur – that was singled out for high praise by the *New York Times*. Hughes's effort left her in a state of complete exhaustion (she called it a nervous breakdown) and forced her to take an extended rest in 1912, but she was present at the annual CWPC meeting in Edmonton. Her association with the CWPC would effectively end with that meeting as she would leave the country for long periods right up until her death. As for Peggy Watt, she had retired from active journalism and opened an antique shop. But these original architects of the CWPC had established a strong foundation upon which others could build.

Well-known writers like Nellie McClung, Emily Murphy, and E. Cora Hind picked up the gauntlet from the founders and made the club into a respected and powerful entity. At the Edmonton meeting in 1913, these three women emerged as prominent leaders. As the influence of the western wing of the CWPC grew, participation in the east declined. The membership list for 1913 shows only a handful from Montreal and only one French Quebecer – Eva Le Boutillier Marchand – Alice Asselin's sister. Even though she is listed as a member, there is no evidence she ever wrote for a newspaper.

At the Edmonton meeting, the group elected Emily Murphy national president. A major force in the feminist movement, Murphy wrote under the pseudonym "Janey Canuck" and would become the first female magistrate in the British Empire. At that meeting, too, club member Nellie McClung, a powerful suffragette, a journalist, and an orator, read a selection of her writings. More than a decade later, McClung and Murphy would become part of the Famous Five, joining three other women to press the *Persons* case, through which Canadian women would finally be recognized as persons under the law.

At that 1913 meeting, Cora Hind, a highly respected agricultural reporter for the *Manitoba Free Press*, imparted valuable tips in a talk entitled "New Lines of Work for the Newspaper Woman." Having transcended the boundaries of the Woman's Page with her crack reporting on crop yields, Hind was the ideal person to discuss opportunities that female journalists might consider. In a talk entitled "The Equipment of the Woman Journalist: Keeping up with the Times," Isabel A.R. MacLean, editor of the women's page of the *Vancouver Daily Province*, gave advice that remains remarkably applicable to the journalism field today: "A presswoman's value increases in proportion with the development of her own character and mentality and ability with which she responds to the need of her time. She must be prepared for her age. She must never stop growing."[5] In addition, Elizabeth Parker, who wrote for the *Manitoba Free Press*, gave a paper entitled "The Art of Book Reviewing." So motivating were the presentations that the women suggested that, at future meetings, more time be allotted to similar discussions and that all papers given at general meetings be archived.

At the same meeting in Edmonton, the CWPC made a move that would distinguish it for years to come. In Canada at the time, unemployment insurance and disability insurance did not exist. The CWPC established a beneficiary fund "to assist any infirm, ailing, or needy member in temporarily straitened circumstances" and sustained it with a yearly grant equivalent to 15 percent of the national membership fees and open to donations from members and friends.

Inspiration for the fund may have come from the Vancouver branch of the CWPC. In March of 1913, the Vancouver branch took charge of funeral arrangements for a member, E. Pauline Johnson, a celebrated poet and daughter of a Mohawk chief. Johnson had become internationally famous for giving a series of readings extolling Aboriginal heritage – readings that today might be called "spoken word" performances – but she had been ill for a year with terminal breast cancer and died penniless. Members of the Vancouver branch stepped in during the last stages of her illness. When the Duke of Connaught, third son of Queen Victoria, visited the dying Johnson in the hospital, the Vancouver branch sent a blue and gold silk kimono for her to wear.[6] When she died, branch members arranged a memorial for her. Johnson was so beloved in the city that flags flew at half-mast and her ashes were buried in Stanley Park on what would have been her fifty-second birthday.

In Edmonton in 1913, club women formally voted to set up a national fund to take care of their members and to make their first beneficiary grant of twenty-five dollars to a Winnipeg charity. The Beneficiary Fund would later be maintained at a stable sum of $3,500 and become the longest-running club initiative. It was administered in a confidential manner, paying the medical expenses of a member who had suffered a stroke and purchasing an electric typewriter for another member who was afflicted with arthritis.[7]

Even in the early days, benefits of membership were far-reaching, as corresponding secretary Margaret Fairbairn, art critic at the *Toronto Star*, noted in 1913. It was comforting to be able to tap into the reservoir of friendship and information that club membership provided, she remarked, even when travelling abroad, as the CWPC had affiliations with press clubs in other parts of the world. "This bond of comradeship has been helpful in many ways and a stimulus to better work," Fairbairn said.[8] Another form of networking came courtesy of the *Canadian Courier*, a weekly newspaper based in Toronto that, beginning in 1910, granted the women a full page for CWPC news once a month. Later, a club newsletter would be established that would eventually evolve into a quarterly publication called *Newspacket*, in which the achievements of club members could be reported.

The women also gave a boost to fellow members by writing about the accomplishments of their colleagues. For example, in her column in the *Mail and Empire*, Kit Coleman, who once threatened to take legal action against an impetuous young Peggy Watt, now lauded a book Watt published in 1907. "I rejoice to see my friend's book and to hear on all sides praises of it," Kit wrote: "It breathes enthusiasm for our great West, our sunset land. Bright and cheerful writings these from the pen of one of Canada's cleverest newspaper women."[9]

Little did the women at the 1913 triennial in Edmonton imagine that the next general meeting of the CWPC would not take place for another seven years. And little did club historian Katherine Hughes realize that the precious letters she had requested of the founders, dealing with the club's formation, would be misplaced and never recovered. Not long after the Edmonton meeting, the First World War began and national meetings were suspended. Divisions emerged as well. Nationalist sentiments during the war split the women and may have further alienated French journalists in Quebec, many of whom did not support the war effort. Indeed, even two prominent Winnipeg journalists were ostracized for their anti-war stance. Lillian Beynon-Thomas of the *Winnipeg Free Press* and her sister Francis Beynon, women's editor of the *Grain Growers Guide*, became pariahs in Winnipeg for their pacifist beliefs. They were forced to resign from their jobs and were black-balled from the CWPC.

It was a divisive time for the country and for the CWPC. Yet, during that interval, regional branches continued to form. When the next national gathering took place in Montreal in 1920, two years after the war ended, club membership had ballooned to 350, reflecting, in great part, the changing status of women in the field since the turn of the century. Women were now writing for almost every newspaper in Canada. During the First World War, although still confined in large measure to the women's pages, women were nevertheless given an opportunity to fill spots formerly occupied by men and to take on reporting jobs once denied them: they began covering suburban and city beats. Their professional scope had widened.

At the 1920 triennial, held at the Ritz Carlton Hotel in Montreal, the CWPC membership list showed a marked increase in members from Ottawa and the Maritime provinces, perhaps because the meeting place was more accessible to these people than previous meetings had been. There was also a notable spike in the number of members from Montreal, and French-Canadian membership rose for the first time since the club's founding in 1904. Original member Irene Currie Love (who was now married to journalist Eldred Archibald) helped organize the 1920 triennial, having moved east to Montreal from Calgary before the war. Writing under the penname "Margaret Currie" for the women's page of the *Montreal Daily Star*, Currie Love was now the chapter president of the Montreal branch, which served as host for the gathering. A contingent of French-speaking women that probably included the club's first treasurer, Anne-Marie Gleason Hugenin, attended the meeting, and many Quebecers joined the CWPC at this juncture and kept up their membership through the decade.[10]

But it was a prominent member of the English elite, rather than someone from the French community, who acted as a club patron and entertained the presswomen in Montreal. For a musical tea at the home of Lady Julia Drummond, the women dressed up in evening gowns and cloche hats. Drummond, wife of the late senator George Drummond, served as the first

president of the Montreal local Council of Women and was a noted philan-
thropist who had gone to England during the First World War to establish
an information bureau at the London headquarters of the Canadian Red
Cross Society in order to track the wounded and missing. The Montreal
branch of the CWPC, which had a practice of anointing distinguished persons in the city as patrons, made Lady Drummond an honorary member.

Once the business meeting concluded in Montreal, George Ham arranged
for club members to travel to Quebec City and to neighbouring St Anne de
Beaupré. Before leaving Montreal, the women conferred upon Ham, their
long-time honorary president, the new title of active member, qualifying
him as a writer through the publication in *Maclean's* magazine of a series of
sketches pertaining to Winnipeg's boom days.[11] Ham noted: "[I have] been
initiated into the solemn mysteries of the lodge ... I must not divulge the
secret mysteries of the girls' conclave."[12]

The next triennial, held in Vancouver in September 1923, would prove a
sentimental occasion as well as a landmark. After almost twenty years of
steady growth, the women could look back in wonder at the club they had
created and how its prestige had grown. They were able to coax Margaret
"Miggsy" Graham Horton to attend the session as a special guest and hailed
her as the mother of the CWPC. George Ham was there as well. It would be
the last time club members would see either of them.

A glance at the elaborate program for the Vancouver triennial shows how
much the world had changed and how far the women had come. It was filled
with sponsored advertorials about local industries and businesses, from
Purdy's Chocolates to Cascade Beer to the Hotel Elysium – copy that netted
the club members who wrote it several thousand dollars, which they used to
underwrite an elaborate celebration. "Early morning swimming and riding
practices will be arranged for ambitious delegates," members attending the
meeting were told: "Be sure and pack your riding breeches." A private showing of a silent film starring femme fatale Pola Negri was part of the entertainment, along with a reception hosted by the lieutenant-governor and his
wife as well as a luncheon hosted by the CPR and held on board the *Empress
of Asia*. But this was also a working holiday for many. Delegates were as-

sured that workspace had been secured at the Hotel Vancouver for members who wanted to "write copy in peace and mail or wire from the premises."[13]

A triennial of note was staged in 1932, when Kate Simpson Hayes, founding member and, according to Cora Hind, the woman responsible for keeping the CWPC alive in the earliest years, delighted the members by serving as their guest speaker at the Palliser Hotel in Calgary. Now seventy-six, living in Vancouver, and still writing under the penname "Mary Markwell," she called her talk "People I Have Met in Ink Lane" and spoke about encounters with various personalities, from Sitting Bull to the pope. Hayes did not feel up to joining the women on a fact-finding trip to Banff and Lake Louise, having "reached the limitations of my 'juvenility,'" as she explained to Elizabeth Bailey Price, incoming president of the club.[14] But she did tell Price about a conversation she had had with George Ham the last time the two old comrades had met. Ham told her that the day Margaret Graham had shown up in his office asking for free passage on the railway, he had approached CPR president Thomas Shaughnessy with the proposition and was warned against it. "George, you are looking for trouble," Shaughnessy had told him. According to Hayes, Ham told the railway president, "There will be trouble if we don't lend 'em a hand."

Kate Simpson Hayes also confided to Price that it was a miracle the club got off the ground at all following the trip to St Louis. In a speech Price made three years later at the 1935 triennial, she told the membership that, when she had assumed the office of president, Hayes told her a tale "of all the grief that followed in the wake of that first memorable trip."[15] Unfortunately, Price provided no further details.

By the time the CWPC celebrated its fiftieth anniversary in Toronto in 1954, membership exceeded five hundred. It was still the only national press club for women in the world, according to *Saturday Night*.[16] Although a national press club for women in the United States had been formed in 1919, it was based in Washington, DC, and had no regional branches. As the club executives set out to write a brief history of the CWPC for its Golden Jubilee in 1954, they realized they were not only compiling a history of the organization, which had grown so dramatically since 1904, but also a history of

Canada, which, since that time, had gone from being a young undeveloped country to being "an important leader among nations in the world."[17]

The parameters for club membership had expanded over the decades, and by the CWPC's fiftieth anniversary, the club roster included active writers on newspapers and magazines, freelancers, advertising copywriters, and radio commentators who wrote their own scripts. Television was still in its infancy and not yet a factor in club membership. Over 250 members attended the four-day anniversary celebration in Toronto, which, according to a columnist for the *Toronto Telegram*, had all the glamour and glitz of a New York press party. A staggering array of luncheons, dinners, and cocktail parties greeted participants in the club's festivities, sponsored by entities ranging from the Magazine Publishers Association to the Singer Sewing Machine Company, which happened to be celebrating its fiftieth anniversary as well. Simpson's department store ran a full-page ad in the *Globe and Mail* on 22 June, the day the meeting opened:

> For half a century you have taken an active part in the progress of our great country … and we rejoice with you in your outstanding achievements. You have been, and are, the voice of women of Canada … at once kind but firm, always consistent in the fight for better living for all who have elected to make Canada their home. Staunch supporters of our freedoms you come into our homes daily, often nameless, yet so well known that you are like members of our own families. Yes … we salute you, members of the Canadian Women's Press Club, gathered here from the shores of the Atlantic, from the vast Prairie provinces, from the Pacific to uphold the traditions that are yours … and ours … and Canada's.

Members rose early for a breakfast given by Canada's own Elizabeth Arden, who announced a prize of $500 for the best article written on fashion or beauty, and who dispensed her famous Blue Grass cosmetics as favours.[18] A champagne reception and sit-down dinner given by Singer included a fashion show with runway models flown in from New York. Every club member exited the Singer affair with a gold bangle bracelet courtesy of the company.

Interspersed with the parties was a heavy roster of speakers who had made a mark in journalism, particularly in the English-speaking world, including *Good Housekeeping* magazine managing editor Margaret Cousins and A. Davidson Dunton, chairman of the board of the CBC. Also notable on the speaker's roster was a Quebecer, Simonne Daigneault, women's editor of *La Revue Populaire* and the only francophone journalist listed as a featured speaker at the anniversary session. Daigneault would become increasingly influential in the 1960s, sparking a mini-revival of French-Canadian participation at the national level.

Members invited Peggy Watt to be their special guest at the fiftieth anniversary gala. Watt, then seventy-five, was thought to be the only member of the Sweet Sixteen still alive. In reality, Alice Asselin and Amintha Plouffe were also alive and living in Montreal; however, since ties with the French women on the trip to St Louis had lapsed so many years before – or perhaps because the two had never developed a journalism profile – the executive may not have considered it important to track them down. In retrospect, the omission of these two members of the original sixteen can perhaps be seen as another clue to the mystery concerning the CWPC's inability to build a strong presence among French Canadians.

After the triumphant Golden Jubilee, the CWPC's success across English Canada continued unabated. Members had been frustrated that no newswomen were included on a journalistic tour of British war sites after the Second World War, but in 1950 they were pleased when nine members of the CWPC were invited to tour British industrial sites with an eye to suggesting how manufacturers might make their products more appealing to Canadian consumers. It was not the trip they had lobbied for, but it represented the first time club members had been officially asked to travel beyond Canadian borders.[19]

In 1955, the women took matters into their own hands. The CWPC sponsored an overseas tour that would provide an opportunity for the women to do some reporting on foreign affairs. The club chartered an airplane and flew seventy-two members to the United Kingdom, Europe, and the Union of Soviet Socialist Republics. The trip was a coup for the CWPC. It took place at the height of the Cold War, when access to the USSR was off limits. CBC broadcaster Marjorie McEnaney brought a movie camera and a suitcase full of film, and, upon her return, the footage was quickly turned into a documentary for *CBC Newsmagazine*, showing viewers a USSR they had not seen for two decades.[20] The Canadian journalists had been told not to expect to meet any government higher-ups during their visit to the USSR; but, while attending a reception at the Canadian Embassy on Canada Day, they were caught off guard as Soviet foreign minister Andrei Gromyko entered with two first deputy premiers.[21]

As the CWPC expanded its reach, members sought to help female journalists outside of Canada expand their parameters. In 1967, to celebrate Canada's Centennial, the CWPC brought thirty-three women journalists from other countries to Canada for a month-long visit. In 1968, club membership reached its zenith at 680. But the brightest moment in club history would soon become its darkest. By June 1971, at the club's twenty-fifth general meeting at the Royal York Hotel in Toronto, members were stunned to learn that their numbers had dropped dramatically to 541 despite the entrance of 140 new members.

A few had predicted the decline and warned that steps must be taken to stem the slide. Although she was not the first to voice concern, Simonne Daigneault, national president from 1962 to 1965 and the first French-speaker since Robertine Barry to hold the top post, was clearly worried when she left office. She noted that members seemed indifferent to improving themselves as professionals. The programming that the various branches offered was not geared to making women become more proficient journalists: the CWPC had become more of a social club than a vehicle for professional advancement.[22] Daigneault accurately forecast that the Woman's Page would soon become a thing of the past and that women would be handed new challenges. "There is a younger generation of presswomen which seems to almost be ignored in our recruiting," she noted: "These are the writers who, ten years from now, will have the big bylines, and we should help them to become highly qualified reporters."[23]

Daigneault also tried to convince the membership to adopt a bilingual strategy in order to expand the CWPC's reach. In her book *No Daughter of Mine*, a history of the club, Kay Rex provides insight into tensions that arose over trying to generate a French presence within the CWPC. As early as 1949, when Daigneault joined the Montreal branch, she lobbied for some French-Canadian programming. In 1950, she and Montreal branch president Madeleine Levanson helped form a branch of the club in Quebec City, trying to convince French-speaking journalists they were welcome. But the branch fizzled out in 1957. Another attempt four years later also proved futile. According to Rex, "The two solitudes were destined never to get together."[24]

In 1951, Laure Hurteau, a long-time writer for the women's pages of *La Presse*, and Solange Chaput-Rolland, a journalist for the CBC who would later be appointed to the Senate, formed a club for French-speaking journalists. Le Cercle des femmes journalistes may have had its genesis in the early 1940s, when Hurteau, then vice-president of the CWPC, was designated to thank, in French, the Right Honourable Mackenzie King at a meeting of female journalists in Ottawa. The women had been invited to Ottawa as part of an effort to prepare the spouses of soldiers for their eventual return from the front.

Evidently, Hurteau felt insufficiently supported at the event, amidst the multitude of English journalists from other provinces, and perhaps had a premonition that French-speaking female journalists needed a group of their own.[25] Under her presidency, Le Cercle des femmes journalistes spread from the Montreal area to the Gatineau region. Talks were initiated with Le Cercle to establish a combined French and English branch of the CWPC; however, according to Rex, given the climate in Quebec during the Quiet Revolution, members of Le Cercle did not see any advantage to amalgamating with the CWPC. And, while a few English-speaking CWPC members joined Le Cercle, joint meetings or exchanges never developed.

In 1955, when the CWPC moved to incorporate, Daigneault suggested adding a French translation of the club name on the registration papers so that the club would be viewed as truly national in scope. However, the Winnipeg branch voted against incorporating bilingually, and the name was never translated.[26] When Daigneault assumed the national presidency in

1962 and visited various branches in the west, she found great resistance to bilingualism. In 1964, she told the Saskatoon branch, in what Kay Rex calls a far-sighted observation, that unless English and French Canada could work together "we [would] all end up losing our sovereignty" to the growing influence of the United States. According to Daigneault, investing in the future meant understanding the other: "Language is the most common medium of understanding. We must learn yours; you, at least many of you, must learn ours."[27]

Not long after this, the downward turn that Daigneault had feared began. The women's movement wrought huge changes and opened all sectors of newspaper work to female reporters. A more level playing field for female journalists seemed to obviate the need for a women's press club. Women journalists did not feel they needed a club devoted only to women's interests, and they certainly did not need a club that seemed increasingly less interested in professional improvement. Furthermore, men's press clubs were beginning to open to women.

At that pivotal 1971 general meeting in Toronto, a highly contested proposal was made to admit men. Put to a vote, it passed, but the move seemed to backfire in the long run. It dismayed many members, some branches left the national club because of it, and, despite opening its doors to men and widening the ranks to accept those working in public relations, membership kept declining. Older members did not renew ties with the club and few newcomers joined. Branches began to fade away and eventually to disband.

In the mid-1990s, barely 160 members remained. In an effort to find a way to carry on, members took a nostalgic trip to St Louis in 1994 to honour the CWPC's ninetieth anniversary and to perhaps spark ideas for keeping the club going. As in the past, the meeting in St Louis featured craft workshops and the theme was "exploring new frontiers," which touched on what was then called the Information Highway. These presswomen were not just looking back; as venturesome as ever, they were looking ahead. But only thirteen women made the trip.

For the CWPC's one hundredth anniversary, long-time members rallied to organize a centennial celebration, which took place in Ottawa in June

2004. They called the event "One Hundred Years of Daring" to honour the courageous women who formed the club and those who followed them. Women from across Canada attended; most had at one time been prominent journalists on newspapers or radio, and now, in their seventies, eighties, or nineties, they remembered the club's glory days and cherished what they had gained from their professional affiliation with it. In many ways, the celebration in Ottawa resembled the triennials of the past. It included a reception at the National Press Club; a panel discussion given by current female journalists on where women stood in 2004; a thought-provoking keynote speech by Marshall McLuhan's son Eric; donation of the CWPC's files to Library and Archives Canada; lunch at the Bayne House, the oldest home in Ottawa; and a banquet at the National Arts Centre.

But amidst the festive celebration, it was quietly announced that the national CWPC would formally fold. Even though the executive officers hoped to revive a press club exclusively for women, a groundswell of support large enough to bring back a national club never materialized. The Media Club of Ottawa remains as the lone branch of a mighty tree whose strong limbs once covered the entire country. It keeps the old club alive, presenting monthly professional programs for those in the field of journalism and communications, offering speakers, workshops, and social events to members. The Media Club of Ottawa's website states that the club originated over a century ago on that fateful trip to St Louis in 1904.

Epilogue

*These were my friends and all have slipped away leaving Canada and
me the poorer, but it is something to have had the privilege of their
friendship and I am sure the Canadian Women's Press Club of today
realizes what it owes to these outstandingly gifted predecessors.*
– Gertrude Balmer Watt[1]

The sixteen women who travelled to St Louis over a century ago wove a collective story that resulted in the Canadian Women's Press Club. But each woman, I discovered through my research, had her own story to tell, although a researcher often finds the story of early women of achievement to be sketchy and incomplete. Here, then, are brief summaries of the lives of the sixteen women who boarded the Canadian Pacific Railway car that travelled to St Louis. I present them in the order of their deaths and include a final look at their patron George Ham.

Robertine Barry

The first female hired as a reporter by a Quebec newspaper and the first vice-president of the CWPC died suddenly in January 1910. Cause of death was then termed "cerebral congestion" – most likely a stroke. She was forty-six, and her death shook club members to the core.

In a short obituary written right after Barry died, *La Patrie*'s Anne-Marie Gleason Huguenin, writing under the penname "Madeleine," rushed to disseminate the news that her colleague and friend had died. She began with the words: "Françoise is dead!" A few days later, an account of Robertine Barry's funeral made the front page of *La Patrie* with the headline: "An Imposing Funeral for a Woman of Letters." The list of mourners included judges, politicians, journalists, and the consul-general of France. Father Raymond Rouleau, a relative on her mother's side of the family, conducted the service (he would later become a cardinal).

Not only had the CWPC lost a founding member, but Robertine Barry's death also dealt a blow to the club's goal of achieving unbroken camaraderie east to west. Without Barry, the chain would miss an important link; no other French-speaking journalist on the St Louis trip stepped forward at that point to take an active role in the club. In 1933, journalist and club member Effie Laurie Storer of Saskatchewan stated that Barry's death created a chasm that early members felt had "never been filled."[2]

Robertine Barry's final year of life can be described as both heartening and heartbreaking. In 1905, the publication she had founded, *Le Journal de Françoise*, had a print run of 4,750 copies, but readership then began to tail off. Barry struggled to keep the publication alive, but because she was suffering from exhaustion she was forced to suspend publication in April 1909 for what she hoped would be a temporary respite.[3]

However, at the same time as her publication teetered, Barry's stature continued to grow. In 1909, when she put *Le Journal de Françoise* on hold, the Quebec government named her inspector of women's work in industrial establishments in recognition of her effort to better the condition of women through her journalism.

George Ham attended Robertine Barry's funeral in the winter of 1910 and was deeply moved by her passing. More than a decade later, he remembered Barry fondly in his memoir. "Françoise was beloved of all, and her charming talk was irresistible," he wrote. "When she passed away, there was many a tear-dimmed eye and many a heavy heart as we reverently laid her to rest."[4] Ham relayed his still-fresh emotions to the women who attended the CWPC's general meeting on 22 June 1910 at the King Edward Hotel in Toronto, where he spoke about the club's loss. He suggested that a donation be made in Robertine Barry's memory to a fund established for survivors of the *Montreal Herald* disaster. On 13 June 1910, thirty-two people had died and many others had been injured when a water tank on the *Herald*'s roof crashed to the basement and caused a massive explosion and fire. Members agreed to contribute twenty-five dollars in the name of the late Françoise Barry, "our well-loved ex-president."

At the same meeting, club president and journalist Marjory MacMurchy, who would marry former *Globe* editor John Willison in 1926, referred emotionally to Barry's death and, alluding to the now shaky Pan-Canadian link her loss had created, admonished members to cherish the national bond among women journalists that the club had forged. Because of Barry's absence, the national bond would be sorely tested. She was the glue that cemented the French-speaking connection, and no strong French-Canadian figure would emerge within the ranks to replace her until Simonne Daigneault became national president of the club in 1962.

With the Robertine Barry Prize, given by the Canadian Research Institute for the Advancement of Women for the best article or column on a feminist topic written in English or French, Barry's name continues to be remembered. A street in the Villeray district north of downtown Montreal was named after her. However, at Notre-Dame-des-Neiges Cemetery in Montreal, where century-old oak trees rim more than a million graves, Robertine Barry's plot has neither headstone nor marker.[5] Only a scraggly patch of grass marks the final resting place of Quebec's first full-time female journalist.

Grace Denison

For reasons she never publicly revealed, Grace Elizabeth Denison did not join the CWPC. By dint of her position on Toronto's *Saturday Night*, Denison's very presence on the train to St Louis lent status to the venture, but she was the only woman among the sixteen who failed to endorse the club with her signature. Nevertheless, she remained a vibrant voice on *Saturday Night* right up until her sudden death in February 1914 at age sixty.

In a memorial tribute, fellow writer Hector Charlesworth said no journalist could equal Denison in the manner she handled social gossip, which was in such a way that it "titillated curiosity without giving offense."[6] Grace

Denison also left a mark in Canadian journalism as one of the country's first female travel writers. Her solo trip to Europe and resultant book, *A Happy Holiday*, made her a pioneer even before she started working for *Saturday Night*.

In a column written about a year before her death, Grace Denison devoted considerable attention to one of the twentieth century's new developments: "the girl journalist." It is not hard to imagine that, in describing this new breed, Denison was describing herself. The girl journalist, she wrote, was "too enterprising to turn to nursing, too independent to long for marriage, too full of strength and life and curiosity and a certain devil may care daring" to accept conventional pursuits as an adequate outlet for her surplus energies. She turned to journalism "as a flower to the sun." By becoming a journalist, Denison wrote, a girl could live her convictions "instead of prating about them." And if she lived her convictions, Denison noted, she would not only become a successful servant of the public but also a success in her own right.[7]

Grace Denison's death shocked her colleagues, who never suspected that, when she handed in her copy five days before, they might not see her again. An indefatigable worker who looked about twenty years younger than her age, she had shown no sign of flagging energy when she had come to the office on that last occasion.[8] On page 1 of the 7 February edition, the editors of *Saturday Night* wrote: "The public has learned with deep regret of the unexpected death of Mrs Grace Elizabeth Denison (Lady Gay), for many years a member of the staff of this journal … During the 23 years that she was connected with this journal she did much to extend its hold on the Canadian community and it may be said that in every home into which this journal goes, she herself had won a personal friend." The cause of Denison's death was not mentioned in the tributes to her made by colleagues, but they intimated that she had a terminal illness she did not reveal.

Kathleen "Kit" Coleman

In 1915, the year following Grace Denison's death, Kathleen Coleman, the first president of the CWPC, died of pneumonia at age fifty-nine. She had been made an honourary member of the press club five years before in recognition of her work on behalf of the organization when it was in its infancy. As an honourary member, she did not have to pay club dues but was entitled to the full benefits of membership. Coleman was a working journalist up until the end and quite famous, but her final years were tinged with monetary woes, poor health, and some regret.

In 1911, in a disheartening dispute over money, Kit Coleman left the *Mail and Empire*, the Toronto paper with which she had been associated for over two decades. Her bosses demanded more copy, at no extra salary, and they continually fought with her over travel expenses. Given her massive readership, Coleman felt she deserved better. She quit.

Colleagues believed that had Kit Coleman worked in the United States, she would have been as esteemed as American advice columnist Dorothy Dix, the highest paid female journalist of her time and the most widely read.[9] Upon leaving the *Mail and Empire*, Coleman syndicated her column in weeklies and dailies across Canada, refusing to sell it to her old employer. She also penned a column for *Canada Monthly* magazine until her death.

Poor health always plagued Coleman, who suffered from eye trouble, bronchial aliments, and depressive episodes.[10] Hints of depression appeared even in a dispatch from the St Louis World's Fair. After describing the icebergs that were part of the North Pole exhibit on the Pike, Kit Coleman suddenly mentioned the "dreadful loneliness" that can descend on any given day. "Then," she wrote with remarkable candour, "it is that suicide apparently becomes the only sane solution, that the getting away from materialism – even by that dreadful opening, seems imperative. Those are the dangerous moments. You see, to be sane means to eat and sleep and 'take the air.' And it is the only wise way. But why did the gods give to poor bound mortals aspirations that are infinite?"[11]

Kit Coleman always felt her own aspirations were never met, even though she reached the pinnacle of her profession and was widely read. Her modern approach, her frank advice, her openness and tolerance, all earned her legions of readers. However, as she neared the end of her life, she felt she had fallen short. The constant grind to produce copy in order to pay the bills prevented her from realizing her loftiest goal: publishing a novel.[12]

Margaret Graham

The so-called mother of the Canadian Women's Press Club died at Montreal's Royal Victoria Hospital of cancer in May 1924. She was fifty-four. A writer until the very end, Margaret "Miggsy" Graham detailed the final days of her life in a poignant letter to her husband.[13] "Albert Dearest," she wrote, "Today the kindly man who has been watching my case for six days, testing all organs etc., but whose good heart will not let him use the chopping axe or carving knife, hands me over to Dr. [Walter] Chipman, skilled in cutting folk into little pieces and then successfully putting them together again." Similar end-of-life accounts appear with frequency today in books and magazines, but Graham's modern approach in documenting her reflections upon life and its final moments aligns with her character as a woman ahead of her time. She writes of plans for her cremation (at Mount Royal Cemetery, Canada's first crematorium) and tells her husband that, while he could hold a memorial service for her at some point: "Be firm in the matter of no service over my body ... believing as I do that sermons and prayers and eulogies over a dead body is paganistic." She also looks back at her former religious beliefs and rues her missionary zeal: "I who started forth at 19 to save the Hindus from Hades. How better to have danced the sunset down the west, [or] danced away the moon." The letter was so powerful that it convinced a family friend, who read it years later, to specialize in palliative care.[14]

Unlike Kit Coleman, Robertine Barry or Kate Simpson Hayes, Margaret Graham did not take an active role in the club she was credited with hatching. Just as surprising, and as inexplicable, she may never have written an article about the trip to St Louis. On George Ham's roster, Graham, a staff writer at the *Halifax Herald*, was listed as representing the *Ottawa Free Press*, probably through an arrangement she had made to freelance for the latter. But no article about the fair appeared in the *Ottawa Free Press* in the summer of 1904. What is more, Kate Simpson Hayes wrote the article about the fair that appeared in the *Halifax Herald*, Graham's own paper. Why did Graham, one of the most skilled and experienced journalists on the trip, fail to write about the fair? Why did she let Kate Simpson Hayes write about it for the *Herald*? Despite extensive interviews and library research, I could find no credible explanation.

Margaret Graham's articles continued to appear in the *Halifax Herald* following the trip to St Louis, but she left daily journalism soon after her marriage to Albert Horton in July 1905. She gave birth to a daughter in 1908, and, that same year, her husband was appointed chief of staff at Hansard, which reported on the Senate debates. Graham never returned to journalism after her daughter was born, and her final association with the CWPC came less than a year before her death, when she was given a free trip to the triennial in Vancouver as "Mother of the Club." She wore a hat for the group photo, in contrast to her hatless appearance in the photo taken on the St Louis trip. However, in both photos she turns her head to the side, the only woman to do so. Perhaps it was her private joke.

Nearly five years after her death, in January 1929, Margaret Graham's husband Albert and daughter Lois, who was then twenty, made a nostalgic trip to Trinidad, where Graham had once ventured as a missionary schoolteacher. They were to drop her ashes at sea. They visited with Graham's former travelling companion, Adella Archibald, who was from a well-known Nova Scotia family and who remained in Trinidad almost forty years after Graham had left.[15] Tragically, as father and daughter made the return trip to Canada, Albert Horton died.[16] In the span of five years, Lois Graham Horton had lost both her parents.

In 1975, Lois Graham Horton made a donation in her mother's name to the Ottawa branch of the CWPC. The first Margaret Graham Award was presented in 1976 for the best feature story in an Ottawa-area newspaper written by a male or female reporter with fewer than three years experience. The award would later go to the top journalism student at an Ottawa-area college or university.

Katherine Hughes

Adventurous Katherine Hughes, who, while attending the St Louis World's Fair wrote for the *Montreal Daily Star* and evinced a deep interest in the welfare of Aboriginal peoples, later took a courageous and unconventional path for a woman. She not only worked as a journalist but also became a controversial activist for a cause that gained her powerful enemies in Canada. She would produce an enduring legacy as a writer before dying in 1925 at age forty-eight.

Moving west from Montreal to Edmonton in 1906 to work for the *Edmonton Bulletin*, Katherine Hughes showed she was far more than a "social editoress," as the paper referred to her. She reported on the cattle roundup after the disastrous winter of 1906–07, when blizzards and frigid weather decimated the herds.[17] She also covered the Alberta provincial Legislature for the paper. However, in 1908, Hughes left daily journalism to become Alberta's first provincial archivist. The *Edmonton Bulletin* announced her departure, stating that it "relinquishe[d] Miss Hughes from its editorial staff with no small measure of regret."

She brought a hands-on approach to her new job as archivist, undertaking a rugged two-month journey through the wilderness of northern Alberta and parts of British Columbia by stage coach, river boat, and canoe and keeping a detailed account of the landscape and the people she met. Katherine Hughes had been approached as early as 1904, the year of the St Louis trip, to write the life story of Father Albert Lacombe, a missionary priest from Quebec who was known as the Black-Robe Voyageur and who had pioneered Catholic settlements and schools in the west. In 1908, Lacombe again asked her to help him out after church superiors ordered him to set down his remarkable story. She had already written a biography of her uncle, Father Cornelius O'Brien, entitled *Archbishop O'Brien: Man and Churchman*, and the timing was right for a new undertaking. Hughes now lived in the west, the land Lacombe had explored as a daring young missionary in the 1850s, and Edmonton was close enough to Lacombe's mission in St Albert, where the Father Lacombe Chapel still exists today, to visit the priest with frequency.

Father Lacombe ministered to Aboriginal groups and acted as their intermediary with the outside world. He claimed a trace of Aboriginal blood, and he respected the Métis, Cree, and Blackfoot peoples and learned their languages. No doubt Katherine Hughes greatly admired him. He smoothed the way for the Canadian Pacific Railway as it expanded westward in the

1880s, serving as chaplain for the railway construction crews and even intervening when land surveyors for the CPR mistakenly appropriated a piece of Aboriginal land. Thus, Hughes asked former CPR titan Sir William C. Van Horne to write the preface for her book on Lacombe. An accomplished artist, Van Horne also created a poignant painting to accompany his preface. Katherine Hughes and Sir William Van Horne would collaborate again, but not with the same happy outcome.

Hughes's book on Father Lacombe was hailed as one of the best biographies of 1911 in Canada and the United States. A reviewer for the *New York Times Review of Books* stated: "[A] good biographer is 'rarer than hen's teeth,' but Miss Hughes is one. Out of her book stands a figure as compelling as any in history. She has painted him like an artist ... She has literally written history like a novel."[18] Her monumental effort took a toll on Hughes's health. In a letter to a Roman Catholic Church authority, she wrote that, in addition to cystitis, an inflammatory condition in the urinary tract and bladder, her "long threatened nervous breakdown seem[ed] to have come."[19] Members of the CWPC learned from the club newsletter dated 17 February 1912 that Katherine Hughes had "left for Honolulu for two months of complete rest after a somewhat severe breakdown."[20]

By the time the CWPC held its 1913 triennial in Edmonton, where she gave the historian's report, Katherine Hughes was feeling well enough to accept an appointment as assistant to the agent general for Alberta, based in London, England. The *Edmonton Bulletin* noted the elevation: "Miss Hughes has shown herself capable of doing a man's work on more than one occasion."[21] The move would auger a startling change and eventually transform Hughes from a highly regarded public servant into what many viewed as a traitor to her country.

In London, in 1914, Katherine Hughes befriended figures in the Irish separatist movement and decided to learn Gaelic.[22] That same year, on a visit to London, William Van Horne approached Hughes to help him write a history of the CPR; however, before they could begin work, he suddenly died. His children then asked Hughes to instead write their father's life story.[23] By 1916, Katherine Hughes was back in Montreal, living close to the Golden

Square Mile mansion where Van Horne had resided and gathering material for a biography of the railway tycoon. At the same time, she was becoming one of the most vocal advocates in Canada for Irish self-determination. George Ham made a tongue-in-cheek comment in his 1921 memoir, describing Hughes as "now trying to free Ireland with that distinguished person of Spanish parentage [who was] born in the United States, de Valera." Éamon de Valera was the president of the unilaterally declared "Irish Republic," and Ham's remark hinted at how controversial Hughes's stance had become.

With the First World War still raging, the influential publication *Saturday Night* commented on a speech Katherine Hughes made in Montreal that was sympathetic to Sinn Fein, a movement the magazine referred to as pro-German and anti-British. The article, which appeared in March 1918, noted that Hughes had a "pleasing journalistic gift" but suggested that she could certainly find more productive work than "exploiting a cause which ha[d] meant the loss of hundreds of British lives." It continued: "The Sinn Fein movement … is an aid to the enemy – and as such is not to be countenanced by those who would have the Allies win."[24]

As Katherine Hughes travelled the country expounding what the *Manitoba Free Press* termed the "Sinn Fein doctrine," her stance became more controversial. The *Morning Bulletin* (Edmonton) reported that her presence at the Pantages Theatre drew a hostile reception when she stated that the British army's occupation of Ireland had done more damage than had the German army's occupation of Belgium. The theatre was "rocked … with violent argument for a considerable time" after someone asked Hughes "what Ireland was doing while the Canadian boys were giving up their lives at Paschendale [sic]."[25]

This was the atmosphere swirling around Hughes as she completed her first draft of the biography of Van Horne in 1920 and gave it to the railway titan's son, Richard "Bennie" Van Horne, who then handed it to former McGill University official Walter Vaughan to polish. The book now completed, Hughes moved to Washington, DC, to establish an organization to lobby for the Irish cause, later returning to Canada to rally Irish Canadian support for de Valera. At some point in 1920, she was stunned to learn that her biography of Van Horne had been published – without her knowledge and without her name attached. Walter Vaughan had been credited as sole author of *The Life and Work of Sir William Van Horne*. In his preface, Vaughan all but admitted that he had not done the actual research or writing: "Much of this volume … is frankly based on Miss Hughes's material and wherever it has been possible I have used and adopted her rough material."[26]

It was a bitter pill. Katherine Hughes knew her political stance had cost her the authorship, but she had no money to fight the Van Horne family. She sailed to Australia on behalf of the Irish cause and, on her return, joined her sister, who had moved to New York. She never again felt comfortable in Canada. She died of stomach cancer and was buried, a pauper, in an unmarked grave at St Raymond's cemetery in the Bronx.[27]

In Catholic circles in Edmonton, Katherine Hughes was memorialized as a humanitarian who had left an enduring mark in western Canada by writing the life of Father Lacombe and founding Edmonton's chapter of the Catholic Women's League, which aided indigent women. She was lauded for her "sympathetic attitude towards mankind" and her bravery in defending the cause of Irish self-determination when "the lending of one's name risked bringing upon one the charge of sedition."[28] The true cost of Katherine Hughes's stance is inestimable. Had she been properly credited with Van Horne's biography, she might have died famous rather than all but unknown.

George Ham

On a beautiful fall afternoon in 1927, newspaperwomen from Nova Scotia to Manitoba gathered at Windsor Station in Montreal to unveil a bronze plaque engraved with a likeness of George Henry Ham, rendered by renowned portrait artist Victor Long. They presented the tablet to CPR president Edward Beatty as other railway officials stood by. Another group of women journalists had already gathered in Whitby, Ontario, for the dedication of a porch donated by the CWPC and built onto St John's (Anglican) Church, where Ham was buried in the adjacent graveyard.

George Henry Ham, the club's loyal friend and benefactor, died in 1926 at age seventy-nine following a long illness. For the presswomen, it was a loss keenly felt.

The plaque unveiled at Windsor Station expressed their gratitude and admiration in just two sentences: "This tablet is erected by the Canadian Women's Press Club in grateful recognition of his services as their founder and friend. He was a gallant gentleman and great of heart." Attending the ceremony were three women who had been in St Louis. Founding club members Irene Currie Love, Kate Simpson Hayes, and Mary Dawson relayed recollections of Ham and his generous acts to the nearly one hundred clubwomen present.

Irene Currie Love called Ham "the laughing philosopher – the Democritus of the twentieth century," comparing him to the ancient Greek philosopher known for placing a value on cheerfulness. She praised Ham's ability to see the good in everybody. With his loss, she said, "There is something lacking in the scheme of things."[29] Mary Dawson told the crowd no person did as much as Ham to improve the status of women journalists in Canada. Current club president Mae Clendenan of London, Ontario, noted that, while the women were extremely pleased to memorialize Ham with a plaque at Windsor Station and a portico at the church in Whitby, perhaps the finest memorial to Ham was a club that spread from sea to sea and, at that time, numbered over four hundred women: the CWPC.

Mary Dawson

Mary Adelaide Dawson, given the nickname "Happiness" (a name that stuck) by George Ham when the CWPC was founded in 1904 remained a working journalist until her death in 1932 due to complications from a fractured vertebrae. She was fifty-two. When she died, she had just finished a second term as president of the Toronto branch of the CWPC. It was ironic (and spoke volumes about the prejudice against working wives) that her obituary listed her specialty as homemaking when she was a career journalist with no children who had married C.H.J. Snider, the associate editor of the *Toronto Evening Telegram*, the paper for which she worked.[30]

Not long after the trip to St Louis, Dawson began writing a column for the *Toronto Evening Telegram* specifically designed to entice women readers. "Market Day Hints" proved a popular feature. It was widely copied and remains a staple in some Canadian newspapers even today, advising readers on the best buys for the week. She also inaugurated a feature for the Saturday paper entitled "Do You Remember Away Back When?"

She would make her name on a big news story in April 1912, when she was sent to meet the ship *Carpathia*, which brought survivors of the *Titanic* into New York harbour. She alone in the press corps pierced the cordon that blocked reporters from arriving passengers. Mary Dawson had the "happy inspiration," as press colleagues described it, to ask a doctor connected with one of the ambulances to take her along.[31] "I did not throw myself in front of an ambulance," she later stated, "but just stopped in front of it sudden like – just held it up and persuaded the doctor in charge that if I failed in the assignment, all Canadian newspaperwomen would be discredited."[32]

In 1919, covering the Winnipeg General Strike, Dawson managed to get her stories through to the *Toronto Evening Telegram* by filing her copy from Minnesota in order to circumvent Canadian telegraphers in Calgary and Edmonton who were in sympathy with their colleagues in Winnipeg.[33] Upon her death, a rival paper, the *Mail and Empire*, remembered Mary Dawson as someone who always lent a hand to rookies in the business: "Seasoned journalist that she was, she never forgot that once she was a 'cub.'"[34]

Léonise Valois

After the St Louis trip, steady work in journalism failed to materialize for Léonise Valois, who had represented *Le Canada* on the trip. Interestingly, this fiercely independent woman, who was self-supporting and who refused to marry someone whom she did not love, would re-emerge as a journalist later in life and use her distinctive voice and strong reporting skills to write sporadically for newspapers and magazines in Quebec almost up until her death at age sixty-seven in 1936. In between, she would earn a literary distinction that would forever belong to her when she became the first woman to publish a volume of poetry in Quebec.

Returning from the St Louis World's Fair with no permanent journalism position in sight, Léonise Valois ultimately took a job with the post office, which had been arranged for her by her first love and now prominent politician, Rodolphe Lemieux. She remained at a branch in east end Montreal from 1907 until her retirement in 1929. She never stopped writing, however, gathering reams of poems that she had penned over the years into a volume of verse entitled *Fleurs Sauvages*. Published in 1910, this volume put her on the literary map in Quebec.

In 1922, as an independent single woman, she proudly bought a house on Greene Avenue in Westmount, which later became the site of the Double Hook bookstore (now Babar Books). She also began writing for *La Terre de chez nous*, a weekly agricultural newspaper aimed at the farm community that had a pro-Catholic and anti-women's suffrage stance. This seems at odds with Valois's earlier position at *Le Monde illustré*, where she had her first journalism job and where she advocated for women's rights.[35] However, like many of her colleagues on the trip to St Louis, Valois lobbied for improvements in education and better wages for women while backing away from endorsing their right to the vote.

In November 1931, her work as woman's page editor for *La Terre de chez nous* came to an abrupt halt. A car running a red light hit a motorcyclist, who hit Valois as she was exiting the bank in her neighbourhood. She was in a coma for sixty-three days, and, when she emerged, her physical and cognitive capacities were impaired; however, she slowly recuperated. She was able to publish a second book of poetry in 1934 entitled *Feuilles tombées*.

Shortly before her death from uterine cancer, Léonise Valois took a final stand for women. In her last will and testament, she challenged the laws on succession. At that time, if a married woman inherited money in Quebec, her husband had to endorse the cheque. Valois specified that the capital derived from the sale of her home should be divided among her surviving sisters and that the signature of their respective husbands should not be required.[36]

Marie Beaupré

Marie Beaupré, the distinguished Villa Maria alumna who represented *La Presse* in St Louis, died in 1942 at an old-age home run by nuns on Ste Catherine Street in Montreal. She was sixty-nine. While she had been a public figure earlier in the century, she had gradually faded from view as a journalist.

The lengthy article Beaupré wrote in *La Presse* following the St Louis trip did not run until 6 August 1904, a full six weeks after the women returned. But perhaps it was timed to coincide with a publicity stunt typically favoured by the newspaper: *La Presse* sponsored its own trip to the world's fair on the Grand Trunk Railway in August 1904. The Grand Trunk line competed directly with the CPR by offering "fast express trains" to the world's fair. When *La Presse* announced its promotional trip to St Louis, so many travellers signed up that a second railway car had to be added. One wonders how the CPR and George Ham regarded the placement of Marie's Beaupré's article, given that the promotional trip sponsored by *La Presse* was arranged by the CPR's competitor.

Beaupré's affiliation with *La Presse* continued to grow following the trip to St Louis, and she seemed to have a bright future as a journalist in Quebec. She was a member of the Association des journalistes canadiens-français (AJCF), and, in 1905, she landed what appeared to be a permanent job editing the woman's page of *La Presse*. Her photograph appears in a publicity shot with the paper's full-time staff, and she is the only female journalist in the photo. Writing under her penname "Hélène Dumont," Marie Beaupré announced her arrival on the paper's weekly *Page des Dames* on Saturday, 11 February 1905. Two weeks later, she seemed to be making her own mark on the page. Under the stylized headline "Propos Féminins," she wrote a provocative sentence in large type: "Tous les hommes sont frères: ne faut-il pas que toutes les femmes soient soeurs?" (All men are brothers: are not all women sisters?)

Marie Beaupré replaced Woman's Page editor Édouardina Lesage, otherwise known as Colette, who left the paper in early 1905. When Beaupré took her place, it appeared that *La Presse* was grooming her to become a permanent fixture. In a letter written in February 1905 to Marie Gérin-Lajoie (Antoinette Gérin-Lajoie's sister-in-law), which is part of the Gérin-Lajoie collection at the Centre d'archives de Montreal, Beaupré said her new duties at *La Presse* were keeping her chained to the office. But Beaupré's writing disappears from the page at the end of 1905 and Colette's byline suddenly reappears. Did serious-minded Marie Beaupré feel boxed in by having to oversee a page of society gossip and fashion coverage? Did she displease the editors at *La Presse*? Or had she only been given a temporary post in the first place? The answer remains a mystery.

It is clear that Marie Beaupré then changed course completely. By 1907 she had inherited a small private school for girls started by long-time educator and sometime journalist Hermine Lanctôt.[37] The *Bulletin du parler français au Canada* (May 1913) reported that Beaupré "obstinately remain[ed] aside" from daily journalism, indicating that she had made a deliberate choice to cut herself off from the profession. For nearly two decades after that, Beaupré's listing in the city directory describes her as a schoolteacher. She gave private lessons in French, English, math, and religion. However, she continued to write for *Le Foyer*, which published articles for women on topical subjects as well as church-related material in the form of edifying poems and essays. A highly successful magazine partially due to its massive distribution through the Roman Catholic Church, it would provide a home for Beaupré's work for almost twenty-five years.

In the 1930s, Marie Beaupré began working on a book that focused on her fascination with piety. She wrote a biography of recluse Jeanne LeBer who was born in 1662, the daughter of a rich Montreal merchant, and who renounced every material possession to live alone and in silence. Beaupré was urged to document the story of the first recluse in French Canada by priest and historian Lionel Groulx. The book, *Jeanne LeBer: Première recluse du Canada Français, 1662–1714*, was published in 1939, with a preface by Groulx. One reviewer noted the difficulty of writing about a recluse who left so few traces: "Such poor documentation, that to talk about her, we must mostly insist on the framework."[38] In a sense, the same could be said about Marie

Beaupré. Apart from her attraction to religious affairs, no clear portrait of Beaupré emerges. Only an evanescent outline of this once promising journalist survives.

Both Marie Beaupré and her mother Mélina, who died only a few years before her daughter, were buried in a large plot belonging to the Desaulniers family at Notre-Dame-des-Neiges Cemetery. Mélina's sister had married Arthur Desaulniers and Gonzalve Desaulniers, a poet, may have edited the newspaper that provided the first publishing venue for a young Marie Beaupré, but this cannot be verified.

Anne-Marie Gleason

Using today's terminology, Anne-Marie Gleason seemingly had it all. The first treasurer of the CWPC, she was the only woman out of sixteen in St Louis to have a child, a successful marriage, and a long productive career in journalism. She started her own magazine, wrote a book about women, and penned some three thousand columns and articles before her death in 1943 at age sixty-eight. At one point, she would become the most famous female journalist in Quebec.

Shortly after the trip to St Louis, Gleason confirmed her place as a rising star among journalists in Quebec with her election to the board of the Association des journalistes canadiens-français. The organization had a rousing start but apparently expired around 1907. For reasons that could not be discerned, she would not renew her bond with the CWPC in those early years, although there are indications she rejoined at the time of the triennial in Montreal in 1920.

In October 1904, just months after the St Louis trip, Anne-Marie Gleason married Quebec-born Dr Wilfrid Huguenin, a physician of independent wealth who ceased the practice of medicine to live off the fortune he had inherited from an uncle. In 1905, the couple had their only child, a daughter they named Madeleine. The couple shared a passion for the arts. In 1915 they opened their home to a group of experimental writers, architects, and musicians who created an arts magazine called *Le Nigog*, named for an instrument used by Aboriginal people to spear salmon. The magazine folded after only twelve issues,[39] but perhaps its demise and the absence of a replacement were tied to Gleason's decision to leave *La Patrie* in 1919 and start her own publication, *La Revue moderne*, considered one of the most literary and artistic magazines of its time. In September 1919, Anne-Marie Gleason wrote a series of letters to well-known writers and intellectuals in Quebec, soliciting their contributions to the planned magazine. She noted that she was attempting to create "a national sentiment truly Canadian" with the publication and vowed to pay them for their efforts. "We know the value of intellectual work," she wrote: "We will never publish an article we don't pay for."[40] *La Revue moderne* was extremely successful and would become the French edition of *Chatelaine* in 1960.

Anne-Marie Gleason supported Canada's role in the First World War and served as president of the French section of the Red Cross. The governments of France and Belgium both recognized her efforts.[41] She lobbied in print for the preservation of the French language and for the betterment of women in education and the workplace. But she faced great obstacles when it came to embracing a feminist agenda. Church authorities such as Monsignor Louis-Adolphe Paquet and leading thinkers such as Henri Bourassa regarded feminism as a menace to family life and society.[42]

Even after the federal franchise was accorded to all Canadian women, there was virulent opposition in Quebec to granting women the right to vote in provincial elections. "That the innovation of the woman in politics be more or less acceptable in certain countries is possible," stated Senator L.-O. David, "but here, in our province, our national and social destinies oppose it and demand that nothing distract her from the sacred duties imposed on her by the family."[43]

In 1924, Anne-Marie Gleason's husband died. Five years later, her daughter, just twenty-three years old, died suddenly from what was termed a cardiac lesion. The shocking loss was announced on the front page of *La Patrie*, where Gleason had worked for almost two decades. It was a devastating blow. Anne-Marie Gleason retired from active journalism, although she would not abandon it. In 1938, using her formidable reporting skills, she published

Portraits de femmes. The book paid homage to ninety-five important women in Quebec history through a series of short biographies, and she dedicated it to her daughter.

Portraits de femmes would prove to be Gleason's lasting contribution to journalism, providing a cogent survey of special women in the province, many of them unrecognized. Anne-Marie Gleason herself is barely remembered today, although a street in east end Montreal near the intersection of rue Honoré-Beaugrand and rue Hochelaga is named rue Madeleine-Huguenin.

Antoinette Gérin-Lajoie

Preoccupied by the educational exhibits at the World's Fair in St Louis, Antoinette Gérin-Lajoie pursued her passion for hands-on learning until her dying day in May 1945 at age seventy-four. She never returned to journalism, but her journalistic effort in St Louis remained close to her heart. Among the private papers archived after her death were letters of praise from the assistant editor of the lively Quebec City daily *L'Événement* urging her to continue writing for the paper after the St Louis trip. She had kept these for four decades.

Gérin-Lajoie was torn between writing and teaching. Shortly before the St Louis trip, plans were in the works to bring a school of domestic science to Montreal. Caroline Béïque, who engineered the idea and directed the woman's sector of the Société Saint-Jean-Baptiste, asked Gérin-Lajoie to enrol in a specialized training program in household science, or what we would now call "home economics," given in Fribourg, Switzerland.

Antoinette Gérin-Lajoie studied in Switzerland from 1905 to 1906, joining a fellow Quebecer, Jeanne Anctil, who had also been recruited by Béïque. Antoinette Gérin-Lajoie and Jeanne Anctil, who would later be credited with bringing authentic French cuisine to Canada, then returned to Montreal, where they jointly supervised l'École ménagère, which formally opened in 1907 in the presence of Quebec premier Lomer Gouin. The school offered a day course for full-time students, a night course for the general public, and teacher training in the domestic sciences, including bookkeeping, housekeeping, dressmaking, and cooking. The school struggled financially at the start, and Gérin-Lajoie was so committed to her work that she did not draw a salary for two years.

In 1910, Antoinette Gérin-Lajoie left the school to teach home economics at another school in Montreal, l'Académie Marchand. She returned to l'École ménagère upon the death of Jeanne Anctil in 1926 and became director. In 1936, Antoinette and her niece Marie Gérin-Lajoie, a nun, expanded the program by opening a school of family and social education at l'Institut Notre-Dame du Bon-Conseil on St Joseph Street in Montreal. Middle-class young women of that era remember taking cooking classes at l'Institut as almost a rite of passage before marriage.[44]

Highly admired by family members, Antoinette Gérin-Lajoie is remembered as a woman of extraordinary energy who was perceived by her younger nieces and nephews as vigorous and contemporary even as she aged.[45] She retired in 1942 but continued to live with the nuns at their residence on St Joseph Street until her death three years later.

Irene Currie Love

The youngest woman of the St Louis contingent carved a highly successful journalism career that spread over four decades. Irene Currie Love served as the Woman's Page editor and advice columnist for the *Montreal Daily Star* from 1914 until her death in 1945 at age sixty-four. Her last column, written from a hospital bed, appeared in the *Star* the day of her funeral under her penname "Margaret Currie."[46]

Marrying journalist Eldred S. Archibald in 1912, Love moved to Montreal because of his job. In a twist, she would ultimately have the more visible journalistic presence in the city as a columnist dispensing advice that was free of ethnic and religious discrimination and winning fans not just among readers but also among local doctors and ministers, who called her page an influential source of "social service work" in an increasingly multicultural Montreal.[47] Her open-minded approach in her column echoed the same thoughts she had expressed in the articles written from St Louis, where she had marvelled at the handiwork produced by foreign cultures that many Canadians considered uncivilized.

Irene Currie Love's long-running advice column had its genesis shortly after the outbreak of the First World War. While visiting a friend at the *Montreal Daily Star*, she was shown a letter from a reader who related how she was conserving food during strenuous times. Currie Love suggested to the paper's managing editor that the *Star* should field similar ideas from readers to help the war effort. A few days later, she was hired to undertake the assignment. The response was overwhelming. "Margaret Currie" was soon writing a full-page column and answering questions on every subject imaginable.[48]

In 1924, acceding to the requests of her readers, Irene Currie Love published a compendium of her advice columns, which she called "chats." She added household hints, beauty tips, and a voluminous number of recipes and simply entitled the book *Margaret Currie – Her Book*. She dedicated it "in all humility" to her correspondents over the past ten years. Currie Love's "chats" covered everything from gossip ("So few people in the world have sufficiently accurate memories to report a speech correctly, that it is better not to report it at all" (37) to the high incidence of unsuccessful marriages ("the world, in 999 cases out of a thousand, blames the woman, without pausing to investigate the reasons pro and con" [41]).

In an interview given shortly before she died, Irene Currie Love, who never had children, was asked to provide advice to aspiring journalists. Her reply echoed the down-to-earth style she had maintained in her journalism. "High-falutin' language is not essential, but grammatical English is," she stated: "Never forget that you are writing for Mr and Mrs Jones and the Jones family. If you can get it across to them, you can get it across to everyone. Anyone can 'sling the dictionary' and use dollar words, but you must make the everyday reader get what you mean, for he is the backbone of newspaper and magazine circulation."[49]

Kate Simpson Hayes

Were it not for Kate Simpson Hayes, the CWPC might never have gotten off the ground after the St Louis trip.[50] As the club's first secretary, working out of George Ham's office in Montreal, Hayes almost singlehandedly took on the responsibility for planning the next meeting, recruiting new members, gathering corporate sponsors, and arranging for the CPR to provide transport to Winnipeg in 1906.

Of all the women on the trip, she turned out to be the most prolific writer. She penned books, plays, poetry, and songs as well as innumerable newspaper and magazine articles. She was a working journalist longer than any woman on the trip, still contributing to newspapers up until a few years before she died of a heart attack in January 1945 in Victoria, British Columbia. She was eighty-eight.

A trailblazer in the journalism field, and the first librarian for the Legislature of the Northwest Territories – an 1895 photo shows a comely Kate Simpson Hayes surrounded by male civil servants and government officials – she was staunchly independent when most women were not. For that reason it is fascinating to ponder why she adamantly clung to the notion that marriage and motherhood were a woman's true calling. Despite her extensive travels and exposure to leading feminist thinkers, Hayes often displayed a stance in her writing that completely contradicted the reality in which she herself lived.

From 1900 through 1906, Hayes wrote for the *Free Press* in Winnipeg under the penname "Mary Markwell." She made extended trips to England in 1906 and 1911 on behalf of the CPR to assist in the immigration of female settlers to Canada, and she enjoyed a major literary coup when a prestigious New York publishing house picked up her book of short stories entitled *Derby Day in the Yukon*, for which she used the pseudonym "Yukon Bill." Her publisher, George Doran, whose stable would include Virginia Woolf, O. Henry, and Joyce Kilmer, told Hayes he was captivated by her book and addressed her in correspondence as M. Markwell, Esq. – a male. There is no evidence that Doran ever learned her true identity.[51]

But despite her success, Hayes had not gotten over her lover Nicholas Flood Davin, who had died of a self-inflicted gunshot wound in 1901, nor could she ever forget a secret they shared. In 1904, the year of the St Louis trip, Hayes told author Henry J. Morgan, who was attempting to write a biography of Davin: "sometimes I think I'll die, remembering it all."[52]

Given the moralistic stance she took in her columns, it is hard to believe that, in the 1890s, Kate Simpson Hayes had borne two children out of wedlock, both fathered by Davin. During the final stages of each pregnancy, Hayes left Regina, ostensibly to travel, while continuing to send articles to the *Leader* from other cities. She gave up both children, placing the first in private care and the second in a Roman Catholic orphanage in Manitoba. She refused to divorce Charles Bowman Simpson in order to marry Davin and deemed it more socially appropriate to give up the "illegitimate" children than risk scandal by divorcing her husband and marrying her lover. For the rest of her life, Hayes would not publicly acknowledge either child she had with Davin.[53]

Frustrated by Hayes's refusal to get a divorce, Davin married twenty-one-year-old Eliza Reid of Ottawa and began searching for the son and daughter he had with Hayes. He managed to find six-year-old Henry Arthur, whom his new wife agreed to raise as their nephew, but efforts to find daughter Agnes were foiled when the nuns at the orphanage learned of the search and hid the young girl.[54] Henry Arthur was killed fighting in Belgium in 1916 during the First World War. Agnes did not discover the true circumstances of her birth for nearly three decades. Agnes's discovery deeply troubled Kate Simpson Hayes, who wanted her secret kept at all costs.

For her part, Agnes longed for Hayes's formal acknowledgment of maternity and an introduction to her half brother and sister, Hayes's "legitimate" children. Kate Simpson Hayes would not hear of it. She felt she had done the best for Agnes under the circumstances and wanted both to protect her own reputation and to shield her two legitimate children from shame. Letters exchanged between Agnes and Hayes show tensions growing as the latter increasingly feared disclosure and the former lobbied for openness. Communication was ultimately cut off.[55]

Kate Simpson Hayes made her mark in journalism as one of the first female journalists in western Canada and a vivid and witty writer. She made a contribution to Canadian culture as one of the first women to achieve any degree of literary stature in that part of Canada. She continued to work until the end of her life, writing an advice column when she was nearly seventy for the *Winnipeg Tribune*. She never stopped promoting herself as a writer and hustling for a living. Legendary *Winnipeg Free Press* editor J.W. Dafoe, in a 1935 letter that begins "My dear Mary Markwell," sanctioned her proposal to serialize her recollections of pioneer life in Saskatchewan. She was almost eighty years old at the time.

Hayes was eighty-two when she wrote to American novelist Fannie Hurst complimenting her on her short story entitled "Mama and Papa." Hurst's reply politely acknowledged Hayes's own stature: "As an author," Hurst wrote, "you must well realize to what extent that kind of appreciation gives the scribe courage to go forward."[56]

Cécile Laberge

Cécile Laberge would never become a journalist after writing about the St Louis World's Fair for the Quebec City newspaper *Le Soleil*. But the fiery musician would take a stand for the rights of women, serving briefly in the 1920s as president of the Provincial Franchise Committee (Comité provincial pour le suffrage féminin), which fought the clerics and politicians opposed to suffrage for women.[57] And, before her death in 1948 at age eighty-seven, Cécile Laberge would undertake a labour of love that combined a life-long passion for music with a latent journalistic impulse.

Laberge would document the fifty-year history of the Ladies' Morning Musical Club with a book she wrote in English: "I have often been asked by members of the Ladies' Morning Musical Club and by musicians whom I number among my friends to write an account of the Club's musical activities ... I am writing these recollections through love and gratitude to the organization which has given me so much musical joy."[58] Due in part to Laberge, club president for nine years and head of the concert committee for eight years, musicians of international renown, including soprano Lotte Lehmann, violinist Jascha Heifetz, and guitarist Andres Segovia, were brought to Montreal to perform in an unbroken series of weekly concerts. A poignant moment occurred when Laberge learned that contralto Marian Anderson, in Montreal to perform for the club, had been refused entry to her hotel because of her colour. She rushed to bring Anderson, an African-American, to her home.[59] The Ladies' Morning Musical Club became a formidable institution in Laberge's lifetime. Membership grew to over twelve hundred, with a waiting list of two hundred. The club still exists today, holding concerts in Pollack Hall on the McGill University campus.

In her book about the club, Cécile Laberge details encounters with world-class performers; a move from humble quarters at the YMCA to the Ritz-Carlton Hotel as the club's prestige grew; and the establishment of a scholarship enabling young women to study at the Juilliard School of Music in New York. The best parts of the memoir describe a few harrowing close calls in the effort to keep the club's string of weekly Thursday concerts unbroken in the face of illness, inclement weather, and problems with transport and visas. One of these close calls involved Amintha Plouffe's sister Eva. At nine o'clock on the morning of a concert slated to start at eleven, Laberge learned that the principal number on the program, Debussy's violin sonata, would have to be scratched because the violinist was ill. "There was only one person who could save the day," she wrote: "In those days we had no telephone communication so I had to travel three miles in a sleigh, with a slow horse, to reach the home of Miss Eva Plouffe. 'Please change your frock and come to the Club,' I entreated, as I entered her home. I explained in brief what had happened. Miss Plouffe said she had not played that particular music for some time. 'Debussy can be played with wrong notes,' I said, 'Do come quickly!'"[60]

She also writes with understated humour about Italian pianist Adriano Ariani, brought to Montreal in the dead of winter. As the hands of the clock approached concert time, the artist had not yet appeared. A club member was dispatched to the Windsor Hotel, where the musician was staying. Snowflakes were softly falling, and the pianist was found at a window admiring the fairy-tale landscape. "What a beautiful country," he exclaimed. "Yes," came the answer, "but the ladies are waiting to hear you play your all-Chopin programme!"[61]

In 1908, Cécile Laberge would marry for a third time, to Arthur Léger, whose cousin Paul-Émile would become world famous as a cardinal. A family joke recounts that her granddaughter, at age six, asked Laberge which one of her three husbands she would like to join in Paradise. Her answer went unrecorded.

Alice Asselin

Alice Asselin, who died in 1954 at age seventy-seven, never wrote anything about the St Louis trip, nor was an article about the fair ever published in her husband's newspaper *Le Nationaliste*. Her descendants had no idea she had travelled to St Louis with a group of female journalists in 1904, and they did not think she had any time, as a young wife and mother, to pursue an interest in writing after the trip. Indeed, following the St Louis venture, Asselin resumed a hectic routine. By 1910, she had given birth to four sons and lived anything but a quiet existence.

Her husband Olivar, a crusading journalist, was often in the eye of a storm. Gérard Dagenais, editor of Olivar Asselin's selected works, called him "the greatest and most celebrated master of French thought in Canada." Journalism colleague Omer Héroux called him "the greatest journalist of his time in Canada."[62] But his journalism frequently put him at odds with the powerful. He was sued for libel a number of times and imprisoned twice, once for slapping Louis-Alexandre Taschereau on the floor of the National Assembly in 1909 when the future premier of Quebec publicly questioned his sanity.

Alice Asselin, as best as can be learned, dutifully raised the children and provided moral and emotional support for her husband. Whether their marriage was a happy one is hard to discern. Olivar was frequently absent; money problems dogged the family because Olivar's income was not steady; and there appeared to be little opportunity for Alice to carve a space for herself other than as her husband's helpmate.

During the First World War, Olivar, who had vehemently opposed any participation in a war that involved Britain, did an about-face and volunteered for service in the Canadian army, forming a regiment of French-Canadian volunteers to fight overseas. After his service, Olivar continued to write for many publications, including *La Revue moderne*, founded by Anne-Marie Gleason. He also served as editor-in-chief of *Le Canada*.

But a major interest in his life involved his charitable undertakings. He and Alice coalesced as a couple around these endeavours. Olivar used his journalistic talents to lobby for a shelter and a hospital to serve the city's elderly poor. Alice, too, was passionately committed to helping the indigent. Her niece, Raymonde Marchand Paré, remembers that men would regularly show up at Alice's door on St Hubert Street asking for a job, explaining that they had heard of her reputation for helping people down on their luck.[63]

After Olivar died in 1937, Alice travelled around Europe before the outset of the Second World War. She visited her niece, Raymonde Marchand Paré, who was living in France with her mother (Eva) and attending a private girls high school. Could Alice Asselin have become a journalist given the opportunity? Did she harbour any such ambitions? The questions remain unanswered.

Amintha Plouffe

Amintha Plouffe, who wrote a lively and well-structured account of the St Louis trip for *Le Journal,* a morning daily newspaper in Montreal, died in July 1962 at the age of ninety-two. Her story about the World's Fair was a joy to read and was better written than were the articles penned by several of her colleagues. However, Amintha Plouffe never became a journalist. It appears she never wrote for *Le Journal* again, and, when the paper folded in 1905, it is possible that Plouffe's aspirations died with it. It is probable that no full-time position on a newspaper was offered to her after the St Louis trip. As an unmarried woman, Amintha Plouffe could not support herself without steady work: freelance writing paid little and could not guarantee financial stability.

After the trip, Amintha Plouffe continued to be listed in the Montreal city directory as a stenographer until the age of seventy-five. Her sister Eva Plouffe, the famed pianist, won wide acclaim and moved to New York City. Eva's accomplishments overshadowed Amintha's, but it is not hard to imagine that Amintha might have been a successful journalist had the opportunity arisen. She was a skilled writer.

Nearing age eighty in 1950, Amintha Plouffe moved to a Catholic old-age
home on Ste-Catherine Street in Montreal called Foyer Notre-Dame-de-
Lourdes. This was where Marie Beaupré had lived before her death in 1942
and where Félicité Angers, who used the nom-de-plume "Laure Conan" and
was Quebec's first female novelist, lived between 1910 and 1923.[64]

Gertrude Balmer Watt

Gertrude "Peggy" Watt, who had represented the *Woodstock Sentinel-Review*
in St Louis and then became a pioneering female journalist in Alberta, was
the last of the Sweet Sixteen to pass away. She died in hospital in Edmonton
in 1963 after she had fallen and broken her hip. She was eighty-four.

Peggy Watt and husband Arthur Balmer Watt broke new ground in
journalism when they left Woodstock for Edmonton, where Arthur started
the *Saturday News* and Peggy edited the Woman's Page in the early 1900s.
Peggy Watt, an amateur actress, also wrote drama criticism for the *Edmonton Daily Capital* and the *Alberta Homestead*, both of which were established
by her husband. She drew acclaim for two books of essays on frontier life: *A
Woman in the West* (1907) and *Town and Trail* (1908).

Peggy Watt left daily journalism when Arthur Watt joined the *Edmonton
Journal* in 1912 as assistant editor. Arthur would eventually become editor-
in-chief and guide the paper to a Pulitzer Prize for public service in 1938.[65]
It would mark the first time the Pulitzer was given to a newspaper outside
the United States. The Pulitzer committee recognized the *Edmonton Journal* for editorial leadership in defending freedom of the press by vigorously
campaigning against a provincial bill that would require newspapers to print
government-ordered rebuttals of information it deemed incorrect.

According to Peggy Watt's grandson Tom Radford, despite Arthur's success, Peggy believed he had given up his independence by working for a
paper he did not own. Peggy Watt would never do the same; instead, she
turned a hobby into a job and opened an antiques store. She contributed to

newspapers, magazines, and radio through the years and liked to say she found her topics in the lives of the people who brought antiques into her store.[66] "Arthur had a wonderful newspaper career, but lost his independence," said Radford. "Peggy lost her career, but kept her independence."[67]

Radford said his grandmother was dearly loved by her family and friends but unforgiving when crossed. After arguing with her sister, Peggy Watt never spoke to her again. Her dislike of CWPC member Emily Murphy, the first female magistrate in Canada, was so strong she would spit out the car window when she drove through an Edmonton park that bore Murphy's name. And while Watt had three children, the mothering role did not come easily to a woman whose own mother had abandoned the family. Her daughter (Radford's mother) suffered a nervous breakdown as a child and was sent to board at a convent.

In 1954, Peggy Watt was the honoured guest at the CWPC's fiftieth anniversary celebration. She wrote a detailed memoir for the anniversary program and patiently helped CWPC historians unravel the club's earliest days, providing precious information and a window onto the journey that established the foundation for every women who entered journalism in Canada for decades to come. With Peggy Watt's death, the story of the founders would come to a close. But their effort on behalf of women journalists would live on, and today it resounds in newsrooms across the country.

NOTES

INTRODUCTION

1 Anne-Marie Gleason, "Les Excursions," *La Patrie,* 27 June 1904. All quotes from the French press are translated into English in this text.
2 Cook and Mitchinson, *Proper Sphere,* 6.
3 *London Advertiser,* 2 July 1904. A front-page story trumpeted the views of G. Stanley Hall, eminent psychologist and president of Clark University in Worcester, Massachusetts, who told a national conference on education in the United States that higher education for women and co-education are to blame for "race suicide."
4 Fiamengo, *Woman's Page,* 14–15.
5 Edmund S. Hoch, "Features of the Exposition," *National Magazine,* vol. 20, no. 3, June 1904, available at <www.philsp.com/homeville/FMI/t1014.htm>.
6 Kathleen (Kay) Mathers to Mae Clendenan, 27 April 1954, Library and Archives Canada, Media Club of Canada, Golden Jubilee Packet Correspondence 1953–54, file 17-3.
7 Ham, *Reminiscences,* 153.

CHAPTER ONE

1 Rutherford, *Victorian Authority,* 9.
2 Ibid., 3.
3 See <http://www.canadianencyclopedia.ca/index.cfm?PgNm=TCE&Params=A1ARTA0005724>.
4 Lang, *Women Who Made the News,* 8.
5 Cruise and Griffiths, *Lords of the Line,* 272.
6 Rutherford, *Victorian Authority,* 13.

7 Cruise and Griffiths, *Lords of the Line*, 13, 1, 65.

8 Ibid., 62, 278–83.

9 Ibid., 283, 311.

10 Notes by Mary Hamer, 2007, <http://www.kipling.org.uk/rg_ladysnows1.htm>, taken from *Letters of Rudyard Kipling*, vol. 2 (London and New York: Macmillan, 1990).

11 Author unknown, *(Winnipeg) Free Press*, 9 June 1906.

12 Ham, *Reminiscences*, 152.

13 Wilson et al., *Canadian Education*, 316.

14 Fergusson, *Story of the Nova Scotia Teachers Union*, 23. Dr Fergusson, a former math and science teacher who served as executive director of the Nova Scotia Teachers Union from 1970 to 1984, began researching the life of Margaret Graham forty years ago.

15 "NSTU Conference Room Has Been Named," *The Teacher* 40 (December 2001): 8. Graham's words are inscribed on a plaque in the Halifax offices of the Nova Scotia Teachers Union, where a conference room is also dedicated to her memory.

16 M.H.W., *Sun* (New York), 14 February 1897. The book in question was compiled by the Honourable James D. Richardson and published in Washington, DC, by the Government Printing Office.

17 Norman H. Fergusson, "Margaret Graham Revealed," *The Teacher* 41 (November 2002): 12; Norman H. Fergusson, "Margaret Graham Revealed (Part 2)," *The Teacher*, 41 (December 2002): 5.

18 M.G., *Halifax Herald*, 14 June 1904. Unless otherwise indicated, all Graham quotes are from this source.

19 Gosselin, *Les journalistes québécoises*, 57. Robertine Barry expressed this opinion in a speech to the Fedération nationale Saint-Jean-Baptiste in 1907.

20 Wilson et al., *Canadian Education*, 334.

21 Ibid., 333.

22 Rex, *No Daughter of Mine*, 6.

23 Newspaper article from the *Calgary Herald*, 25 June 1932, Library and Archives Canada, Media Club of Canada, Canadian Women's Press Club, Jubilee Packet Correspondence 1953–54, 17-3.

24 See Canadian Human Rights Commission website at <http://www.chrc-ccdp.ca/en/getbriefed/1900/population.asp>.

25 Ibid.

26 Maguire, "Convention and Contradiction," 31. Maguire explains the fascinating "contradiction" that made Hayes so intriguing: she believed domesticity was the

foundation for a strong nation despite the realities of her own life, and she clung to that ideal.

27 Morgan, *Canadian Men and Women* (1912 ed.), 516. Three women on the St Louis trip – Robertine Barry, Kate Simpson Hayes, and Grace Denison – were included in Morgan's first volume (1898 ed.), which documented 2,891 impressive living Canadians. His second volume (1912 ed.) contained 7,900 sketches.

28 Argan et al., *Regina*, 10–11.

29 Ibid.

30 Government of Saskatchewan website, Arts and Culture, History. See <www.gov.sk.ca>.

31 Irene Gardiner Price, newspaper article from an unidentified publication, June 1932, Library and Archives Canada, Media Club of Canada, Canadian Women's Press Club scrapbooks, vol. 24, file 1.

32 Morgan, *Canadian Men and Women* (1898 ed.), 247.

33 Maguire, "Convention and Contradiction," 36.

34 Morgan, *Canadian Men and Women* (1898 ed.), 451.

35 Kate Simpson Hayes spells "Clarke's Crossing" with an "e."

36 Early Canadiana Online, scanned from a CIHM microfiche of the original publication held by Library and Archives Canada. Available at <http://www.canadiana.org/cgi-bin/ECO/mtq?doc=30325>.

37 Maguire, "Convention and Contradiction," 65–7.

38 John Sanford, "Queen of the Sob Sisters," *Maclean's*, 15 January 1953.

39 Canadian Human Rights Commission website. Available at <http://www.chrc-ccdp.ca/en/getbriefed/1900/population.asp>.

40 Ham, *Reminiscences*, 153.

41 Kate Simpson Hayes, "Woman's World," *Manitoba Free Press*, 9 July 1904.

CHAPTER TWO

1 Morgan, *Canadian Men and Women* (1898 ed.), 54. Morgan's entry for Robertine Barry was prefaced by this quote.

2 Hélène Pelletier-Baillargeon, biographer of Olivar Asselin, telephone interview, 8 August 2007.

3 Carrier, "Barry."

4 Anne Carrier, personal interview at the Chateau Ramezay in Montreal, June 2005.

5 Desjardins, *Robertine Barry*, 36.

6 Denault and Lévesque, *Éléments*, 50.

7 Danylewycz, "In Their Own Right," 6.

8 Ibid., 177, 179.

9 Desjardins, *Robertine Barry*, 94.

10 In 1878, Beaugrand published his best-known work, a novel about French-Canadian emigrants entitled *Jeanne la fileuse*. He founded *La Patrie* in 1879. He ran for mayor in 1885, at age thirty-six. Michael Bliss, in his book entitled *The Plague: A Story of Smallpox in Montreal*, notes that the handsome and perfectly bilingual Beaugrand enjoyed widespread support in the English community. Beaugrand argued that public health was the great question of the day. Ironically, he would face one of the gravest health crises in Montreal history when, after he was elected, smallpox infested the city and claimed more than three thousand lives.

11 Desjardins, *Robertine Barry*, 144–5.

12 Bliss, *The Plague*, 15.

13 Ibid., 16.

14 Boivin and Landry, "Françoise et Madeleine," 231.

15 The Bank of Canada's inflation index only goes back to 1914, but $100 at that time would be equal to $1,900 in 2009. Please see <http://www.bankofcanada.ca/en/rates/inflation_calc.html>.

16 Anne Carrier, recounting Barry's words in a personal interview at the Chateau Ramezay in Montreal, June 2005.

17 Morgan, *Canadian Men and Women*, 54 (1898 ed.). *Fleurs champêtres* would be reprinted again in the 1920s and the 1980s.

18 Hugh Fraser left provisions in his will to establish a free library, museum and gallery; the Fraser Institute opened in 1885. The Institute received a $1 million donation in the 1950s from J.W.A. Hickson. See www.fraserhickson.ca.

19 Lemire and Boivin, *La vie littéraire au Quebec*, 220.

20 Wyczynski, *Émile Nelligan*, 156.

21 Publication information provided by Alice Cocunubova, archiviste de reference, Centre de recherche en civilization canadienne-française, Bibliothèque Morisset Université d'Ottawa.

22 Wyczynski, *Émile Nelligan*, 160.

23 Green, "Literary Feminists," 135.

24 Prepared for the Paris Exposition by the Conseil National des Femmes du Canada, 1900.

25 Green, "Literary Feminists," 128–9.

26 Cambron, *La vie culturelle*, 324.

27 Huguenin, *Portraits de femmes*, 63.

28 Cambron, *La vie culturelle*, 121.

29 The street address no longer exists, but the building would have been located behind the present-day courthouse in Old Montreal.

30 Cambron, *La vie culturelle*, 15.

31 Robertine Barry, *Women in the Book Trade*, Library and Archives Canada, available at <http://www.collectionscanada.gc.ca/women/002026-281-e.html>.

32 Gertrude Balmer Watt (Peggy), "Fifty Years Back," Library and Archives Canada, Media Club of Ottawa Fonds, *Golden Jubilee Newspacket*, June 1954.

CHAPTER THREE

1 Irene Currie Love's speech, in "Unveiling of The Canadian Women's Press Club Memorial Tablet to Colonel George Henry Ham," 1927, 4–5, Canadian Pacific Archives.

2 "Off to the Fair: CPR takes Canadian Newspaper Women on a Jaunt," *London Advertiser*, 17 June 1904.

3 Personal interview and e-mail, Cynthia Cooper, Curator, Costumes and Textiles, McCord Museum of Canadian History, 25 August 2009.

4 Newton MacTavish, "George Ham: Sketch of a Gentleman on Whom the Sun Never Sets," commissioned by the CPR, Canadian Pacific Archives.

5 Kate Simpson Hayes, "Woman's World," *Manitoba Free Press*, 2 July 1904. Unless otherwise indicated, all Hayes quotes are from this source.

6 A. Plouffe, "Excursion à Saint-Louis," *Le Journal*, 2 July 1904. Unless otherwise indicated, all Plouffe quotes are from this source.

7 Ham, *Reminiscences*, 7.

8 Hart, *Selling of Canada*, 70 (obtained from Canadian Pacific Archives, Montreal).

9 Heintzman, "Struggle for Life," 38–43.

10 Forget's daughter, feminist Thérèse Casgrain, led the suffrage movement in Quebec, became a radio journalist, and later entered provincial politics. She was appointed to the Senate by Prime Minister Pierre Trudeau.

11 Warren, *Léonise Valois*, 125. Great-niece of Valois and an established poet herself, Warren tapped family archives to paint a fine portrait of her great-aunt as well as a picture of a woman writer living at the turn of the last century.

12 Ibid., 125–6.

13 Ibid., 134.

14 Ibid., 28, 37–8.

15 Ibid., 89. The quotes are drawn from a letter to her sister composed the year Valois began writing steadily for *Le Monde illustré*.

16 Pierre-Georges Roy, *À propos de Crémazie*, 265–6. Gleason wrote a fictionalized account of the final moments in the life of French-Canadian poet Octave Crémazie, who died an exile in France.

17 McKenzie Porter, "The Pulse of French Canada," *Maclean's*, 15 March 1954. The stunt took place in March 1901.

18 Beaupré's father died when she was three. Her widowed mother, Mélina, later married Alphonse Christin, a lawyer whose family made a fortune bottling and selling soft drinks. Alphonse Christin was related to Quebec provincial premier Honoré Mercier, and in a letter written around the time of his marriage, Christin solicited a job from Mercier, disclaiming in a postscript that he was a rich man. (See Fonds Famille Mercier, "Documents du cabinet du Premier ministre," microfilm no. 10429). But there's no doubt that Christin provided Mélina and her daughter a step up financially. Marie was sent, along with her new stepsister, to Villa Maria, where all students lived on the premises.

19 Marie Beaupré, monographie, courtesy of the Archives Congrégation de Notre Dame.

20 Ibid.

21 The sessional papers for the government of Canada, 5th session, 8th Parliament, 1900 Vol. I, Part II. The report of the auditor general, (p Q 12), states that Beaupré translated a 73-page report.

22 Lanthier, *Monklands Then*, 29.

23 Telephone interview with Tony Cashman, 14 August 2008. Cashman, a radio journalist in Edmonton in the 1950s and 1960s and a historian with Alberta Government Telephones (now Telus), heard stories about Hughes from his mother (a journalist) and other family members. When Hughes died, Cashman's mother wrote her obituary.

24 Rutherford, *Victorian Authority*, 53.

25 Today the reserve is called Akwesasne. It encompasses parts of Quebec, Ontario, and New York State.

26 Letter from Katherine Hughes to "His Lordship" (Bishop Émile-Joseph Legal), 7 November 1901, courtesy of the archives, Catholic Archdiocese of Edmonton.

CHAPTER FOUR

1 François Hone, "Un siècle et demi de documents historiques: La fascinante petite histoire de nos familles Jules Hone-Antoine Gérin-Lajoie: La grande histoire très souvent dramatique de l'agence de voyages," 1977, Montreal, Fonds Bibliothèque et

Archives nationales, MICB7259 GEN. Source of the anecdote regarding the death of Cécile Laberge's brother.

2 Ibid.

3 Danielle Badeaux Edgell, telephone interview, 29 August 2009. Napoléon Lefebvre's last will and testament was supposed to leave Cécile a fully furnished house and a pension that would carry her for life; however, according to Danielle Badeaux Edgell, Cécile Laberge's great-granddaughter, Napoléon inserted a clause stipulating that if Cécile should remarry, she was not to get a penny. When Cécile later met the love of her life, she had to choose between love and money. She gave the inheritance to her children.

4 Léger, *Fifty Years*. Laberge wrote the history of her beloved club in 1942. Formed in 1892 to give local women a performance space and an opportunity to study and appreciate music, the Ladies Morning Musical Club met every Thursday morning at the YMCA, then located on Dominion Square, where the women heard performances by noted musicians, sometimes accompanied by lectures about the work.

5 Interview with Danielle Badeaux Edgell.

6 Vida Bruce, trans., introduction to Gérin-Lajoie, *Jean Rivard*, 9–10. According to Bruce, at the turn of the nineteenth century, newspapers like *Le Canadien* were a mouthpiece for those concerned with using constitutional means to ensure the survival of the French fact in Canada. "To write for a reading public," Bruce states, "was ultimately to be an advocate of survival."

7 Vida Bruce, trans., in Gérin-Lajoie, *Jean Rivard*, 12–13. *Jean Rivard* claims to be the true story of a young man who, after the death of his father, leaves school and, in order to support himself, his mother, and his eleven siblings, buys a parcel of uncleared land and becomes extremely successful through hard work, honest dealings, and perseverance. *Jean Rivard* incarnates an agrarian myth that was to dominate French-Canadian literature for decades. An overarching theme in the novel is that to be patriotic is to cherish the rural community.

8 Jean Dumont to Antoinette Gérin-Lajoie, 29 June, 2 July, 10 July 1904, Centre d'archives de Montreal, P3, 1886–mai 1945.

9 Gosselin, *Les journalistes québécoises*, 57. At the triennial in 1938, journalist Ishbel Ross told the Canadian Women's Press Club that her research showed that a surprisingly large number of American journalists had started as stenographers.

10 Mimeault, *John Le Boutillier*.

11 Second-hand accounts lean towards Alice's working in city hall, but employment records were destroyed when the building burned down in 1922 so the accounts could not be verified. Alice's niece, Raymonde Marchand Paré, believes she may have worked in the post office.

12 Wade, "Olivar Asselin," 141.
13 Interestingly, Hélène Pelletier-Baillargeon, Olivar Asselin's biographer, who was privy to letters exchanged between Alice and her husband, doubts she had the writing ability to pen an article about the World's Fair. (Hélène Pelletier-Baillargeon, telephone interview, 8 August 2007).
14 Alice Asselin's niece (Raymonde Marchand Paré) and her grandson (André Asselin), multiple personal interviews and e-mails, 2007–8.

CHAPTER FIVE

1 Kate Simpson Hayes (Mary Markwell), "Woman's World," *Manitoba Free Press*, 2 July 1904. Unless otherwise indicated, all Hayes quotes in this chapter are from this source.
2 Ibid. Hayes wrote in detail about the actual train excursion.
3 Hector Charlesworth, "The Late Grace E. Denison," *Saturday Night*, 8 February 1914.
4 Lang, *Women Who Made the News*, 201.
5 Charlesworth, *Candid Chronicles*, 93.
6 Ibid., 92–3.
7 Jean Graham, "The Late Grace E. Denison," *Saturday Night*, 8 February 1914.
8 Kröller, *Canadian Travellers*, 25.
9 Charlesworth, *Candid Chronicles*, 92.
10 Ibid.
11 Minko Sotiron, entry on John Ross Robertson, *Dictionary of Canadian Biography Online*, http://www.biographi.ca/009004-119.01-e.php?BioId=41796.
12 Rutherford, *Victorian Authority*, 77.
13 Ibid., 53–5.
14 Gertrude Balmer Watt, "Fifty Years Back," Library and Archives Canada, Media Club of Ottawa Fonds, *Golden Jubilee Newspacket*, June 1954, 2.
15 Charlesworth, *Candid Chronicles*, 94.
16 Barbara M. Freeman, entry on Kit Coleman, *Dictionary of Canadian Biography Online*, http://www.biographi.ca/009004-119.01-e.php?&id_nbr=7365
17 Ibid.
18 Freeman, *Kit's Kingdom*, xv.
19 Ibid.
20 Ibid.
21 Ibid.
22 Ted Ferguson, *Kit Coleman*, 5, 12.

23 Freeman, *Kit's Kingdom*, 8. See also Downie, *Passionate Pen*, 141. Downie cites a discussion triggered by an article in the *New York Herald* in which several women writers asserted that their editors were only interested in "fads, follies and personal gossip" on the women's pages and that they refused to publish anything else.

24 Freeman notes that, while Kit's accreditation for the war seems to represent a giant leap for women, in fact "she played a secondary role to that of her male colleagues, consistent with women's lack of status in the profession in general." See Freeman, *Kit's Kingdom*, 4.

25 Forster, *100 Canadian Heroines*, 69.

26 Fiamengo, "Woman's Page," 133.

27 Telephone interviews with documentary filmmaker Tom Radford, grandson of Arthur and Peggy Balmer Watt, November 2008. Radford grew up in a renovated garage behind his grandparents' house in Edmonton.

28 Lei, "Material Culture," 96, 100, 104.

29 Watt, "The Mirror," *Weekly Sentinel-Review*, 18 February 1904.

30 The *Sentinel-Review* published Meek's letter in full on 17 March 1904.

31 Telephone interviews with Tom Radford: "She (Peggy) was the original devil's advocate, not having a foot to stand on, she would take someone on ... I always had the sense of him [Arthur Balmer Watt] trying to reign her in."

32 *Sentinel-Review*, 17 March 1904.

33 Watt, "Fifty Years Back."

34 Ibid.

35 Irene Currie Love, "Reminiscences," in *The Collegiate*, London: The Collegiate Institute, 1903. Copy held by the London Central Library, London, Ontario.

36 Arthur Ford, "Over the Week-End," *London Free Press*, 15 October 1945.

37 Rex, *No Daughter of Mine*, 7.

38 Ford, "Over the Week-End."

39 Hayes, "Woman's World."

40 "Unveiling of the Canadian Women's Press Club Memorial Tablet to Colonel George Henry Ham," 1927, 4–5, Canadian Pacific Archives.

CHAPTER SIX

1 Robertine Barry, "Impressions d'une exposition," *Le Journal de Françoise*, 16 July 1904. In their dispatches, several women on the trip used the image of a genie conjuring a fairyland. Unless otherwise indicated, all Barry quotes in this chapter are from this source.

2 Jackson, *Meet Me in St Louis*, 27. See also, Fox and Sneddeker, *Palaces to the Pike*, 5.

3 Grace Denison, "Lady Gay's Column," *Saturday Night*, 2 July 1904.

4 Kate Simpson Hayes (Mary Markwell), "Woman's World," *Manitoba Free Press*, 2 July 1904. Unless otherwise indicated, all Hayes quotes in this chapter are from this source.

5 Barry, "Impressions d'une exposition."

6 Official Photographic Company, *Greatest of Expositions*.

7 Anne-Marie Gleason (Madeleine), "À Travers l'exposition universelle: Impressions féminines," *La Patrie*, 2 July 1904. Unless otherwise indicated, all Gleason quotes in this chapter are from this source.

8 Marie Beaupré (Hélène Dumont), "Causerie de voyageuse," *La Presse*, 6 August 1904. Unless otherwise indicated, all Beaupré quotes in this chapter are from this source.

9 Gertrude Balmer Watt (Peggy), "At the Fair," *Woodstock Sentinel-Review*, 2 July 1904. Unless otherwise indicated, all Watt quotes in this chapter are from this source.

10 Amintha Plouffe (A. Plouffe), "Excursion à St-Louis," *Le Journal*, 2 July 1904. Unless otherwise indicated, all Plouffe quotes in this chapter are from this source.

11 Oxley, "Canada at the Fair," 18–19.

12 Official Photographic Company, *Greatest of Expositions*, 69.

13 Kathleen (Kay) Mathers to Mae Clendenan, 27 April 1954, Library and Archives Canada, Media Club of Canada, Golden Jubilee Packet Correspondence 1953–54, file 17-3.

14 Rademacher, *Still Shining*, 18; and Jackson, *Meet Me in St Louis*, 24.

15 From Our Own Reporter (Mary Dawson), "Ripple from St Louis," *Evening Telegram*, 2 July 1904. Unless otherwise indicated, all Dawson quotes in this chapter are from this source.

16 Ibid.

17 Gleason, "À Travers l'exposition."

18 Birk, *World Came*, 56.

CHAPTER SEVEN

1 Kate Simpson Hayes (Mary Markwell), "Woman's World," *Manitoba Free Press*, 2 July 1904. Unless otherwise indicated, all Hayes quotes in this chapter are from this source.

2 Fox and Sneddeker, *From the Palaces*, 221.

3 Amintha Plouffe (A. Plouffe), "Excursion à St Louis," *Le Journal*, 2 July 1904.

4 Léger, *Fifty Years*, 11. Belgian violinist Eugène Ysaÿe made his Canadian debut at the club only after Belgian friends in Montreal repeatedly reassured him that his money would be guaranteed.

5 Ham, *Reminiscences*, 154.

6 Ibid., 155.

7 Jackson, *Meet Me in St Louis*, 74.

8 Robertine Barry, "Impressions d'une exposition," *Le Journal de Françoise*, 16 July 1904.

9 Maguire, "Convention and Contradiction," 27–8.

10 Pelletier-Baillargeon, *Marie Gérin-Lajoie*, 29–30. See also Michael R. Haines and Steckel, *Population History*, 568.

11 Anne-Marie Gleason (Madeleine), "À Travers l'exposition universelle: Impressions féminines," *La Patrie*, 2 July 1904.

12 Ohl, *Louis Cyr*, 431.

13 See <http://www.biographi.ca/009004-119.01-e.php?BioId=41341&query=>.

14 See <http://www.virtualsk.com/current_issue/giant_beaupre.html>.

15 Jackson, *Meet Me in St Louis*, 100.

16 *Canadian Magazine*, October 1904, 508.

17 Valverde, *Age of Light*, 104–8.

18 Rutherford, *Victorian Authority*, 160.

19 See Canadian Human Rights Commission website at <http://www.chrc-ccdp.ca/en/getbriefed/1900/population.asp>.

20 Ibid.

21 Fiamengo, *Woman's Page*, 133.

22 Canadian Human Rights Commission website at <http://www.chrc-ccdp.ca/en/getbriefed/1900/population.asp>.

23 Fiamengo, *Woman's Page*, 141.

24 Cook, *The Regenerators*, 82.

25 Irene Currie Love (Nan), "Of Interest to Women," *London Advertiser*, 2 July 1904. Unless otherwise indicated, all Love quotes in this chapter are from this source.

26 Jackson, *Meet Me in St Louis*, 101–2.

27 Ibid., 104.

28 Letter from Katherine Hughes to "His Lordship" (Bishop Émile-Joseph Legal), 7 November 1901, courtesy of the archives, Catholic Archdiocese of Edmonton.

29 Katherine Hughes, "Films from the Fair," *Montreal Daily Star*, 2 July 1904. Unless otherwise indicated, all Hughes quotes are from this source.

30 Antoinette Gérin-Lajoie (A.G.L.), "Huit jours à l'exposition," *L'Événement*, 18 July 1904.

31 Léonise Valois (Attala), "Au Retour d'un voyage sans égal à Saint-Louis, Mis. [sic]," *Le Canada*, 4 July 1904.

32 Cécile Laberge, "Nos Femmes journalistes à l'Exposition de St-Louis," *Le Soleil*, 4 July 1904.

33 Grace Denison, "Lady Gay's Column," *Saturday Night*, 2 July 1904.

CHAPTER EIGHT

1 Léonise Valois (Attala), "St-Louis, Chicago et Detroit," *Le Canada*, 9 July 1904. Unless otherwise indicated, all Valois quotes in this chapter are from this source.

2 Robertine Barry (Françoise), "Impressions d'une Exposition," *Le Journal de Françoise*, 16 July 1904. Unless otherwise indicated, all Barry quotes in this chapter are from this source.

3 Gertrude Balmer Watt (Peggy), "The Mirror," *Woodstock Sentinel-Review*, 18 August 1904 (unless otherwise indicated, all Watt quotes in this chapter are from this source); and Irene Currie Love (Nan), "Of Interest to Women," *London Advertiser*, 16 July 1904.

4 Currie Love, "Of Interest to Women."

5 Grace Denison, "Lady Gay's Column," *Saturday Night*, 2 July 1904.

CHAPTER NINE

1 Amintha Plouffe (A. Plouffe), "Excursion à St-Louis," *Le Journal*, 2 July 1904. Unless otherwise indicated, all Plouffe quotes in this chapter are from this source.

2 Marie Beaupré (Hélène Dumont), "Causerie de voyageuse," *La Presse*, 6 August 1904.

3 Rutherford, *Victorian Authority*, 230–1.

4 George Murray, "A Notable Journalistic Career," *Canadian Magazine*, 32 (1908–09): 418.

5 Desmond Morton, *A Military History of Canada*, 114.

6 Grace Denison, "Lady Gay's Column," *Saturday Night*, 2 July 1904.

7 Beaulieu and Hamelin, *La presse québécoise*, 187.

8 Kate Simpson Hayes (Mary Markwell), "Woman's World," *Manitoba Free Press*, 2 July 1904. Unless otherwise indicated, all Hayes quotes in this chapter are from this source.

9 Kathleen Blake Coleman (Kit), "Piking," *Mail and Empire*, 9 July 1904. Unless otherwise indicated, all Coleman quotes in this chapter are from this source.

CHAPTER TEN

1 Antoinette Gérin-Lajoie, "Huit jours à l'exposition," *L'Événement*, 18 July 1904. Unless otherwise indicated, all Gérin-Lajoie quotes in this chapter are from this source.
2 Allan Greer, "The Pattern of Literacy in Quebec, 1745–1899," *Histoire sociale/Social History*, 9 November 1978, 297.
3 Olsen, "Fair Connections."
4 Kate Simpson Hayes (Mary Markwell), "Woman's World," *Manitoba Free Press*, 2 July 1904.
5 Maguire, "Convention and Contradiction," 135.
6 Kate Simpson Hayes (Mary Markwell), "Woman's World," *Manitoba Free Press*, 9 July 1904. All Hayes quotes in this paragraph are from this source.
7 Maguire, "Convention and Contradiction," 136.
8 Freeman, *Kit's Kingdom*, xv.
9 In his *Mighty Women: Stories of Western Canadian Pioneers*, Grant MacEwan notes that Davin's critics were quick to comment (probably incorrectly) that "Kate talked him into that one," 37.
10 From Our Own Reporter (Mary Dawson), "Ripple from St Louis," *Evening Telegram*, 2 July 1904.
11 Irene Currie Love (Nan), "Of Interest to Women," *London Advertiser*, 16 July 1904. Unless otherwise indicated, all Love quotes in this chapter are from this source.
12 Amintha Plouffe (A. Plouffe), "Excursion à St-Louis," *Le Journal*, 2 July 1904.

CHAPTER ELEVEN

1 "Bribery of a Chicago Juror," *New York Times*, 18 October 1894.
2 "Will Ostracize Mrs Springer," *Chicago Daily Tribune*, 21 May 1904; and "Women to Talk of Feud," *Chicago Daily Tribune*, 23 May 1904.
3 Green, "Illinois Woman's [sic] Press Organizations," 79.
4 Morgan, *Canadian Men and Women*, 250.
5 Léonise Valois (Attala), "St-Louis, Chicago et Detroit," *Le Canada*, 9 July 1904. Unless otherwise indicated, all Valois quotes in this chapter are from this source.

6 Gertrude Balmer Watt (Peggy), "The Mirror," *Woodstock Sentinel-Review*, 9 July
   1904. Unless otherwise indicated, all Watt quotes in this chapter are from this
   source.

7 Léonise Valois (Attala), "St-Louis, Chicago et Detroit," *Le Canada*, 9 July 1904.

8 See award ceremony presentation speech by Ragnvald Moe on 10 December 1913 at
   <http://nobelprize.org/nobel_prizes/peace/laureates/1912/press.html>.

9 Platt, *Shock Cities*, 468.

10 Marie Beaupré (Hélène Dumont), "Causerie de voyageuse," *La Presse*, 6 August
   1904.

11 Kathleen "Kit" Coleman, "Down the Pike: The Passion Play and Other Wonders,"
   Mail and Empire, 2 July 1904.

CHAPTER TWELVE

1 For background information on the club and some of its early members, Marzolf,
   "Detroit Women Writers," helped me flesh out what had only been a list in Amintha
   Plouffe's story.

2 Amintha Plouffe (A. Plouffe), "Excursion à St-Louis," *Le Journal*, 2 July 1904. Unless otherwise indicated, all Plouffe quotes in this chapter are from this source.

3 Léonise Valois (Attala), "St-Louis, Chicago et Detroit," *Le Canada*, 9 July 1904.
   Unless otherwise indicated, all Valois quotes in this chapter are from this source.

4 Kate Simpson Hayes (Mary Markwell), "Woman's World," *Manitoba Free Press*, 9
   July 1904. Unless otherwise indicated, all Hayes quotes are from this source.

5 Freeman, *Kit's Kingdom*, 138.

6 Yvan Lamonde, "Case Study: *Tante berceuse,*" included in *The History of the Book in
   Canada*, see http://books.google.ca/books?id=4nHT2uoovSMC&pg=
   PA159&lpg. Also "La revue canadienne," p. 420–4, see http://www.archive.org/
   stream/p1revuecanadien48montuoft

7 Ruth Hammond, former women's editor of the *Toronto Star*, interviewed on camera
   in 2005 by Isabel Warren for *Women of Daring*, a short video produced by Linda Kay.
   Hammond said that Ham told the woman: "You girls ought to get together more
   often and talk to each other. You women are terrific, you've got big jobs to do."

8 Ham, *Reminiscences*, 153.

9 Grace Denison, "Lady Gay's Column," *Saturday Night*, 2 July 1904. Unless otherwise indicated, all Denison quotes in this chapter are from this source.

10 Kathleen "Kit" Coleman, *Mail and Empire*, 25 June 1904. Unless otherwise indicated, all Coleman quotes in this chapter are from this source.

11 Kit Coleman, *Mail and Empire,* 13 August 1904.

CHAPTER THIRTEEN

1 Kit Coleman, *Mail and Empire,* 25 June 1904.
2 Kate Simpson Hayes, *Manitoba Free Press,* 9 July 1904.
3 Letter from Robertine Barry to Kate Simpson Hayes, courtesy of the Saskatchewan Archives Board, R 2.15, SAB microfilm.
4 Rex, *No Daughter of Mine,* 92.
5 Ibid.
6 Cook and Mitchinson, *Proper Sphere,* 168.
7 Ibid., 6.
8 Ibid., 168.
9 Telephone interview with Tom Radford, grandson of Peggy Watt, November 2008.
10 Conversations with Raymonde Marchand Paré at her home in Outremont, Quebec, in the spring of 2008. Madame Marchand Paré remembered her mother spoke about the trip out west (especially meeting Mackenzie King), but she never mentioned writing about it.
11 Robertine Barry, "Winnipeg," *Le Journal de Françoise,* 2 July 1906.
12 Barry, "Winnipeg."
13 For historical information on the CPR train station in Winnipeg, see <http://www.gov.mb.ca/chc/hrb/prov/p076.html>.
14 Cameron, *New North,* 9–10.
15 Barry, "Winnipeg."
16 *Morning Telegram,* 6 June 1906, available at: http://manitobia.ca/cocoon/launch/en/newspapers/TMT/1906/06/09/16/Ar01600.pdf/Olive.
17 Barry, "Winnipeg."
18 Rex, *No Daughter of Mine,* 174.
19 Linda L. Hale, *Dictionary of Canadian Biography Online,* <http://www.biographi.ca/009004-119.01-e.php?BioId=41384&query>.
20 Cameron, *New North,* 26.
21 Robertine Barry, "L'Ouest lointain," *Le Journal de Françoise,* 21 July 1906.
22 Press clipping from the St John, New Brunswick, *Evening Times,* 30 June 1906, Library and Archives Canada, Media Club of Canada, Canadian Women's Press Club scrapbooks, vol. 43-1.
23 Ibid.
24 Barry, "L'Ouest lointain."

25 Reminiscences written in 1933 by Effie L. Storer. She donated her scrapbook to the Canadian Women's Press Club. See Library and Archives Canada, Media Club of Canada, Canadian Women's Press Club, vol. 23-1.

26 Desjardins, *Robertine Barry*, 152.

27 Société historique de la Côte-Nord, Robertine Barry Fonds, PO93/003.02/003.

28 Cook, *Regenerators*, 65–6.

29 Stacey, *Very Double Life*, 163.

30 Desjardins, *Robertine Barry*, 199, 206.

31 Barry, "L'Ouest lointain."

32 Ibid.

CHAPTER FOURTEEN

1 Ham, *Reminiscences*, 154.

2 Gosselin, *Les journalistes québécoises*, 108.

3 "Fifty Years Back," Canadian Women's Press Club Golden Jubilee Newspacket, 1904–1954, p. 28, Library and Archives Canada (hereafter LAC), Media Club of Ottawa Fonds.

4 Ibid.

5 *Triennial Report*, LAC, MG 28, Media Club of Ottawa Fonds, vol. 46, 22.

6 "Fifty Years Back," 29.

7 Rex, *No Daughter of Mine*, 223.

8 *Triennial Report*, 11.

9 Gertrude Balmer Watt, in "Fifty Years Back," Canadian Women's Press Club Golden Jubilee Newspacket, 1904–1954 (June 1954), LAC, Media Club of Ottawa Fonds.

10 Gosselin, *Les journalistes québécoises*, 137. Gosselin lists Anne-Marie as a member from 1920 to 1923, but this could not be confirmed by other sources consulted.

11 Historian's report prepared by Florence N. Sherk, Minute Book, 1909–32, p. 26, LAC, MG 28, I 232, vol. 1, pt. 1.

12 Ham, *Reminiscences*, 153.

13 Triennial Convention of the Canadian Women's Press Club, 24–26 September 1923, LAC, MG 28, I 232, vol. 61.

14 Scrapbook of Elizabeth Bailey Price, handwritten letter from Kate Simpson Hayes, dated Friday afternoon [1932], written on Canadian Pacific Railway stationary, LAC, Media Club of Canada Fonds.

15 Ibid.

16 *Saturday Night*, 10 July 1954.

17 Marjorie S. Oliver, president of the CWPC, Golden Jubilee Newspacket, 1904–1954, foreword, LAC, Media Club of Ottawa Fonds.

18 "Fifty Years Back," 15.

19 Rex, *No Daughter of Mine*, 188–90.

20 Ibid., 208–9.

21 Ibid., 209–11.

22 Ibid., 250–1.

23 Ibid.

24 Ibid., 154.

25 Cercle des femmes journalistes, *Vingt-cinq* à *la une*, 96–7.

26 Rex, *No Daughter of Mine*, 156.

27 Ibid.

CHAPTER FIFTEEN

1 Gertrude Balmer Watt (Peggy), "Fifty Years Back," Canadian Women's Press Club Golden Jubilee Newspacket, 1904–1954 (June 1954), 2, Library and Archives Canada, Media Club of Canada Fonds.

2 Reminiscences and early reports, LAC, Media Club of Canada Fonds, vol. 18, file 22.

3 Huguenin, *Portraits des femmes*, 63.

4 Ham, *Reminiscences*, 155.

5 It is unclear why the grave has no marker; the family may not have had money to pay for a headstone, or if a marker did exist, it may have been destroyed.

6 Charlesworth, *Candid Chronicles*, 92.

7 Grace Denison, "Lady Gay's Column," *Saturday Night*, 16 November 1912.

8 Charlesworth, *Candid Chronicles*, 94.

9 Lang, *Women Who Made the News*, 51.

10 Freeman, *Kit's Kingdom*, 10.

11 Kit Coleman, "Piking," *Mail and Empire*, 9 July 1904.

12 Freeman, *Kit's Kingdom*, 10. Freeman also writes that Kit had written a novel but that it was never published.

13 Letter from Margaret Graham to Albert Horton, dated 8 April 1924, provided by Margalo Grant Whyte, Margaret Graham's granddaughter. All quotes in this section come from this source.

14 E-mail from Margalo Whyte, granddaughter of Margaret Graham, 29 August 2009.

15 Information on Adella Archibald provided by Dr Norman Fergusson, who, from a relative in Nova Scotia, obtained Archibald's diary, in which she documents the

arrival of Graham's family members. Unfortunately, in later life, Archibald reworte the diary and discarded the original, likely altering some of her earlier writings and impressions. E-mail from Dr. Fergusson, 13 August 2011.

16 E-mail from Margalo Whyte, 29 August 2009.

17 Dempsey, introduction to "The Last Great Roundup." Hughes's piece originally ran in the *Edmonton Bulletin* on 22 June 1907.

18 "Bayard of the Wilderness: Father Lacombe, 'The Black-Robe Voyageur,'" *New York Times Review of Books*, 31 December 1911, copy located in City of Edmonton Archives.

19 Katherine Hughes to "My Lord" (Bishop L'Égal), 21 December 1911, Archives of the Catholic Archdiocese of Edmonton.

20 Scrapbook, clippings presented to the Vancouver branch of the Canadian Women's Press Club by Pat Groves, October 1928, LAC, MG28-12, Media Club of Canada Fonds, vol. 47, file 9.

21 "Miss Hughes to Go to London as Reid's Assistant," *Edmonton Bulletin*, 20 August 1913, copy located in City of Edmonton Archives.

22 Pádraig O Siadhail, "Hughes, Katherine Angelina," Dictionary of Canadian Biography, available at http://www.biographi.ca.

23 Knowles, *Telegrapher to Titan*, 9. See also Katherine Hughes to Bishop "My Lord" (Bishop L'Égal), 6 December 1915 and 9 June 1916, Archives of the Archdiocese of Edmonton.

24 "At five o'clock: Katherine Hughes lectures on the Sinn Fein movement," *Saturday Night*, 30 March 1918.

25 "Irish Republic Gets a Mixed Greeting Here," *Morning Bulletin* (Edmonton), 16 August 1920, copy located in City of Edmonton Archives.

26 Siadhail, "Hughes."

27 Ibid.

28 Helen Gorman Cashman, "Katherine Hughes Humanitarian," *Western Catholic*, 30 April 1925, copy located in Archives of the Archdiocese of Edmonton.

29 "Unveiling of The Canadian Women's Press Club Memorial Tablet to Colonel George Henry Ham," 1927, 4–5, Canadian Pacific Archives.

30 Obituary for Mary Dawson Snider, *Toronto Evening Telegram*, 6 September 1932.

31 Scrapbook, clippings presented to the Vancouver branch of the Canadian Women's Press Club by Pat Groves, October 1928, LAC, MG28-12, Media Club of Canada Fonds, vol. 47, file 9.

32 Lang, *Women Who Made the News*, 252–3.

33 Ibid., 253.

34 Obituary of Mary Dawson Snider, *Toronto Evening Telegram*, 6 September 1932.

35 Warren, *Léonise Valois*, 163.

36 Ibid., 261.

37 Georges Bellerive. *Brèves apologies de nos auteurs féminins*, 1920, available at http://www.archive.org/details/brvesapologiesoobelluoft.

38 A.L., "Jeanne Leber [sic]," *L'Action Nationale* 15, 4 (1940): 295. Available at <http://bibnum2.banq.qc.ca/bna/actionnationale//fp/1940/p5637.htm>.

39 Armand and Bernadette Guilmette, *The Canadian Encyclopedia*. See <http://www.thecanadianencyclopedia.com/index.cfm?PgNm=TCE&Params=AIARTA0005753>.

40 "Correspondance avec, entre autres, Madeleine," Bibliotheque Nationale du Quebec, Fonds Albert Ferland, P783, S3.

41 Ouimet, *Biographies Canadiennes-Françaises*, 145.

42 Boivin and Landry, "Françoise et Madeleine," 239.

43 David, "La Jeunesse et l'avenir", 42.

44 Personal interview with Andrée Gérin-Lajoie, Antoinette's niece through marriage to Paul Gérin-Lajoie, former education minister of Quebec, 3 August 2009.

45 E-mails from Denyse Gérin-Lajoie, Antoinette's niece, 4 August 2009.

46 Arthur E. Ford, "Over the Week-End," *Free Press* (London), 15 October 1945.

47 Lang, *Women Who Made the News*, 167.

48 Ibid.

49 Ford, "Over the Week-End."

50 Reminiscences and early reports, LAC, Media Club of Canada Fonds, vol. 18, file 22.

51 George H. Doran to M. Markwell, Esq., 29 October 1910, Saskatchewan Archives Board.

52 Maguire, "Convention and Contradiction," 51.

53 Ibid., 39.

54 Ibid., 42.

55 Ibid., 203.

56 Fannie Hurst to Mary Markwell, 8 December 1938, Saskatchewan Archives Board.

57 Obituary of Cécile Léger (formerly Laberge), *Montreal Daily Star*, 6 April 1948.

58 Léger, *Fifty Years*, 5.

59 Danielle Badeaux Edgell, telephone interview, 29 August 2009.

60 Léger, *Fifty Years*, 23.

61 Ibid., 21.

62 McDougall, *Canada's Past and Present*, 135.

63 Interview with Raymonde Marchand Paré, May 2008.

64 See <http://www.biographi.ca/009004-119.01-e.php?&id_nbr=8007>.
65 See description of holdings for Arthur Balmer Watt, University of Alberta Archives.
66 *Toronto Evening Telegram*, 23 June 1954.
67 Telephone interviews with Tom Radford, November 2008.

BIBLIOGRAPHY

Argan, William, Pam Cowan, and Gordon Staseson. *Regina: The First 100 Years.* Regina: *Leader-Post* Carrier Foundation, 2002.

Beaulieu, André, and Jean Hamelin. *La presse québécoise.* Vol. 4: *1896–1910.* Québec: Les Presses de l'université Laval, 1979.

Beaupré, Marie. *Jeanne LeBer: Première recluse du Canada Français, 1662–1714.* Montréal: Éditions ACF, 1939.

Bellerive, Georges. *Brèves apologies de nos auteurs féminins.* Québec: Librairie Garneau, 1920.

Birk, Dorothy Daniels. *The World Came to St Louis.* St Louis: Bethany Press, 1979.

Bliss, Michael. *Plague: A Story of Smallpox in Montreal.* Toronto: HarperCollins, 1991.

Boivin, Aurélien, and Kenneth Landry. "Françoise et Madeleine: Pionnières du journalisme féminin au Québec." *Voix et images* 4, 2 (1978): 233–43.

Bonville, Jean de. *La presse québécoise de 1884 à 1914: Genèse d'un média de masse.* Québec: Les Presses de l'université Laval, 1988.

Brun, Josette, ed. *Interrelations femmes-média dans l'Amérique française.* Québec: Les Presses de l'université Laval, 2009.

Burt, Elizabeth V. "Challenges in Doing Women's History." *Clio* (newsletter of the History Division of the Association for Education in Journalism and Mass Communication) 31, 1 (1998): 1–8.

– ed. *Women's Press Organizations: 1881–1999.* Westport, CT: Greenwood, 2000.

Cambron, Micheline, ed. *La vie culturelle à Montréal vers 1900.* Québec: Les Éditions Fides et la Bibliothèque nationale de Québec, 2005.

Cameron, Agnes Deans. *The New North.* New York and London: D. Appleton and Company, 1912.

Camp, Walter Mason, Earl A. Averill, and Orville Haydn Reynolds. *Railroad Transportation at the Universal Exposition, St Louis, Missouri*. Chicago: Chicago Railway and Engineering Review Co., 1904.

Carrier, Anne. "Barry, Robertine." *Dictionnaire biographique du Canada*. Vol. 13. Québec: Les Presses de l'Université Laval, 1994.

– "Une pionnière du journalisme féministe québécois: Françoise, pseudonyme de Robertine Barry." MA thesis, Université Laval, 1988.

Carrier, Hervé. *Le sociologue canadien Léon Gérin, 1863–1951*. Montréal: Les Éditions Bellarmin, 1960.

Cercle des femmes journalistes. *Vingt-cinq à la une: Biographies*. Montréal: Éditions La Presse, 1976.

Charlesworth, Hector. *Candid Chronicles*. Toronto: Macmillan, 1925.

Cleverdon, Catherine L. *The Woman Suffrage Movement in Canada*. Toronto: University of Toronto Press, 1950.

Cook, Ramsay. *The Regenerators: Social Criticism in Late Victorian English Canada*. Toronto: University of Toronto Press, 1991.

Cook, Ramsay, and Wendy Mitchinson, ed. *The Proper Sphere: Woman's Place in Canadian Society*. Toronto: University of Toronto Press, 1976.

Cordery, Stacy A. *Alice: Alice Roosevelt Longworth, from White House Princess to Washington Power Broker*. New York: Penguin, 2007.

Crean, Susan. *Newsworthy: The Lives of Media Women*. Toronto: Stoddart, 1985.

Cruise, David, and Alison Griffiths. *Lords of the Line: The Men Who Built the CPR*. Toronto: Penguin, 1988.

Currie, Margaret (pseudonym for Mrs Eldred Archibald or Irene Currie Love). *Margaret Currie: Her Book*. Toronto: Hunter-Rose Co., 1924.

Danylewycz, Marta. "In Their Own Right: Convents, an Organized Expression of Women's Aspirations." In *Rethinking Canada: The Promise of Women's History*, ed. Veronica Strong-Boag and Anita Clair Fellman, 161–81. Mississauga: Copp Clark Pitman, 1991.

– *Taking the Veil: An Alternative to Marriage, Motherhood, and Spinsterhood in Quebec, 1840–1920*. Toronto: McClelland & Stewart, 1987.

David, L.-O. (Laurent-Olivier). *La jeunesse et l'avenir*. Montréal: Librairie Beauchemin, 1926.

Demolins, Edmond. *Anglo-Saxon Superiority: To What Is It Due?* London: Leadenhall Press, imprint of Charles Scribner and Sons, 1898.

Dempsey, Hugh A., ed. Introduction to "The Last Great Roundup" (reprint of an article by Katherine Hughes first published in the *Edmonton Bulletin*, June 1907). *Alberta Historical Review* 11, 2 (1963): 1–7.

Denault, Bernard, and Benoît Lévesque. *Éléments pour une sociologie des communautés religieuses au Québec*. Montréal: Presses de l'Université de Montréal/Université de Sherbrooke, 1975.

Denison, Grace E. *A Happy Holiday*. Toronto: N.p., 1890.

Desgagné, Raymond. "Françoise (Robertine Barry)." *Saguenayensia* 2, 3 (1960): 73–5.

Desjardins, Sergine. *Robertine Barry: La femme nouvelle*. Éditions Trois-Pistoles, Notre-Dame-des-Neiges, 2010.

Des Ormes, Renée (pseudonym of M.-L. Turgeon née Ferland). *Robertine Barry: En litérature Françoise – pionnière du journalisme féminin au Canada, 1863–1910*. Québec: L'Action Sociale, 1949.

Downie, Jill. *A Passionate Pen: The Life and Times of Faith Fenton*. Toronto: Harper-Collins, 1996.

Driver, Elizabeth. *Culinary Landmarks: A Bibliography of Canadian Cookbooks, 1825–1949*. Toronto: University of Toronto Press, 2002.

Éthier-Blais, Jean, ed. *Émile Nelligan: Poésie rêvée et poésie vécue*. Ottawa: Le Cercel du Livre de France, 1969.

Felteau, Cyrille. *Histoire de* La Presse: *Le livre du peuple, 1884–1916*. Tome 1. Montréal: Éditions La Presse, 1983.

Ferguson, Ted. *Kit Coleman Queen of Hearts: Canada's Pioneer Woman Journalist*. Toronto: Doubleday, 1978.

Fergusson, Norman. *The Story of the Nova Scotia Teachers Union*. Armdale, NS: Nova Scotia Teachers Union, 1990.

Fiamengo, Janice. *The Woman's Page: Journalism and Rhetoric in Early Canada*. Toronto: University of Toronto Press, 2008.

Forster, Merna. *100 Canadian Heroines*. Toronto: Dundurn, 2004.

Fox, Timothy J., and Duane R. Sneddeker. *From the Palaces to the Pike: Visions of the 1904 World's Fair*. St Louis: Missouri Historical Society Press, 1997.

Françoise. *Fleurs champêtres suivi d'autres nouvelles et de récits et Méprise: Comédie inédite en un acte* (Édition préparée et présentée par Gilles Lamontagne). Montréal: Fides, 1984.

Freeman, Barbara M. *Kit's Kingdom: The Journalism of Kathleen Blake Coleman*. Ottawa: Carleton University Press, 1989.

Gérin, Léon. *Antoine Gérin-Lajoie: La resurrection d'un patriote canadien*. Montreal: Éditions du Devoir, 1925.

Gérin-Lajoie, Antoine. *Jean Rivard*. Trans. Bruce Vida. Toronto: McCelland and Stewart, 1977.

Giroux, Rollande. *Bibliographie de Léonise Valois (Atala)*. Montréal: École des Bibliothécaires de l'Université de Montréal, 1947.

Gosselin, Line. *Les journalistes québécoises, 1880–1930.* Québec: Collection RCHTQ Études et Documents, 1995.

Gray, Charlotte. *Mrs King: The Life and Times of Isabel Mackenzie King.* Toronto: Penguin, 1997.

Green, Mary Jean. "The 'Literary Feminists' and the Fight for Women's Writing in Quebec." *Revue d'études canadiennes* 21, 1 (1986): 128–43.

Green, Norma Fay. "Illinois Woman's [sic] Press Organizations, 1885–Present." In *Women's Press Organizations, 1881–1999,* ed. Elizabeth V. Burt, 75–88. Westport, CT: Greenwood, 2000.

Greenaway, Roy. *The News Game.* Toronto/Vancouver: Clarke, Irwin, 1966.

Grisé, Yolande, Réjean Robidoux, and Paul Wyczynski. *Émile Nelligan: Cinquante ans après sa mort.* Montréal: Fides, 1993.

Haines, Michael R., and Richard Hall Steckel, ed. *A Population History of North American.* London: Cambridge University Press, 2000.

Ham, George. *Reminiscences of a Raconteur.* Toronto: The Musson Book Company Ltd., 1921.

Hart, E.J. *The Selling of Canada: The CPR and the Beginnings of Canadian Tourism.* Banff: Altitude Publishing Ltd., 1983.

Heggie, Grace, and Gordon R. Adshead, eds. *Saturday Night: The First 50 Years – 1887–1937.* Toronto: Micromedia, 1987.

Heintzman, Ralph. "The Struggle for Life: The French Daily Press of Montreal and the Problems of Economic Growth in the Age of Laurier, 1896–1911." PhD diss., York University, 1977.

Huguenin, Madeleine. *Portraits de femmes.* Montréal: Éditions La Patrie, 1938.

Hughes, Katherine. *Father Lacombe: The Black-Robe Voyageur.* Toronto: McClelland and Stewart, 1920.

Jackson, Robert. *Meet Me in St Louis: A Trip to the 1904 World's Fair.* New York: HarperCollins, 2004.

Kaiser, Ken, and Merrily Aubrey, eds. *In the Promised Land of Alberta's North: The Northern Journal of Katherine Hughes (Summer, 1909).* Calgary: Alberta Records Publication Board, Historical Society of Alberta, 2006.

Kesterton, W.H. *A History of Journalism in Canada.* Toronto: McClelland and Stewart, 1967.

Knowles, Valerie. *From Telegrapher to Titan: The Life of William C. Van Horne.* Toronto: Dundurn, 2004.

Kröller, Eva Marie. *Canadian Travellers in Europe, 1851–1900.* Vancouver: UBC Press, 1987.

Lacourcière, Luc, ed. *Poésies complètes: 1896–1899.* Montréal and Paris: Fides, 1952.

Lamonde, Yvan. "Case Study: *Tante berceuse.*" In *The History of the Book in Canada: 1840–1918*, online project, p 159.

Lamoureux, Diane. *Citoyennes? Femmes, droit de vote et démocratie.* Montreal: Éditions due remue-ménage, 1989.

Lang, Marjory. *Women Who Made the News: Female Journalists in Canada, 1880–1945.* Montreal and Kingston: McGill-Queen's University Press, 1999.

Langlois, Yvon. *Blanche orchidée: Jeanne LeBer.* Montréal: Congrégation Notre Dame, 1997.

Lanthier, Helen. *Monklands Then, Villa Maria Now.* Montréal: Congrégation Notre Dame, 2004.

Leacock, Stephen. *Leacock's Montreal*, rev. ed. Toronto: McClelland and Stewart, 1963.

Léger (formerly Laberge), Cécile. *Fifty Years of Musical Recollections.* Montreal: Victoria Press Ltd., 1942.

Lei, Christine. "The Material Culture of the Loretto School for Girls in Hamilton, Ontario, 1865–1971." *Historical Studies* 66 (2000), 92–113.

Lemieux, Pierre H. *Nelligan et Françoise: L'intrigue amoureuse la plus singulière de la fin du 19e siècle québécois.* Lévis: Fondation littéraire Fleur de Lys, 2004.

Lemire, Maurice, et Denis Saint-Jacques, eds. *La vie littéraire au Québec, 1870–1894: Je me souviens.* Tome 4. Québec: Les Presses de l'Université Laval, 1999.

– *La vie littéraire au Québec, 1895–1918: Sois fidèle à ta Laurentie.* Tome 5. Québec: Presses de l'Université Laval, 2005.

MacEwan, Grant. *Mighty Women: Stories of Western Canadian Pioneers.* Vancouver/Toronto: Douglas and McIntyre (Greystone Books edition), 1995.

Maguire, Constance Anne. "Convention and Contradiction in the Life and Ideas of Kate Simpson Hayes." MA thesis, University of Regina, 1996.

Major, Robert. *The American Dream in Nineteenth-Century Quebec: Ideologies and Utopia in Antoine Gérin-Lajoie's Jean Rivard.* Toronto: University of Toronto Press, 1996.

Marzolf, Marion. "Detroit Women Writers, 1900–Present." In *Women's Press Organizations: 1881–1999*, ed. Elizabeth, V. Burt, 59–62. Westport, CT: Greenwood, 2000.

Matos-Andrade, Maria-Eugenia de. "Biographie et bibliographie descriptive de Madeleine, 1875–1943." Thèse de Diplôme d'Études Supérieures, Université de Montréal, 1970.

McDougall, Robert L., ed. *Canada's Past and Present: A Dialogue*. Toronto: University of Toronto Press, 1965.

Mimeault, Mario. *John Le Boutillier, 1797–1872: La grande époque de la Gaspésie*. L'Anse-au-Griffon: Corporation du Manoir Le Boutillier, 1993.

Morgan, Henry J. *The Canadian Men and Women of the Time*. Toronto: W. Briggs, 1912 [1898].

Morin, Lisette. "Madeline Gleason-Hugenin: Un demi-siècle d'écriture au féminin," *Revue d'histoire du Bas-Saint-Laurent* 5, 3–4 (1978): 28–31.

Morton, Desmond. *A Military History of Canada*. Toronto: McClelland and Stewart, 1999.

Mount, Nicholas James. *When Canadian Literature Moved to New York*. Toronto: University of Toronto Press, 2005.

Murolo, Priscilla. *The Common Ground of Womanhood: Class, Gender, and Working Girls' Clubs, 1884–1928*. Urbana: University of Illinois Press, 1997.

Official Photographic Company. *The Greatest of Expositions Completely Illustrated*. St Louis: Samuel Myerson Printing Co., 1904.

Ohl, Paul. *Louis Cyr: Une épopée légendaire*. Outremont: Libre Expression, 2004.

Olsen, Deborah. "Fair Connections: Women's Separatism and the Lewis and Clark Exposition of 1905." *Oregon Historical Quarterly* 109, 2 (2008): 174–203.

Ouimet, Raphaël, ed. *Biographies Canadiennes-Françaises*. 5th ed. Montréal: Ouimet, 1925.

Oxley, J. Macdonald. "Canada at World's Fair," *National Monthly of Canada* 5 (1904): 14–23.

Pelletier-Baillargeon, Hélène. *Marie Gérin-Lajoie*. Montréal: Boréal Express, 1985.

– *Olivar Asselin et son temps: Le militant*. Tome 1. Montréal: Fides, 1996.

– *Olivar Asselin et son temps: Le volontaire*. Tome 2. Montréal: Fides, 2001.

– *Olivar Asselin et son temps: Le maître*. Tome 3. Montréal: Fides, 2010.

Platt, Harold. *Shock Cities: The Environmental Transformation and Reform of Manchester and Chicago*. Chicago: University of Chicago Press, 2005.

Rademacher, Diane. *Still Shining! Discovering Lost Treasures from the 1904 St Louis World's Fair*. St Louis: Virginia Publishing Co., 2003.

Rex, Kay. *No Daughter of Mine: The Women and History of the Canadian Women's Press Club, 1904–1971*. Toronto: Cedar Cave, 1995.

Roy, Pierre-Georges. *À propos de Crémazie*. Québec: Éditions Garneau, 1945.

Rutherford, Paul. *A Victorian Authority: The Daily Press in Late Nineteenth-Century Canada*. Toronto: University of Toronto Press, 1982.

Saint-Pierre, Jocelyn. *Histoire de la tribune de la presse à Québec, 1871–1959*. Montréal: VLB éditeur, 2007.

Sanders, Byrne Hope. *Emily Murphy Crusader ("Janey Canuck")*. Toronto: Macmillan, 1945.

Skelton, O.D. *Life and Letters of Sir Wilfrid Laurier*. Vol. 1. Toronto: Oxford University Press, 1921.

Stacey, C.P. *A Very Double Life: The Private World of Mackenzie King*. Toronto: Macmillan, 1976.

Stephenson, Marylee, ed. *Women in Canada*. Don Mills: General Publishing Company, 1977.

Strong-Boag, Veronica, and Anita Clair Fellman. *Rethinking Canada: The Promise of Women's History*. Mississauga: Copp Clark Pitman, 1991.

Tausky, Thomas E. *Sara Jeannette Duncan: Novelist of Empire*. Port Credit, ON: P.D. Meany Publishers, 1980.

Valverde, Mariana. *The Age of Light, Soap, and Water: Moral Reform in English Canada, 1885–1925*. Toronto: McClelland and Stewart, 1991.

Wade, Mason. "Olivar Asselin." In *Canada's Past and Present: A Dialogue*, ed. Robert L. McDougall, 134–79. Toronto: University of Toronto Press, 1965.

Warren, Louise. *Léonise Valois, femme de lettres: Un portrait*. Montréal: l'Hexagone, 1993.

Widdows, P.F. *Émile Nelligan: Selected Poems*. Toronto: Guernica, 1995.

Wilson, J. Donald, Robert M. Stamp, and Louis-Philippe Audet. *Canadian Education: A History*. Scarborough: Prentice Hall, 1970.

Wyczynski, Paul. *Album Nelligan: Une biographie en images*. Montréal: Éditions Fides, 2002.

– *Émile Nelligan: Biographie*. Saint-Laurent: Bibliothèque québécoise, 1999.

– *Nelligan, 1879–1941: Biographie*. Montréal: Éditions Fides, 1987.

INDEX